Free Speech and
the Pornography Debate

Free Speech and the Pornography Debate

A Gender-Based Approach to Regulating Inegalitarian Pornography

Lynn Mills Eckert

LEXINGTON BOOKS
Lanham • Boulder • New York • London

Published by Lexington Books
An imprint of The Rowman & Littlefield Publishing Group, Inc.
4501 Forbes Boulevard, Suite 200, Lanham, Maryland 20706
www.rowman.com

6 Tinworth Street, London SE11 5AL, United Kingdom

British Library Cataloguing in Publication Information Available

Library of Congress Cataloging-in-Publication Data Available
Library of Congress Control Number: 2020940433

ISBN 978-1-4985-7260-6 (cloth)
ISBN 978-1-4985-7262-0 (pbk)
ISBN 978-1-4985-7261-3 (electronic)

For my father, in loving memory

Contents

Introduction

At the broadest level, this book is about the epistemology of law while at the narrowest vantage it is concerned with the possibility of placing gender-based regulations on inegalitarian pornography. In making a case that epistemology can help us find our way through the highly contentious debate about regulating pornography, I examine free speech categories, concepts, and rules. Everything from how to define pornography, to whether pornography constitutes speech or a practice, to whether it harms concerns epistemology. By examining the highly contested legal debate about the regulation of pornography through an epistemic lens, the book project hopes to reveal insights into competing claims about the proper role of speech in our society, pornography's harm, the relationship between speech and equality, and whether law should regulate and, if so, upon what grounds.

EPISTEMOLOGY: DEFINING A PARTICULAR UNDERSTANDING

In examining the legal debate about pornography from an epistemic lens, the book adopts a particular approach to epistemology, one that both problematizes and retains notions of truth and objectivity while recognizing that desire and power play a role in producing knowledge.[1] It recognizes the linguistic turn in philosophy as well as where "an epochal shift in philosophy and social theory [has taken place] from an [traditional] epistemological problematic, in which mind is conceived as reflecting or mirroring reality, to a discursive problematic, in which culturally constructed social meanings are accorded density and weight.[2] Relying on studies and measures of harm alone will not end the debate about porn's regulation. The empirical variables rest upon the social construction of meaning and the way that construction informs the epistemological understanding of the problem. The discursive problematic ranges from the social construction of sexuality, masculinity, femininity, freedom of speech, harm, and equality. Such an understanding of epistemology, which in colloquial terms means the study of "how we know what we know," borrows from the criticisms of the sociology of knowledge, feminist epistemology, continental theory's understanding of meaning and interpretation, critical theory, and poststructuralism.[3] In varying degrees, those criticisms have demonstrated that none of us have a God's-eye-

1

view-from-nowhere and that the ability of humans to access the unfiltered truth isn't possible. In short, we are fallible, bringing our own cultural, historical, and social biases or prejudgments with us when attempting to validate or invalidate truth claims. Our ability to establish truth upon a solid metaphysical foundation isn't possible.[4] These insights should influence legal discussions about porn's meaning, the categories law deploys, whether it harms, standards of evidence and appropriate regulations, if any. Truth matters, but it may be a moving target depending on context and power. Moreover, law may have to respond to the idea that we have no access to enduring truths, requiring law to accommodate changes as material conditions and context changes.[5]

Despite conceding that truth has no solid metaphysical foundation from which to tell us definitively porn's meaning and its harms, the book, nonetheless, seeks to retain a concept of truth and to provisionally discover a "truth" about pornography in its current historical form. Those committed to social justice must rely upon truth, even a problematized version of truth, to fight oppression.[6] Without truth, claims about discrimination rest upon the whims of those in power rather than on the objective ability to demonstrate harm. At the same time, Western culture has used claims to "truth" and "objectivity" to brutalize and oppress minority groups.[7] A social epistemology grounded in coherentism and attentive to the relationship between truth and power should provide insight into how and why false claims of objectivity prevailed at particular moments in history while recognizing the need to recoup and remedy those failings that brought us far short of authentic "truth." For example, such an understanding of epistemology should help to navigate the competing claims within the debate about pornography regarding which group has more power—pornographers or feminists. It should help us reconsider how to conceptualize and measure harm claims about pornography. It should help us define pornography as a practice, even though that practice isn't static.

My hope throughout this project is that the very same heterogenous combination of theories that led philosophers such as Linda Alcoff, Nancy Fraser, and Satya Mohanty, to name just a few, to analyze the failings of more traditional, foundationalist accounts of epistemology will be applied to free speech law and the pornography debate. Through the application of feminist epistemologies, continental philosophy, poststructuralism, critical theory, egalitarian liberalism, the sociology of knowledge, and phenomenology, I will attempt to place the debate about pornography's regulation on a different terrain. This is no easy feat. Many of the underlying presumptions of these theories are at odds. Yet the argument about the utilization of competing theories relies upon far more auspicious scholars who have already done the heavy intellectual lifting in determining where these theories can complement one another. I attempt to apply those theories to First Amendment law and the pornography debate.

Such an approach to epistemology, as I understand it, entails several different assumptions worth highlighting and scrutinizing. The first is that knowledge and power are interconnected, which is to say that we must analyze power as an influence in determining knowledge.[8] To be clear, power is not reducible to knowledge, but it plays an integral and analyzable role involving such considerations as who sets criteria for knowledge claims, to whose account is plausible, and to which groups receive resources enabling the very production of knowledge.[9] Law is a site of knowledge production where legal precedents validate a specialized kind of truth. Knowers are always already socially, historically, and culturally embedded, and that embeddedness brings with it certain assumptions, biases, and prejudgements from which we are not free. Whose insights are predominately embedded in the law? Which narrative is stronger in shaping our understanding of modern free speech doctrine? In the conversation about pornography and its effects, which group deploys power to shape discursive understandings and legal outcomes? As Margaret Attwood remarks about the porn industry's claims to powerlessessness, for example, "it is hard to feel that porn is the excluded other when it is so prevalent and so present in public."[10] Can a self-conscious analysis of the relationship between power and knowledge help us to come to conclusions about the relationship of power in this debate and how it influences what we know and validate in law regarding pornography?

These insights concerning our prejudgments and biases come from a tradition of continental philosophy called hermeneutics, which developed from the desire to interpret ancient texts, especially biblical texts. The ability to understand those texts rests upon a fusion of cultural horizons between the reader in the present and the text from the past. As a modern reader of an ancient text, we have limited abilities to embrace the nuanced subtleties of language, practices, and culture from a bygone age. Instead, we do our best to interpret by bringing our modern prejudgements intermixed with tradition to bear on the past. Some prejudgements produce interpretations that must be ruled out given what we know about a past culture. Other prejudgments produce disruptive meanings, which "pull us up short" from the text.[11] In such instances, we are made aware of our biases and must grapple with them.

In the debate about pornography, no one escapes these cultural horizons and prejudgments of which we are inextricably a part. The meaning we attach to pornography must be scrutinized with an awareness of social locatedness within a cultural horizon as well as an awareness of our prejudgements. Our social locatedness within a horizon is always specified by variables such as our gender, race, class, and sexuality. For example, within our current cultural horizon, we are far more willing to recognize racism within the genre of pornography and less willing to discuss sexism within the industry.[12] The question becomes *why*? What about our social locatedness and the context makes one unequal aspect of the genre more recognizable and problematic than another?

In both instances—the interconnection between knowledge and power and our social, cultural, and historical embeddedness—we are reminded that knowledge and truth are provisional and their justifications are very much a social affair. Where new information presents itself that better coheres with our web of meanings, we revise knowledge as we know it. An analysis of porn and its harms requires similar attentiveness to concerns about patriarchal power and its distorting effects on law, culture, and epistemology as well as the ways in which pornography as a discourse has evolved due to market and technological changes, reactions to cultural shifts, and critiques of the genre from feminists and others.[13] Pornography as a practice may not be monolithic, although some versions of it may be more dominant and problematic than others.

The second assumption requiring some explanation is that I borrow insights from the sociology of knowledge. A sociology of knowledge approach can make visible the gap between how we *actually* produce knowledge and how we *should* or *purport to* produce knowledge. It is Thomas Kuhn's *The Structure of Scientific Revolutions* which demonstrates that science's actual practices and experimental character are quite different than the dominant theoretical accounts of science producing knowledge.[14] In too many traditional accounts of epistemology, how knowledge *is* produced is quite different from the ideal of how it *should be* produced. In Kuhn's work, traditional scientific models of knowledge posit the displacement of old theories with the replacement of new theories as a linear, progressive march toward adopting paradigms that better explain phenomena.[15] Instead, with the introduction of new paradigms or new models of knowing, entrenched interests hold out to protect old models because of their investments in time, money, and intellectual capital. In an even broader application of the sociology of knowledge, power, desire, and the tendency to conserve beliefs play a role in producing knowledge rather than just the notion that we adopt new paradigms when they offer better explanations. More accurate theories of knowledge will account for the insights from the sociology of knowledge, analyzing elements like power as ineliminable, while retaining the need for epistemology. The book applies this sociology of knowledge approach to demonstrate the ways that we already both regulate pornography and acknowledge its problematic effects without fully admitting it and openly and honestly weighing free speech concerns in the zoning cases. How can we be more truthful about pornography, about its diversity, it potential transgressiveness, and its problematic variants? A first step would be to recognize what we already acknowledge but attempt to obscure in the zoning cases.

To be clear, the argument that is developed through the comparison between zoning and civil damage ordinance is not one that supports zoning as a regulatory policy option. The comparison is meant to highlight what we will say and not say about pornography. It is meant to reveal the obfuscations and doctrinal contortions and denials within free speech law about pornography and its harms rather than a rigorous argument in favor of zoning, which would necessarily entail a broader conversation about gentrification and the role of racism prevelent in the history of zoning law. Such an undertaking is simply not the focus of the book.

The understanding of epistemology utilized in this book also embraces the poststructural insight about the multiplicity of meaning, namely, that texts (including pornography broadly speaking) have no one meaning. As a discourse, pornography continues to evolve and diversify, making it difficult to see the genre as monolithic. Not all pornography falls into the problematic variety that would contribute to maintaining inequality. This book attempts to make a pro-regulation argument that is aimed at the most violent, degrading, and dehumanizing variety of pornography, which will be referred to broadly as inegalitarian pornography. This is the variety of pornography that Canada, Scotland, the United Kingdom, and other nations with strong free speech traditions have attempted to regulate. At the same time, the book recognizes the debate among pro-sex and anti-porn feminists concerning pornography's multiple meanings. In that debate, porn studies scholars suggest that pornography may produce a multiplicity of meanings, where, for example, ostensibly heterosexual representations may be read through a transgressive queer lens.[16] Scholars such as Thomas Waugh or Emily Shelton produce analyses of mainstream heterosexual porn through the loci of queer culture finding that "straight sex in porn is anything but just straight."[17] Nonetheless, as interesting and as provocative as these analyses are, we can recognize that some meanings may have more relevance than others—or, put differently, not all interpretations are equally compelling. As Tim Stuttgen suggests, porn remains dominated by "white straight men, selling their boring and heteronormative desires through the ideas of liberalism and democracy."[18] Stuttgen makes an important point using rather sharp and provocative language. In essence, despite a diversity of pornographic offerings, the most dominant form remains the heteronormative, white, straight, male variety. Not only does that variety remain dominant, but we can agree on the generally accepted mainstream meaning of those representations. Put differently, as a matter of law, public meanings remain the basis upon which we adjudicate given a particular context, history, and set of power relations. The question remains whether the content-neutrality principle within free speech doctrine operates in such a manner to allow nuanced consideration of context, history, and power in assessing harm and determining which subset of pornography deserves regulation.

Finally, the last point to emphasize is that given the provisional nature of truth, we must be open to differing perspectives. Where these views fit into a web of meaning and better cohere, we must refine our knowledge claims. Such an approach means that we must be open to hearing from groups historically excluded from both the processes of producing knowledge rather than only privileging the elite groups who set standards for determining valid knowledge claims. Those on the front line of experience, where immutable characteristics such as race and sex have precluded their contributions, should be heard as we attempt to both know and understand. Standpoint matters in how we experience life, particularly in societies where racism, sexism, classism, homophobia, and other kinds of oppression persist.[19] If we truly want a fuller account of the truth, those marginalized voices must be heard. Moreover, individuals with such diverse backgrounds must be part of the very groups that determine the criteria for valid knowledge claims. Diversity, even multiculturalism, then, is continuous with epistemology rather than at odds with it.[20]

One of the more contentious elements in the debate over regulating pornography concerns who precisely is marginalized: pornographers, women, people of color, gays and lesbians, or those working in the sex industry. We need to hear from all of these groups in order to get a fuller account of the truth without giving any one group epistemic privilege. Law must better reflect the reality of pornography in the culture as best we can understand it or lose respect.[21] Some groups experience the potential for regulation as threatening and retrogressive while others understand potential regulation as a commitment to equality. Can epistemology help us to navigate through the debate?

EPISTEMOLOGY AND THE LAW: CONTENT-NEUTRALITY, CAUSALITY, AND DISCURSIVE EFFECTS

What does this understanding of epistemology specifically entail for my analysis of law and pornography? It means that the first step in my attempt to understand the pornography debate in US law will be to ask a series of questions closer to a sociology-of-knowledge approach. What makes it possible for pornography to exist in the inegalitarian form and to thrive? What institutions, structures, rules, beliefs, discourses, and ideologies must be in place to justify and defend inegalitarian pornography? What conditions would need to change in order to understand it differently and perhaps for it to transform? In essence, the first step is to bracket the moral claims about the rightness or wrongness of pornography regulations and determine whether we regulate pornography and, if we do, how and why?

The sociology-of-knowledge approach yields important insights about how and why we regulate porn and what law is willing or unwilling to say about it. Interestingly, in the modern era, law rarely uses obscenity to regulate porn but instead draws upon zoning law. Those different regulative approaches (obscenity, zoning, civil damage approaches) apply varying categorical choices, concepts, and language. One chapter will examine the varying categorical choices in both the zoning and civil damage cases regulating pornography, analyzing their implications for regulations. Another chapter will linger on the language used to describe adult establishments and nude dancing, to uncover the banal meanings hidden from us due to our familiarity.

After examining the categorical choices and language of the zoning and nude dancing cases, the next chapter analyzes free speech doctrine itself. Specifically, I will examine the assumptions underlying a core element of modern free speech doctrine, namely, the content-neutrality principle. The content-neutrality principle holds that government may never regulate speech based upon a like or dislike of the message. The guiding purpose of the principle is to prevent government from making a judgment about speech: its rightness or wrongness. Government can and should remain neutral in evaluating speech in our democracy. This indeed is a noble principle, one worth preserving. Yet, intentions that inform the categories of law sometimes deviate from how those categorizations operate in practice. I will argue that content-neutrality in practice is non-neutral when it comes to evaluating the harms from pornography and hate speech. An espistemological approach described earlier in the introduction will help us to understand how and why the current understanding of content-neutrality is profoundly biased.

More specifically, I will explore how the content-neutrality principle effectively functions as both a gender and racially coded category, preventing any serious evaluation of harm claims stemming from speech that implicates Fourteenth Amendment concerns. Instead of upholding values of neutrality in assessing such inegalitarian forms of speech, content-neutrality functions in an ahistorical and acontextual manner, stripping away the ability to assess meaning and negative effects from language. As we know, harm remains one of the principal rationales to constitutionally regulate speech under US free speech doctrine. If speech harms, as in the case of libel, we regulate. Language, its meaning and effects, is deeply contextual, depending upon power, history, and culture. Any process that prohibits a weighing of such factors operates in a de facto non-neutral manner.

Embedded in modern free speech doctrine and its central tenet, the content-neutrality principle, is a particular understanding of speech that I will examine as well. Despite advances in philosophy about the nature of language and how it shapes our reality, free speech doctrine remains mired in a libertarian understanding of speech. The classic colloquial description of that perspective is embodied in the old children's saying "sticks and stones may break my bones but names will never hurt me." In this view, speech is distinctive from the real world of action. Yet poststructural theory provides an alternative understanding of speech through the concept of discursive effects. Following from that view, discourse creates more than hurt feelings. Instead, it generates ideological, material, and epistemic effects. The very concept of discursive effects challenges not only the libertarian understanding of speech but also dislodges the causal criteria to prove harm. Under the civil damage ordinance approach advocated by Catharine MacKinnon and Andrea Dworking in *American Booksellers v. Hudnut* (1985), the content-neutrality principle would not prevent government from regulating pornography *if* harm could be causally proven. Yet, in *Hudnut*, pro-regulation advocates find themselves in a catch-22: to narrowly define the kind of porn that harms is to reference its gendered, misogynistic, and violent content. Once the definition references content, it triggers the content-neutrality principle. If the content-neutrality principle is operative, the only way to prove harm is causally. Under a theory of discursive effects, speech produces serious effects or harms about which egalitarian liberals should be concerned, but not in a causal manner. Causality, as Foucault tells us, is a mystification: an unattainable ideal beyond the grasp of even the hard sciences.

While the concept of discursive effects may better explain how porn harms than sophisticated causal accounts or speech-act theory, the fact remains that law is conservative in its reliance on precedent. Free speech precedent in cases involving pornography regulation (and hate speech) does not rely upon a poststructural understanding of speech or discursive effects.[22] Instead, I will contend, arguments that present courts with harm claims about pornographic speech (or hate speech) rely upon precedents that invoke outdated understandings of speech. Yet the claim I wish to make in the pages that follow is that we must re-read a seminal case, *Brown v. Board of Education* (1954), through the lens of speech and, specifically, from the framework of discursive effects. Such a re-reading depends upon Charles Lawrence's radical re-interpretation of *Brown* as a case primarily about speech. Lawrence argues that the expressive elements inhering in the practice of segregation (i.e., the message of white supremacy) harms more than the actual act of segregating individuals. The sting, humiliation, and harm from segregation is expressive, particularly in instances where the pro-segregation advocates attempted to provide equal facilities, eliminating the potential for facial discrimination.[23] I want to extend Charles Lawrence's profound and ground-breaking insight about *Brown* as speech, placing it within the context of discursive effects. Lawrence, in his argument, highlights Warren's concerns about the effects of segregation on the hearts and minds of young black children. For Lawrence, those effects are the harms from a white supremacist message. Those harms, in my view, are better understood as discursive effects. In Lawrence's re-reading of *Brown* we see the very linguistic turn in philosophy mentioned at the beginning of the introduction. Segregation becomes a discursive problematic, the social construction of meaning, and it is accorded density and weight.[24]

With the concept of discursive effects, we have a more extensive understanding of how discursive practices effect or hurt "the hearts and minds" of young black children and we have a better ability to understand the extent of those harms on citizenship outside of the confining and distorting frame of causality. Reframed from the lens of discursive effects, Warren's moving language in *Brown* is describing the ideological, material, and epistemic effects of a white supremacist message. The mechanism of those devastating harms is not causal and they do not, I will argue, rest upon speech-act theory.

If Lawrence is correct and *Brown* should be properly understood as speech, then I hope to utilize that radical reinterpretation in two ways. First, I want to suggest that embedded in US law are arguments, however brief or momentary, that may be recouped, highlighted, and reapplied to incorporate an understanding of harmful speech of the kind in inegalitarian pornography by deploying the concept of discursive effects. Such an understanding of harmful speech in terms of discursive effects, I will contend, is compatible with US law and its liberal philosophical foundations. By connecting discursive effects to a well-established precedent (*Brown*), it is possible to avert concerns about the conservative nature of precedent. In effect, a new paradigm of discursive effects helps us to better understand a case long ago decided and more effectively elucidates the precise reasons why expression helped to maintain inequality in the case of segregation in violation of the Fourteenth Amendment. Second, I want to attempt to apply this theory of discursive effects to pornography regulation. *Brown*, understood as a case about expression that produces discriminatory discursive effects, can and should help us understand and evaluate the claim that inegalitarian pornography harms women's citizenship rights.

It is in the latter part of the book where the shift from a sociology-of-knowledge approach to an epistemic approach becomes relevant. Linda Martin Alcoff in her seminal work on epistemology, *Real Knowing: New Visions of Coherence Theory*, writes that, like Marx, she believes there shouldn't be an absolute separation between how we actually justify our beliefs and the way in which we *should* justify them. The distance between epistemology and the sociology of knowledge on that view closes or should close. In terms of the book's argument, the distance between how and why we regulate pornography in the zoning cases and the arguments rejected in *Hudnut* should close. In both the zoning approach to regulating pornography and the *Hudnut* case, law finds that pornography generates adverse secondary effects or harms, including those aimed specifically at women. Yet in one set of cases, the gender-based arguments concerning pornography are submerged in larger concerns about zoning to protect property, while in the other the gender-based concerns frame the entire case.[25] The former set passes constitutional muster while the latter case is struck down as legislation aimed at thought control.[26] The distance between how we *do* regulate pornography's harm in the zoning cases and how we *should* regulate pornography as a civil rights matter in *Hudnut* should close. The sociology-of-knowledge approach helps us to recognize that gap, while epistemology in the way advanced in the preface helps us to close it.

Alcoff explains why we must maintain a separation between the sociology of knowledge and epistemology. She contends that epistemology shouldn't simply be reduced to a sociology of knowledge approach. We need an epistemology that enables us to analyze and critique our actual ways of coming to know even as they reveal biases.[27] Only epistemology helps us to evaluate competing knowledge claims in ways that are defensible and based upon reason, even if that understanding of reason is problematized by power and desire. What the sociology of knowledge has taught is that actual operations concerning power in producing knowledge shouldn't remain silently unanalyzed. Yet knowledge claims can't simply be reduced to sociological concerns about power relations, desire, and the conservation of beliefs. Reason, truth, and objectivity matter if we are to remain committed to democratic ideals of justice and fairness and a constitutional form of government premised on public justification. Where we can point out that past knowledge claims are contradictory, distorted by power relations, or at odds with reality, we may revise them.

In that same spirit, my own analysis is no "view-from-nowhere." The argument advanced here is just as fallible and embedded in a particular cultural horizon with hidden (and unhidden) prejudgments as the perspective embedded in free speech doctrine and the feminist debate about pornography regulation. The same critiques that I level at these various knowledge claims can and should be leveled at my own argument.

My position throughout the book is to remain committed to the principles of liberalism engrained in US constitutional law. This may sound like an odd claim given that I depend upon philosophical positions critical of the very ideas of truth, objectivity, and reason, which are so central to the liberal enlightenment tradition. Nonetheless, these philosophical critiques of liberalism throw into relief the provisional nature of truth and our inherent fallibility in accessing it. Problematizing these concepts gives us the hope of accounting for such biases and remaining humble in the face of proclaimed certainties while retaining truth, reason, and objectivity as criteria for assessing knowledge claims. At a minimum, even compromised understandings of reason and truth are better than the alternative: namely, the criteria of might makes right. In our system, might equates to the forces of capitalism, patriarchy, homophobia, and white supremacy rather than fairness, equality, and justice.[28] Those forces are particularly relevant in analyzing the place of pornography in maintaining inequality. Liberalism as a theory is supple enough to embrace critiques of reason while simultaneously relying upon a more problematized and realistic understanding of reason for the operation of just law.

This commitment to liberal constitutional law as a means to address the inequalities of pornography separates my approach from someone like Catharine MacKinnon.[29] Liberal law, especially the egalitarian variety, can conceptually recognize and redress the harm from pornography. While MacKinnon and Dworkin used liberal law as a vehicle to regulate pornography in *Hudnut*, the approach failed. MacKinnon's larger theoretical work critiques liberalism's ability to address the roots of gender inequality. MacKinnon is not alone among feminists in rejecting the notion that liberalism can address the regulatory issues surrounding pornography. Carol Smart writes:

> The aim of "fitting" feminist ideas on pornography into a legal framework that might be "workable" (in narrow legal terms) or politically "acceptable", means that many of the subtle insights and complexities of feminist analysis are necessarily lost. The framework (whether civil or criminal) requires that we fit pornography, or the harm that pornography does, into existing categories of harms or wrongs. Hence, we are left with a focus on degrees of actual violence or the traditional (non-feminist) concern with degrees of explicitness which are the mainstay of obscenity laws.[30]

This book aims to explain how liberal legal categories are subject to rupture and change in ways that embrace these feminist insights. Not only can liberal law redress the harms from inegalitarian porn but it can also embrace a more realistic understanding of how speech actually operates. Speech, I will argue, is best understood through the theory of discursive effects rather than a simplistic libertarian notion. I assert that the philosophical assumptions underlying the categories within liberal free speech law can evolve in such a way to apply reasonable regulations on inegalitarian pornography. It can recognize different varieties of pornography while finding that some deserve protection while others require regulation. In short, liberalism can fully embrace the gender equality rationale as a basis to regulate inegalitarian pornography. The book is, in part, a road map as to how liberalism can do so.

Moreoever, liberal law can recognize and redress the gendered harms from pornography based upon its commitment to reason, which is also entailed in an epistemological approach. Where inconsistencies and contradictions nag, not just in constitutional law, but also in the pursuit of knowledge more generally, we must refine them. We cannot engage in such a refinement if all knowledge is reduced to sociology or ideology. Stephen Macedo in *Liberal Virtues* writes:

> Where we have no good reasons for the distinctions and discriminations we draw, we have anomalies or inconsistencies calling, not for bland acceptance, but for further reflection and perhaps revision in our thinking.[31]

Reason, even a problematized version, one where truth is always provisional and interconnected to power and desire, holds out a hope that we may govern and, in this case, regulate not out of intolerance, puritanism, or pruience, but out of a commitment to equality, fairness, and dignity. Epistemology provides a method to help us separate pretextual harm-based arguments favoring pornography regulation from authentic ones. We cannot, however, currently assess the role of pornography in undermining women's unequal citizenship rights without more closely examining the content-neutrality principle, the causal standard of harm, and the need for a new paradigm to understand speech and its effects.

NOTES

1. Nancy Fraser, *Unruly Practices: Power, Discourse, and Gender in Contemporary Social Theory* (London: Polity Press, 2004). Linda Alcoff, *Real Knowing: New Versions of the Coherence Theory* (Ithaca, NY: Cornell Univ. Press, 2008). Steve Fuller, *Social Epistemology* (Bloomington: Indiana University Press, 2002). Sandra Harding, *Science and Social Inequality: Feminist and Postcolonial Issues* (University of Illinois Press, 2006). While this is not a debate about the intricacies of epistemology, the insights of these other scholars provide a fresh perspective on the problem of determining what pornography is, whether it harms, and whether to regulate.

2. Nancy Fraser, "Pragmatism, Feminism, and the Linguistic Turn," in *Feminist Contentions: A Philosophical Exchange*, ed., S. Benhabib et al. (New York: Routledge, 1995).

3. Linda Alcoff, *Real Knowing: New Versions of the Coherence Theory* (Ithaca, NY: Cornell University Press, 2008). Joseph Rouse, *Knowledge and Power: Toward a Political Philosophy of Science* (Ithaca, NY: Cornell University Press, 1987).

4. Linda M Alcoff, "How Is Epistemology Political?," in *Radical Philosophy* (Philadelphia, PA: Temple University, 1993). Linda Alcoff, "Justifying Feminist Social Science," *Hypatia* 2, no. 3 (1987): pp. 107-120, https://doi.org/10.1111/j.1527-2001.1987.tb01344.x. Linda Alcoff, *Real Knowing: New Versions of the Coherence Theory* (Ithaca, NY: Cornell Univ. Press, 2008). Seyla Benhabib, *Situating the Self Gender, Community, and Postmodernism in Contemporary Ethics* (Polity Press, 2007). Nancy Fraser, *Unruly Practices: Power, Discourse, and Gender in Contemporary Social Theory* (London: Polity Press, 2004). Nancy Fraser tells us that "Belief in philosophical metanarratives tends to decline with the linguistic turn, since to accord density and weight to signifying processes is also to cast doubt on the possibility of a permanent neutral matrix for inquiry."

5. Justice O 'Connor makes a similar point in *Grutter v. Bollinger* 539 U.S. 306 (2003) about the evolving need for affirmative action. In the case, she posits that we may need affirmative action policies for only another 20 years. The changing social context

may make the need for affirmative action policies obsolete and law can and should take account of such a changing context.

6. Seyla Benhabib, *Situating the Self Gender, Community, and Postmodernism in Contemporary Ethics* (Polity Press, 2007).

7. Satya P. Mohanty, *Literary Theory and the Claims of History: Postmodernism, Objectivity, Multicultural Politics* (Oxford University Press, 1998). Nancy Fraser, "Pragmatism, Feminism, and the Linguistic Turn," in *Feminist Contentions*, p.157.

8. Satya P. Mohanty, *Literary Theory and the Claims of History: Postmodernism, Objectivity, Multicultural Politics* Oxford University Press, 1998). Linda M Alcoff, "How Is Epistemology Political?," in *Radical Philosophy* (Philadelphia, PA: Temple University, 1993). Michel Foucault, *Power/Knowledge: Selected Interviews & Other Writings 1972-1977*, ed. Colin Gordon (New York, NY: Pantheon Books, 1980). A. Levin, *Cost of Free Speech: Pornography, Hate Speech, and Their Challenge to Liberalism* (Palgrave Macmillan, 2014).

9. Linda M Alcoff, "How Is Epistemology Political?," in *Radical Philosophy* (Philadelphia, PA: Temple University, 1993). Carol Smart, *Feminism and the Power of Law* (Routledge, 2015).

10. Helen Hester, *Beyond Explicit* (Albany, NY: State University of New York Press, 2015), 9, (in "'Other' or 'One of Us'" in Hester 9).

11. See Alcoff's discussion in Chapter 2 of Linda Alcoff, *Real Knowing: New Versions of the Coherence Theory* (Ithaca, NY: Cornell Univ. Press, 2008).

12. Helen Hester, *Beyond Explicit* (Albany, NY: State University Of New York Press, 2015), 9.

13. Both Tarrant and Hester make this point apparent. The pornography industry has been significantly disrupted by technology reducing entry market barriers. Websites such as Pornhub have both monopolized access to many varieties of pornography and limited the amount of money producers receive. Pornhub offers access to different varieties of pornography as well rather than simply the most inegalitarian and violent forms of which the book is largely concerned. Shira Tarrant, *The Pornography Industry: What Everyone Needs to Know* (Oxford University Press, 2016). Helen Hester, *Beyond Explicit* (Albany, NY: State Univ of New York Press, 2015).

14. Thomas S. Kuhn, *The Structure of Scientific Revolutions* (Chicago, IL: The University of Chicago Press, 2015).

15. Kuhn, *The Structure of Scientific Revolutions* (Chicago, IL: The University of Chicago Press, 2015).

16. Hester, 4.

17. Hester, Shelton 139 in Hester p. 4.

18. Hester quoting Tim Stüttgen, "Before Orgasm: Fifteen Fragments on a cartography of Post/Pornographic Politics," *Post/Porn/Politics: Queer Feminist Perspectives on the Politics of Porn Performance and Sex Work as Cultural Production* Ed. Stüttgen. Berlin: books, 2009. pp. 10–21. Found on page 10 in Hester.

19. Here I am not advocating for a kind of epistemic privilege. While incorporating standpoint experiences where they were previously excluded, it does not follow that those claims need not be evaluated. But the claims should be evaluated under criteria that accounts for biases. See Satya P. Mohanty, *Literary Theory and the Claims of History: Postmodernism, Objectivity, Multicultural Politics* (Oxford University Press, 1998).

20. Satya P. Mohanty, *Literary Theory and the Claims of History: Postmodernism, Objectivity, Multicultural Politics* (Oxford University Press, 1998). Linda M Alcoff, "How Is Epistemology Political?," in *Radical Philosophy* (Philadelphia, PA: Temple University, 1993).

21. Anthony G. Amsterdam and Jerome Seymour Bruner, *Minding the Law* (Harvard Universty Press, 2000).

22. I will explore the relationship homology between hate speech and pornography in later chapters.

23. The Supreme Court famously rejects such an argument in *Sweatt v. Painter* (1950). In the case, the majority opinion argues that even if the tangible facilities at the

Texas law school such as buildings and the number of library books were equal, the intangible features such as the alumni network would never be equal.

24. Nancy Fraser, "Pragmatism, Feminism, and the Linguistic Turn," in *Feminist Contentions: A Philosophical Exchange,* ed., S. Benhabib et al. (New York: Routledge, 1995).

25. A comparison of these two cases will be defended in later chapters.

26. See *American Booksellers v. Hudnut* 771 F. 2d. 323 (7th Cir. 1985).

27. See Satya P. Mohanty, *Theory and the Claims of History: Postmodernism, Objectivity, Multicultural Politics* (Oxford University Press, 1998).

28. See Alcoff, Fraser, and Mohanty.

29. Catharine MacKinnon, *Feminism Unmodified: Discourses on Life and Law* (Harvard University Press, 1987). Catharine A. MacKinnon, *Toward A Feminist Theory of The State* (Harvard University Press, 1989). It is not the only difference from MacKinnon, but it is a significant one. My willingness to use poststructuralist insights, which MacKinnon eschews, is also another difference. At the same time, MacKinnon opens the philosophical terrain upon which I write and, so much of the argument, is simply indebted to her. Tracy E. Higgins, "Gender, Why Feminists Can't (or Shouldn't) Be Liberals," 72 *Fordham L. Rev.* 1629 (2004). Available at: http://ir.lawnet.fordham.edu/flr/vol72/iss5/12.

30. Carol Smart. *Feminism and the Power of Law* (New York: Routledge, 2015), 115.

31. Stephen Macedo, *Liberal Virtues* (New York: Oxford University Press, 1990), 34-35.

I

Sociology of Knowledge: "We Already Regulate Pornography for Gender-Based Reasons without Acknowledging It"

ONE

Regulating Pornography Comparing the Zoning and Nude Dancing Cases to *Hudnut*

The chapter begins with questions set out in the introduction. Those questions owe their significance to the sociology approach to knowledge. Here we ask, *how* do we actually regulate pornography? What reasons do we provide for justifying its regulation, what categorical distinctions do we make within law? In an attempt to answer these questions, we will examine the obscenity, zoning, and civil damage approaches to regulating pornography. In comparing and contrasting these approaches, scrutinizing their foundational assumptions and categorical choices, we will better see what law is willing and unwilling to say about pornography at this historical moment. Of course, in comparing and contrasting these different regulatory approaches, I face many hurdles in advancing the argument. My arguments must address critics who fairly question the appropriateness of comparing these different approaches. The comparison will have to be defended along the way. We will begin with the zoning cases and then the civil damage approach to regulating pornography. The obscenity approach to regulation will largely be discussed within the context of the two approaches that I wish to highlight—the zoning and civil damage approach. In the post–*Miller* era, obscenity approaches to regulating pornography have been unsuccessful and largely abandoned.[1]

The chapter, then, attempts to explain two different approaches to regulating pornography: one unrecognized, and the other rejected by a federal appeals court. In the first set of cases—the zoning cases regulating adult establishments—the Supreme Court has upheld restrictions on adult businesses, arguing that such restrictions attempt to remedy the effects of "erotic" speech rather than the message itself. In the second, regulative approach, a federal appeals court struck down a civil damage ordinance allowing victims of pornography to sue for financial damages. The civil damage case, unlike the zoning cases, defines pornography as a gender-based practice; identifies harms as gender-based; and seeks remedies that are specifically gender-based. In interrogating these two different regulatory approaches, the chapter raises critical questions about the similarities and differences between the two methods. These similarities and differences help us to understand what law will acknowledge and validate about the practice of pornography and its harms and, also, what law leaves unrecognized and invalidated.

THE ZONING APPROACH TO REGULATING PORNOGRAPHY: *YOUNG, RENTON, PAP'S* AND *ALAMEDA BOOKS*

In 1972, the City of Detroit, Michigan, amended an anti-Skid Row ordinance, placing adult theaters into the "regulated uses" category.[2]

Detroit prohibited adult theaters from locating within 1,000 feet of other regulated commercial establishments such as pawn shops or within 500 feet of residential areas, unless adult theaters received a special waiver.[3]

In the decision, the Supreme Court analyzed Detroit's amendment restricting adult theaters as content neutral, finding that Detroit attempted to regulate the *effects* of pornography, not the *content*.[4]

The content-neutrality principle forms the core of modern free speech doctrine, holding that government may not regulate speech based upon a like or dislike of the message.[5]

In the decision, the Supreme Court framed the regulations on adult theaters in terms of zoning rather than free speech law. While the opinion underscored the zoning aspects of the case, its primary concern, the issue that occupied the most space, was whether zoning was a pretext for suppressing unpopular pornographic speech.[6]

Zoning has a long tradition in the United States, and property rights share a preeminent place in the Constitution beside free speech rights. Under the police powers doctrine, textually rooted in the Tenth Amendment, states retain a plenary power to regulate the health, morals, and welfare of the people. In order to invoke police powers, especially when a preeminent right such as free speech is implicated in regulation, governments must demonstrate that they have a compelling state interest in pursuing a particular policy and that the policy is narrowly tailored to the state's objectives.[7]

Protecting property, commerce, and communities certainly falls within the scope of police powers, and courts have long considered zoning an appropriate means to an end. As Justice Lewis Franklin Powell Jr. writes in his *Young* concurrence, "The cases are legion that sustained zoning."[8]

By framing the issue as one about the state's power to zone, the Supreme Court rhetorically displaces substantial free speech concerns. The cases characterize harm as content-neutral *secondary effects*, which are described primarily in terms of injury to property, commerce, and communities.[9]

The secondary-effects doctrine originates in a footnote in *Young*.[10]

The doctrine allows for a less stringent level of review on those regulations justified by the effects rather than the content of speech. A content-neutral regulation is one that "inadvertently regulates speech" and is not designed to specifically target unpopular speech.[11]

Under a secondary effects, content-neutral analysis, government regulation is far more likely to pass constitutional muster. In contrast, a content-based regulation on speech triggers strict scrutiny. The courts question whether the government's motivation is to suppress speech. If a court finds that the government's intention is indeed to suppress unpopular speech, the regulation is struck down. Typically, once a regulation triggers a strict scrutiny analysis, the test becomes outcome determinative. Few regulations survive strict scrutiny. Yet, the "government motivation component" of strict scrutiny is hardly a failsafe method for determining whether the real regulative intention is silencing distasteful expression. Government can easily rephrase regulations targeting unpopular speech into content-neutral terms. For example, local government may impose a time, place, and manner restriction on certain kinds of speech due to an ostensive concern about traffic congestion despite obscuring the real motivation, an underlying dislike of the speech.[12]

The *Young* decision leaves us with some unsettling questions. What is the relationship between adult establishments and pornography? Are we convinced that the secondary effects of adult establishments are indirectly related to the pornography sold inside? Can almost all content-based regulations be redescribed in content-neutral terms? What do these regulations tell us, however indirectly, about pornography's cultural effects? Finally, and more broadly, is the content-neutrality principle the appropriate way to organize free speech doctrine.

In 1980, while considering a zoning ordinance prohibiting adult theaters from locating within 1,000 feet of any residential zone, church or park, or within one mile of a school, the Renton, Washington, City Council placed a moratorium on the licensing of adult entertainment.[13]

In 1981, Renton passed and implemented the zoning ordinance. *The City of Renton v. Playtime Theatres* (1986) defines adult theaters in the same language as *Young*. An adult theater is any enclosed building used for presenting "motion picture films, video cassettes, cable television, or any other such visual media, distinguished or characterized by an emphasis on matter depicting, describing or relating to 'specified sexual activities' or 'specified anatomical areas' . . . for observation by patrons therein."[14]

The Supreme Court upheld the ordinance, reinforcing the plurality decision in *Young*.

The opinion in *Renton* returns to many of the themes in *Young*. *Renton* frames the issue as one principally about police powers and zoning rather than free speech rights, and it refers to the secondary-effects doctrine to justify any "incidental" effects of zoning on speech. At the same time, *Renton* is more far-reaching than *Young*. The opinion in *Renton* amplifies and extends the secondary effects doctrine, which was initially a footnote in *Young*, and it produces a clear majority rather than a fractured plurality.[15]

Renton redefines content neutrality around secondary effects; the content-neutral/content-based distinction turns on whether localities target secondary as opposed to primary effects. As long as localities regulate to combat effects such as increased prostitution but avoid regulating effects directly related to adult entertainment's message, they stay within constitutional boundaries.

The structure of Justice Rehnquist's opinion is similar to the plurality opinion in *Young* in that he spends some time discussing whether the ordinance violates free speech rights and, in particular, whether the ordinance discriminates on the basis of the content. Justice Rehnquist stresses that the ordinance should be analyzed as a legitimate time, place, and manner restriction because it zones rather than bans adult films:

> The ordinance by its terms is designed to prevent crime, protect the city's retail trade, maintain property values, and generally "[protect] and [preserve] the quality of [the city's] neighborhoods, commercial districts, and quality of urban life," not to suppress the expression of unpopular views.[16]

He acknowledges that Renton's ordinance, like the one in Detroit, seems to treat adult theaters differently based on film content:

> At first glance, the Renton ordinance, like the ordinance in *American Mini Theatres*, does not appear to fit neatly into either the "content-based" or the "content-neutral" category. To be sure, the ordinance treats theaters that specialize in adult films differently from other kinds of theaters. Nevertheless, as the District Court concluded, the Renton ordinance is aimed not at the *content* of the films shown at "adult motion picture theaters," but rather at the *secondary effects* of such theaters on the surrounding community.[17]

He invokes the distinction between content and effects to uphold the ordinance. Justice Rehnquist finds that while the ordinance singles out one type of entertainment based on content, the Court may analyze it as content-neutral because the regulation combats effects.

In a more far-reaching passage, Justice Rehnquist defends the constitutionality of the Renton ordinance even if the Court were to categorize it as content-based. Justice Rehnquist writes that even if Renton's ordinance is content based, the city may still constitutionally zone, given the precedent set in *Tinker v. Des Moines School District* (1969).[18]

In that case, the Supreme Court struck down regulations prohibiting children from wearing armbands protesting the Vietnam war. The school district argued that the armbands in a classroom setting would cause disruption. Although the Supreme Court invalidated these restrictions, they did argue that if the school district were to provide factual support for the claim that armbands would disrupt classes, then the school district could potentially regulate.[19]

Justice Rehnquist uses a quote from Justice Powell's *Young* decision to make the point that content-based regulations are sometimes constitutionally permissible under special circumstances and that the zoning cases fall under those special circumstances.

> The dissent misconceives the issue in this case by insisting that it involves an impermissible time, place, and manner restriction based on the content of expression. It involves nothing of the kind. We have here merely a decision by the city to treat certain movie theaters differently because they have markedly different effects upon their surroundings. . . . Moreover, even if this were a case involving a special governmental response to the content of one type of movie, it is possible that the result would be supported by a line of cases recognizing that the government can tailor its reaction to different types of speech according to the degree to which its *special and overriding* [emphasis added] interests are implicated.[20]

Under Justice Rehnquist's interpretation of the *Tinker* ruling, if Renton can reasonably conclude that adult theaters have more substantial effects on the community than other forms of entertainment, the city may treat the adult theaters differently. The "special and overriding interest" reasoning generates greater confusion about what constitutes secondary effects and unavoidably raises questions about the presumably more serious primary effects not mentioned by the Supreme Court.

Critics rightly note that *Renton's* reasoning is troubling on several grounds. First, the secondary effects doctrine lacks analytical rigor and is malleable. The Court in *Renton* finds an arguably content-based law content-neutral because the law is motivated by a permissible content-neutral purpose.[21]

In doing so, the Court confuses whether a law is content based with whether localities have a sufficient purpose for regulation.[22]

Secondary effects doctrine is malleable in another way also. It opens the door for post hoc justifications or, put differently, justifications contrived after the fact.[23]

Legislators may pass laws with the intent to suppress speech, but later justify those regulations in terms of adverse effects. Any law may be rephrased in content-neutral terms despite content-based motivations. Under secondary effects doctrine, the Court evaluates these potentially ad hoc justifications under a lesser standard of review.

Secondly, *Renton* does not take the question of disparate impact seriously. A disparate impact analysis considers whether the content-neutral time, place, and manner restrictions would suppress speech in a substantial de facto manner:

> [T]he actual effect of the Renton ordinance was to confine adult theaters to a small area on which a sewage treatment plant operated, along with a race track, an industrial park, an oil tank farm, and a shopping center.[24]

The Court dismissed the argument, asserting that the City of Renton left enough land available for adult theaters to relocate and that the law does not require the city to offer special deals in the real estate market.[25]

As Justice Brennan notes in his *Renton* dissent, the "special deals" argument misses the point. Most of the land was unavailable or unsuitable for use.

These criticisms of the reasoning in the zoning cases regulating adult establishments are conventional in nature: they respect rather than question the premises of the content-neutrality principle. Despite the conventional nature of the criticism, they raise important points by challenging the intellectual rigor of the secondary effects doctrine. They throw into question the possibility of defining a use with respect to its content while simultaneously denying that the defining content is a direct cause of the adverse effects. Moreover, the critics dispute that speech is only tangentially impacted by the regulations. The unconventional critiques that will be developed later in the book challenge the desirability and workability of a free speech doctrine organized around the content-neutrality principle. They question whether an ahistorical and acontextual approach to evaluating "adverse effects" is bias masquerading as neutrality. The unconventional critiques also challenge the language deployed in the opinions to describe adult establishments. Gender is nowhere mentioned in the definition of a highly gendered practice.

The Supreme Court expands the precedents in the zoning cases in *Barnes v. Glen Theatre* and *City of Erie v. Pap's A.M., tdba "Kandyland."*[26]

In *City of Erie v. Pap's A.M., tdba "Kandyland,"* the Supreme Court upholds an Erie, Pennsylvania ordinance proscribing public nudity.[27]

The de facto effect of this ordinance was to prohibit adult establishments from featuring female nude dancing, expressive conduct usually protected under the First Amendment. Erie premised the ordinance on combating secondary effects such as sexual harassment, prostitution, and the spread of sexually transmitted diseases, and it purportedly targeted the conduct of the nude dancers, not their message. The Supreme Court's approach in *Pap's* is not substantially different from *Young v. American Mini-Theatres* (1976) and *City of Renton v. Playtime Theatres* (1986) or the prior nude dancing decision in *Barnes v. Glen Theatre* (1991).[28]

This line of cases balances a substantial state interest to combat adverse effects with the right to free speech. The Supreme Court's plurality opinion argues that the Erie ordinance, as in *Young* and *Renton,* is content neutral and only minimally affects speech.

Critics may note that, while *Pap's* and the zoning cases share similarities, they differ in one substantial way that invalidates any comparisons. In *Young* and *Renton,* both the cities of Detroit and Renton regulated only adult theaters, distinguishing adult theaters from other theaters on the basis of content. The fact that both cities regulated only theaters showing pornographic movies reasonably undercut the Court's claim that the ordinances were content neutral. In *Pap's,* Erie prohibits public nudity generally rather than targeting nude dancing alone. This general prohibition would seem to dispel the argument that Erie passed the ordinance with the intent to suppress a particular kind of speech, an argument directed at the cities in *Young* and *Renton.*

Justice O'Connor relies on the general nature of the prohibition to prove that Erie's ordinance targets no particular kind of content. Justice O'Connor writes:

> By its terms, the ordinance regulates conduct alone. It does not target nudity that contains an erotic message; rather, it bans all public nudity, regardless of whether that nudity is accompanied by expressive activity.[29]

She makes a distinction between conduct and speech and argues that Erie, unlike Detroit or Renton, does not selectively regulate pornographic entertainment. But does the general nature of the prohibition relieve Erie's ordinance of content-neutrality concerns? Justice Antonin Scalia argues that we have good reason to suspect that the real target of Erie's ordinance is nude dancing, not, for example, streakers at public sporting events.[30]

Even Scalia, who concurs with the majority, doubts that Erie really intended to prohibit all public nudity.[31]

> As far as appears (and as seems overwhelmingly likely), the preamble, the council members' comments, and the chosen definition of the prohibited conduct simply reflect the fact that Erie had recently been having a public nudity problem not with streakers, sunbathers or hot-dog vendors...but with lap dancers.[32]

Moreover, comments from city council members support Justice Scalia's view. They reassured fellow legislators that not all public nudity was prosecutable under the ordinance and that nudity in theater productions, for example, fell outside its reach. The legislative history clearly indicates that lawmakers intended to influence the city's moral climate.[33]

The general nature of the ordinance, then, is questionable both in terms of the motivations that led to the drafting of the ordinance and its disproportionate impacts on nude dancing. First, as Justice Scalia notes, Erie experienced problems primarily with nude dancing rather than other kinds of nudity, and City Council members drafted the ordinance in response to the adverse effects from nude dancing. Second, the ordinance disproportionately impacts nude dancing establishments, not other displays of nudity. If a facially neutral law has a disproportionate impact on a certain category of speech, then we have reason to suspect that the law is non-neutral in application. In *Pap's*, the ordinance primarily affects nude dancing, and legislators even stated that police would apply the law discriminatingly, targeting pornography rather than nude sunbathing.

In sum, opponents of Erie's ordinance rightly question the real target of the general prohibition on public nudity. Erie clearly regulated nude dancing because it produced some unwanted and problematic effects. The fact that nude dancing has substantial, even controversial, communicative dimensions, throws one of the Supreme Court's central framing premises into question. The secondary-effects doctrine enables the Court to evade the issue of nude dancing's communicative dimensions. What does nude dancing communicate and is that message related to the effects Erie attempts to regulate such as increased prostitution or sexual harassment?

For critics, Erie's ordinance is a de facto prohibition on nude dancing, making it comparable to the zoning ordinances in *Young* and *Renton*. Yet, the zoning cases are not identical to *Pap's*. As discussed above, Erie's ordinance is a general prohibition on public nudity, not a zoning ordinance. Despite that difference, both *Pap's* and the zoning cases similarly maintain that the respective cases are about balancing two competing claims—state police powers with free speech rights. In each case, the secondary-effects doctrine is rearticulated. In *Young*, the Supreme Court attributes secondary effects to the location, numbers, and concentration of adult establishments. Justice Stevens writes:

> In the opinion of urban planners and real estate experts who supported the ordinances, the location of several such businesses in the same neighborhood tends to attract an undesirable quantity and quality of transients, adversely affects property values, causes an increase in crime, especially prostitution, and encourages residents and businesses to move elsewhere.[34]

Content (Detroit targeted adult theaters only), location, numbers, and concentration combined together to produce adverse effects.

In *Renton*, the Supreme Court surpassed the *Young* formula, finding that even the existence of one such adult establishment causes adverse effects.[35]

Renton retains only one constant from the *Young* formula—content. That is, adult theaters alone produce adverse effects regardless of their location, numbers, and concentration. Moreover, *Renton* holds that due to the seriousness of the adverse effects generated by adult theaters, government may regulate—regardless of whether those restrictions are content-based or content-neutral—if it factually substantiates those effects.[36]

In *Pap's*, a notable shift in language occurs, which reestablishes a firm separation between primary and secondary effects and obscures the cause of adverse effects. The Supreme Court uses the passive voice to define secondary effects. The passive voice leaves readers unable to determine who or what acts generate the adverse effects. Adverse effects such as "violence, sexual harassment, public intoxication, prostitution, and the spread of sexually transmitted diseases" simply occur.[37]

The *Pap's* articulation of secondary effects doctrine, then, obfuscates a central question—what causes the secondary effects? In *Renton*, the Supreme Court's answer strongly implied content.

What does this definitional shift mean? The *Pap's* definition of secondary effects is a significant moment because it retreats from the logic in *Renton* reviving the primary/secondary-effects distinction:

> Put another way, the ordinance does not attempt to regulate the primary effects of the expression, i.e., the effect on the audience of watching nude erotic dancing, but rather the secondary effects, such as the impacts on public health, safety, and welfare, which we have previously recognized are "caused by the presence of even one such" establishment.[38]

The logic of *Renton* blurs the difference between secondary effects (previously understood as content neutral) and primary effects (previously understood as content-based). It finds the harm from adult theaters serious enough to regulate irrespective of content neutrality. That is, the content-based status of the ordinance no longer automatically means that the regulations will trigger the highest level of scrutiny, thereby invalidating it. By blurring the primary/secondary-effects distinction, *Renton* potentially permits harms previously excluded because they impermissibly referenced content. The primary/secondary-effects distinction maintains a division between the effects cities may combat (harm to property, economic interests, and community) and the effects cities may not constitutionally address (which would presumably include harm to women).

This distinction between content-neutral secondary and content-based primary effects may seem clear in theory, but in practice the line becomes very thin. For example, why is sexual harassment or prostitution a secondary rather than a primary effect? An increase in sexual harassment or prostitution would seem to be directly related to the effect on the audience watching nude dancing, especially since such effects do not "happen to be associated" with other forms of dancing or nudity of a non-pornographic nature. This raises an important subsidiary question: what counts as a primary effect? Is harm to women considered a primary effect, and, if so, is it the only primary effect?

One is left with the sense that the Supreme Court's distinctions have more to do with language games than reason. Increases in prostitution and sexual harassment in Erie are gender-based effects driven by nude dancing's expressive conduct. Moreover, the Supreme Court overlooks the analytical significance of gender's centrality to nude dancing and in doing so produces a tenuous opinion. The use of the passive voice and the primary/secondary-effects distinction in *Pap's* move us away from the central insights momentarily visible in *Renton*. The passive voice and the primary/secondary-effects distinction disassociate pornography from the adverse effects it causes, and it obfuscates the social reality of pornography as an unequal practice.

While *Pap's* shares continuity with the zoning cases in its further articulation of the secondary effects doctrine, it differs in another significant way. *Pap's*, unlike *Young* and *Renton*, muddles the incidental burdens test with secondary effects, creating more confusion about the regulation of pornography. The Court first articulated the incidental burdens test in *United States v. O'Brien* (1968), upholding the conviction of an anti-war protester for burning his draft card.[39]

The Court reasoned that the law, under which the protester was convicted, targeted the nonspeech conduct elements of the symbolic expression, not the antiwar First Amendment elements. O'Brien was free to express his anti-war message but he had to do so without burning his draft card. Under the *O'Brien* incidental-burdens test, a law passes the content-neutrality threshold if the regulation is within government's constitutional powers to enact; the regulation serves a "substantial government interest"; the regulation is unrelated to the suppression of free expression; and the regulation restricts speech no greater than necessary to achieve government's purpose.

The Court applies the incidental burdens test to *Pap's* in two ways. Firstly, the Court defines nude dancing as symbolic expression, holding that the ban on nudity targets the nonspeech element, not the message of the dancers.[40]

Secondly, the *O'Brien* content-neutrality approach evaluates the nude-dancing ordinance as a secondary effects analysis where government addresses the serious problems associated with nude dancing, not its message.[41]

By applying the incidental burdens doctrine, the Supreme Court underscores two points. One, it highlights that the prohibition on public nudity incidentally regulates rather than proscribes nude dancing's message. Two, it correlates adverse effects with the *conduct* of nude dancing rather than the "erotic" *message*. The public nudity ban certainly has the effect of limiting one particular means of expressing the kind of erotic message being disseminated at *Pap's*. But simply to define what is being banned as the "message" is to assume the conclusion. "We did not analyze *O'Brien* as having enacted a total ban on expression. . . . The state's interest in preventing harmful secondary effects is not related to the suppression of expression."[42]

Put differently, the logic of the two approaches, when combined, leads to the conclusion that it is the *conduct* part of nude dancing rather than the "erotic" *message* that causes effects.

By positing that nude dancing's conduct is not integral to its message, the plurality opinion puts forward a puzzling view of pornography. Yet, pornography is distinctive in comparison to other forms of sexual expression in art or literature precisely because of its sexually explicit conduct. Akhil Reed Amar writes:

> Are graphic sexual performances, whether live or on film, with sights and sounds of real-life actors and actresses, more like words (the pure "speech") of Uncle Tom's Cabin, or more like prostitution itself—sex for sale? In the First Amendment, the document's big ideas revolve around democratic deliberation and the freedom of the human intellect; but today's doctrine seems altogether too focused on g-strings, pasties, and sex flicks . . . [43]

Pornography, then, shares characteristics with both speech and prostitution, which is prohibited conduct. While pornography's mixture of speech and conduct characteristics may appear similar to cases such as *O'Brien* or *Clark v. Community for Creative Non-Violence* (1984), I suggest pornography's message is too inextricably bound with conduct in a way that is disanalogous to burning a draft card in protest.[44]

In the most recent zoning case regulating adult establishments, *City of Los Angeles v. Alameda Books, Inc.* (2002), the Court reaffirmed and extended the conclusions from *Renton*.[45]

In 1977, the City of Los Angeles police department issued a study concluding that concentrations of adult establishments correlated with higher rates of robbery, prostitution, assaults, and thefts.[46]

As a result of the study's conclusions, the city passed an ordinance prohibiting adult establishments from locating within 1,000 feet of another adult business or within 500 feet of a park, school, or religious institution.[47]

By 1983, the city realized that the ordinance created a loophole allowing a concentration of different adult uses under one establishment.[48]

In an effort to close the loophole, the city passed another ordinance prohibiting more than one adult use in the same building or structure.[49]

To pass the new ordinance, Los Angeles relied upon the 1977 land use study conducted by the city police department. Alameda Books, who operated an adult arcade and an adult bookstore, challenged the ordinance as a violation of the First Amendment. The District Court found the 1983 ordinance content-based under a strict scrutiny analysis. The Court of Appeals agreed with the District Court upholding the trial court's ruling for different reasons. [50]

The Court of Appeals found that Los Angeles presented insufficient evidence demonstrating a link between adult establishments and adverse secondary effects. Additionally, the Court of Appeals held that irrespective of whether the 1983 ordinance is content-neutral or content-based, Los Angeles demonstrated no substantial government interest in regulating.

The Supreme Court reversed the Court of Appeals, denying summary judgment on First Amendment grounds and remanding the case for further review. [51]

In the plurality opinion, Justice O'Connor writes that *Renton* declined to establish a high evidentiary bar for municipalities attempting to address the adverse effects associated with adult establishments. *Renton* held a correlational standard reasonable for demonstrating a link between speech and a substantial governmental interest. Justice O'Connor argued that shoddy data or poor reasoning would fail to meet *Renton's* evidentiary bar, but explained that some latitude is to be extended to communities experimenting with ways to address negative effects. [52]

Under the *Alameda* plurality opinion, if respondents decline to challenge the city's theory or factual findings, courts will apply intermediate rather than strict scrutiny.

Justice Kennedy's concurrence, however, clarifies an ongoing source of confusion in the zoning cases. According to Justice Kennedy, the earlier Court misled in characterizing the Renton zoning ordinance as content-neutral. [53]

Put differently, the idea that the Renton ordinance was content neutral was a fiction. Nonetheless, Justice Kennedy continues that *Renton's* central holding, even if the ordinance was content based, was sound. *Renton* tells us that the secondary effects doctrine allows for regulations that reduce adverse impacts as long as the overall amount of pornographic speech is not substantially reduced. Courts need not perseverate over whether the ordinance drawn is content-neutral or content-based provided that sufficient alternative avenues of communication are available.

THE CIVIL RIGHTS REGULATIVE APPROACH:
AMERICAN BOOKSELLERS V. HUDNUT (1985)

In 1985, a lower federal court considered the constitutionality of a new type of regulation on pornography, one that aimed to define pornography as a civil rights violation, meaning that pornography discriminates against women. The case, *American Booksellers, Inc. v. Hudnut* (1985), defined pornography as a gender-based practice producing gender-based harms.[54]

The ordinance defines pornography in the following manner:

1. Women are presented as sexual objects who enjoy pain or humiliation; or
2. Women are presented as sexual objects who experience sexual pleasure in being raped; or
3. Women are presented as sexual objects tied up or cut up or mutilated or bruised or physically hurt, or as dismembered or truncated or fragmented or severed into body parts; or
4. Women are presented as being penetrated by objects or animals; or
5. Women are presented in scenarios of degradation, injury abasement, torture, shown as filthy or inferior, bleeding, bruised, or hurt in a context that makes these conditions sexual; or
6. Women are presented as sexual objects for domination, conquest, violation, exploitation, possession, or use, or through postures or positions of servility or submission or display.[55]

Pornography, in the ordinance, is clearly defined with reference to its actual content. The ordinance, despite recognizing that pornography largely objectifies women, noted that the ordinance extended to men, children or transexuals if they were used in any of the ways noted in paragraphs 1-6.[56]

The ordinance seeks to punish those who traffic in pornography; coerce others to perform in pornographic material; and/or force pornography on others.[57]

Moreover, the ordinance provides the right of civil damages for those who can prove that a physical attack was directly caused by a specific piece of pornography.[58]

The civil rights ordinance significantly differed from the traditional approach to regulating pornography, namely obscenity law. Courts consider material obscene if it is offensive and prurient.[59]

In the case of obscenity law, any cultural product—books, magazines, performances, or movies—must be analyzed as a whole.[60]

Under obscenity law, courts may not declare a cultural product obscene by focusing on a problematic part of the overall product. If the cultural product has any literary, artistic, political, or scientific value, even with specific problematic depictions, it is constitutionally protected.

The community determines whether the material constitutes obscenity rather than a national standard set by some faraway courts.

As Judge Frank Easterbrook notes in his opinion in *Hudnut*, the Indianapolis ordinance makes no provision for assessing the material as a whole or considering whether the material has any significant literary, artistic, political, or scientific value. For the writers of the Indianapolis ordinance, noted feminists Catharine MacKinnon and Andrea Dworkin, the cultural value of the material matters little if it discriminates against women.[61]

The Indianapolis ordinance rejected the framework of offensiveness and prurience as well. Both "offensiveness" and "prurience" suggest a prudishness, moral judgement and uptight sensibility about sexuality, nudity, and differences in sexual orientation. This language of "offensiveness" and "prurience" defining obscenity doctrine lends fodder to a familiar American historical narrative, one that depicts Americans as burdened by puritanical prudishness about sex.[62]

Within this narrative, any challenge to the puritanical narrative is progressive and liberatory.

Yet the civil rights approach to regulating pornography interrogates that purportedly transgressive counternarrative about overthrowing sexual puritanism. MacKinnon and Dworkin's civil damages ordinance begins with different conceptual underpinnings about pornography, challenging the idea that pornography is coterminous with sexual liberation. Put more strongly, the introduction of the civil rights approach to regulating pornography suggests that the assumptions underlying obscenity law are wrong and miss the central concern about pornography. Pornography is neither offensive nor liberatory. The civil damage ordinance makes clear that the primary legal concern about pornography is that it discriminates against women.

Catharine MacKinnon and Andrea Dworkin develop the civil rights approach to regulating pornography for yet another reason. In their view, pornography of the sort defined in the ordinance is hegemonic: it is culturally ubiquitous. MacKinnon goes so far as to say that given this cultural hegemony, pornography is mistaken as sex.[63]

If pornography defines our cultural understanding of sex, then obscenity law has a hollow core. It will be unable to recognize any pornographic material as either offensive or prurient. Nor, given the role of technology and digital communication, does it make sense to rely upon a community standard. The hegemony of the pornography industry, in this view, is national in reach, thereby erasing different community standards with reference to judging pornographic content. Under this understanding of inegalitarian pornography as culturally hegemonic, we need no longer delude ourselves that pornography is marginalized and unpopular and that producers are fighting against the repressive powers codified in obscenity law. In short, we do not need to produce more inegalitarian pornography to throw off the shackles of our puritanical sexual repression. Pornography has overtaken the public sphere.[64]

As Michel Foucault notes:

> For a long time, the story goes, we supported a Victorian regime, and we continue to be dominated by it even today. Thus the image of the imperial prude is emblazoned on our retrained, mute, and hypocritical sexuality. . . . What is peculiar to modern societies, in fact, is not that they consigned sex to a shadow existence, but that they dedicated themselves to speaking of it *ad infinitum*, while exploiting it as *the* secret.[65]

The starting assumptions of the Indianapolis ordinance recognize the inversion of power in our cultural narrative about the Victorian prude. Those claiming they are waging a liberatory war on sexuality from a disadvantaged position are not the minority, but the orthodoxy. In Foucault's language, we speak of sexual repression even as we incessantly talk about sexuality. Moreover, one rather narrow version of sexuality has come to dominate and stifle all others.[66]

While MacKinnon and Dworkin have criticized the poststructural philosophical approach Foucault represents, his insights here about the "repression" of a highly successful and hegemonic form of sexual discourse provides another analytical window to assess the feminist case against pornography.

While the civil damage approach throws into relief the problematic assumptions underlying obscenity law and the changing context in which it ineffectively operates, we are left to determine if the civil rights approach can fill a void. Judge Easterbrook provides an answer in striking down the ordinance as impermissibly content-based. In striking down the Indianapolis ordinance, Judge Easterbrook combines among the most compelling and comprehensive arguments defending unpopular speech in First Amendment jurisprudence. In his view, the ordinance amounts to thought control in attempting to impose an orthodoxy on sexually explicit cultural materials. Under the rationale of the ordinance, any material depicting sexual equality is protected while other unequal depictions are invalidated. Government, he argues, should not have power to prohibit the ideas it finds false. Truth is not a precondition for First Amendment protection. Free speech, in fact, is an ally of those seeking political change. Government ought to be neutral in evaluating speech, protecting the speech we hate in order to safeguard the speech we love.

Moreover, the ordinance's definition of pornography fails to provide guidelines distinguishing between Homer's *Iliad*, for example, and *Debbie Does Dallas*. Both present women as submissive objects available for male sexual pleasure. Nor is pornographic speech properly thought of as "low value" under the conceptual underpinnings of the ordinance. To the extent that pornography causes the harms its opponents describe, it is profoundly meaningful. It "influences social relations and politics on a grand scale, [that] it controls attitudes at home and in the legislature."[67]

Finally, Judge Easterbrook notes that pornography may depict women in pain, but "the image of pain is not necessarily pain." Actors dramatize, imitate, perform, and pretend. Acting stages reality; it does not constitute reality.

Nonetheless, in the opinion, Judge Easterbrook makes three concessions to the opponents of pornography. First, he concedes that pornography likely does what opponents say that it does.

> Therefore we accept the premises of this legislation. Depictions of subordination tend to perpetuate subordination. The subordinate status of women in turn leads to affront and lower pay at work, insult and injury at home, battery and rape on the streets. In the language of the legislature, "pornography is central in creating and maintaining sex as a basis of discrimination. Pornography is a systematic practice of exploitation and subordination based on sex which differentially harms women. The bigotry and contempt it produces, with the acts of aggression it fosters, harm women's opportunities for equality and rights [of all kinds]." Indianapolis Code 16-1 (a) (2)[68]

In this passage, Judge Easterbrook acknowledges that speech operates in the manner MacKinnon and Dworkin suggest. Pornography maintains inequality and subordination on the basis of sex. It produces antipathy for women and feeds aggression. Second, Judge Easterbrook allows that opponents may indeed have cause for concern about the nature of sexual responses and the susceptibility of those primal reactions to the ideological message of pornography. He states:

> Sexual responses often are unthinking responses, and the association of sexual arousal with the subordination of women therefore may have a substantial effect.[69]

Yet despite the acknowledgment that viewers might be particularly vulnerable to the subordinating message in pornography, Judge Easterbrook argues that all "cultural stimuli provoke unconscious responses." If we permit the regulation of one type of speech that negatively conditions us, then we would be on the slippery slope to the end of the free speech.[70]

We will more closely examine Judge Easterbrook's rather startling concession to feminist opponents of pornography in later chapters.

The third concession, although qualified, acknowledges that the Court has previously balanced the value of free speech versus the cost of its restriction.[71]

Nonetheless, when the Court presents such a decision-making calculus, it does so by weighing the category of the speech (not the content) against its potential value.[72]

The logic of this statement is precarious and its persuasiveness depends upon uncritical acceptance of the idea that one evaluates content to determine if speech falls into a proscribable category like fighting words, yet in evaluating that content to determine categorization, one does not affirm or reject the speech's message.[73]

The idea that determining the category of speech is separate from evaluating the content of speech is one that the secondary-effects doctrine problematically relies upon.

At this point, the book describes two different ways to regulate pornography. One set of cases, the zoning and nude dancing cases, zone in an effort to combat secondary effects. The other case, *Hudnut*, never made it to the Supreme Court. Instead, a federal court of appeals determined that the regulatory method, a civil rights approach, violated the First Amendment. The book also describes how and why the civil damage ordinance in *Hudnut* is significantly different than obscenity law. Yet, the way I present the cases is not without critique and requires some explanation and defense before moving toward a direct comparison between the two sets, the zoning cases and the civil rights case.

The tutored critic will rightly note that the zoning cases regulate problem land use, namely adult establishments, not pornography, which law understands as speech. The police powers doctrine, derived from the Tenth Amendment, provides states with a plenary power to regulate in the general welfare. Problem land use regulation through zoning clearly falls within the state's charge to regulate in the public good. The secondary effects doctrine buttresses these police powers and the constitutionality of zoning by targeting secondary effects, or put differently, those effects indirectly related to the content sold inside adult establishments. *Hudnut*, a critic would say, is entirely different and incomparable to the zoning cases. *Hudnut* attempts to regulate pornography, not the land use of adult establishments. *Hudnut* targets the primary effects, specifically, those that seem directly related to the content of pornographic speech. The civil damage ordinance defines pornography with direct reference to its content. As a result, law properly categorizes zoning regulations under zoning law and the civil damage ordinance under First Amendment jurisprudence.

Before responding directly to the substance of those fair criticisms, a discussion of the method that permits such comparison of two differently categorized sets of cases is worthy of elaboration. In order to compare the zoning cases to the civil rights case, the book attempts to make the familiar strange.[74]

Philosopher Ludwig Wittgenstein makes this point in a different way. He writes:

> The aspect of things that are most important for us are hidden because of their simplicity and familiarity. [75]

To revisit the familiar with a critical eye—the separate regulatory categorizations of the zoning cases and the civil damage ordinance—the book juxtaposes the past with the present and "decontextualize[s] the obvious only to recontextualize it from a different vantage point."[76]

This means that the book will compare cases that law considers to be significantly different because of the way law categorizes the cases. In this argument, the validity of that deferential legal categorization will be interrogated and challenged rather than assumed. Specifically, the book will compare the zoning and nude dancing cases to *Hudnut* even though, for example, some of the zoning cases such as *Young* predate the feminist critique of pornography. Nonetheless, the purpose of the comparison is to reframe the central issues, to highlight the overlooked gender-based harms, and to move toward a different understanding of pornography and the First Amendment. To re-examine these cases from a different time and vantage point allows a philosophical opening in which to argue that law has missed the central framing issue about inegalitarian pornography: it remains a gender-based practice producing gender-based harms to the community and specifically to women. Nor is inegalitarian pornography simply speech unconnected to the maintenance of gender inequality.[77]

A direct comparison to the two sets of cases promises to throw into relief the ideologically uneven and contradictory reasons law provides to regulate and understand pornography. It will help us to see what we are willing and unwilling to say about pornography as a practice: it is at once liberatory, transgressive, commercial, oppressive, patriarchal and hegemonic.[78]

It will tell us about our ideologically libertarian understanding of free speech doctrine, a doctrine that demands an ahistorical and acontextual understanding of free speech.

Let us approach the critical questions about the way the book presents the two sets of cases directly rather than through a removed discussion of philosophical method. The crucial question posed in plain language is, do we really accept that the zoning and nude dancing cases are not about pornography and free speech? Moreover, in what ways are the zoning cases similar and different from *Hudnut*? As mentioned earlier, critics may argue that the aim and scope of the cases are substantially different. The ordinance in *Hudnut* provided civil damages to women victimized by pornography, while *Young* and *Renton* simply zoned adult establishments. According to this view, the former has a more chilling effect on speech than the latter. Law says *Hudnut* is about speech while the zoning and nude dancing cases are about the state's power to zone to protect the public welfare. Nevertheless, as Amsterdam and Bruner argue, similarity hinges on the axis of comparison one chooses. Determining that similarity is a matter of one's choice of criteria, not nature or inevitability.[79]

One remarkable similarity recognized in the book is that both sets of cases acknowledge that pornography unequivocally harms the community, and, more specifically, women.

Part of the critique, then, of the laws regulating pornography entails an interrogation of categories. Categories are made, not determined in advance. Category choices reveal our values or larger images of reality.[80]

According to Amsterdam and Bruner, for example, underlying categorical divisions between the so-called first and third worlds are notions of progress, modernization, and wealth. Those elements are used in place of different measures such as familial cohesiveness or the vibrancy of informal economies. In law, we distinguish between serious and less serious criminal offenses, acknowledging a difference between murder and robbery. The differing categorizations carry separate sentences, each varying with the severity of the crime.[81]

Categories imply certain commitments, assumptions, and choices. They assign meaning; they authorize some speakers over others. They affect the kinds of analogies we take seriously and, importantly for free speech and pornography, they determine definitions and the kind of evidence deemed sufficient.[82]

While this is inevitable, categories sometimes appear natural and beyond scrutiny. The book will critically examine law's categories as part of an attempt to demonstrate and resolve the inherent contradictions that our culture holds about pornography.

Critics may raise other questions about comparing the two sets of cases. The zoning and the nude dancing cases use the term "effects" while *Hudnut* uses the term "harm." The zoning cases reference the term "adult theater" unlike *Hudnut*, which refers to "pornography." The book argues that while the terms differ semantically, the meanings do not. Terms such as "adult establishments" replace "pornography" and "effects" replaces "harm." If we suspend law's sophisticated distinctions in the zoning and nude dancing cases, one recognizes that adult establishments sell pornography and peripheral effects such as increased rates of sexual harassment are primary gender-based effects.

In terms of the dissimilarity between the two sets of cases, these differences enable law to regulate pornography in the zoning cases without acknowledging it. What do the differences entail? Specifically, in the zoning cases, gender drops out as analytically relevant in describing the practice of pornography and in characterizing the harms generated by the practice. Adult establishments appeal to all adults even though sales data from the industry itself tells us otherwise. Harms like increased rape rates and sexual harassment rates are repositioned as general community harms alongside of property devaluation and the rise of commercial dead zones. Moreover, when the law categorizes these restrictions as regulations about zoning rather than free speech, the evidentiary standards to demonstrate "effects" are laxer. Under zoning law, municipalities must show a correlation between effects and adult establishments rather than causality, as in the case of *Hudnut*. The Court's failure to accurately and precisely define adult establishments and nude dancing as a gendered practice is a classic Wittgensteinian language game, and it has profound cultural, economic, political, and legal consequences.

The book retains the insight that the pornography debate is really an epistemological debate. Categorizing is an indispensable part of human cognition, subject to our hidden assumptions, biases, and prejudgments. Yet, such a recognition of human fallibilism in no way seeks to jettison the concept of objectivity or neutrality in the process of public justification. Nonetheless, "justification of knowledge" is a "social affair," even in law.[83]

We have no transcendent view outside of our historical and cultural context. This means our categories, concepts, and knowledge are fallibilistic and subject to revision. We sometimes need to change our assumptions and refine our particular conceptions with changing social circumstances. This is true of concepts in the study of history, biology, or law. In the case of race, *Brown v. Board of Education* (1954) reversed *Plessy v. Ferguson* (1896) because we came to understand that separate was not equal.[84]

The idea is not to forgo notions of neutrality or objectivity but to ruthlessly scrutinize the criteria we set for our categories and concepts, recognizing that the criteria may change over time as our understanding of pornography, for example, changes.[85]

The concern about criteria separates the book's epistemological approach from a Kuhnian sociology-of-knowledge approach.[86]

The book not only concerns the resistance of free speech categories to change but also is about the criteria law uses to categorize and define pornography. It draws attention to who sets the criteria and whether they are based on the experiences of a particular privileged group.[87]

In free speech doctrine, for example, the standard for "fighting words" is which words would make a man raise his fists.[88]

That standard, which permits regulations on certain kinds of speech, is based on the male experience. Under this standard, women injured by assaultive or defaming speech are effectively discounted for failing to react violently. These categories directly influence the process of public justification or what reasons the larger polity finds legitimate.

CONCLUSION

The purpose of the chapter is to attempt to examine the zoning cases and compare them to the *Hudnut* case from a distancing vantage point—one that attempts to make "the familiar strange." To be clear, the chapter is not making a case that law should utilize zoning as a method to regulate pornography. Rather, the comparison between the zoning approach and the civil damage approach to regulating pornography sheds light on unscrutinized assumptions. The categorical distinctions law makes in distinguishing the two sets of cases is neither inevitable nor natural but instead rests upon a value choice. In comparing the two sets of cases, the chapter proposes to select a different criteria for comparison: namely, both sets of cases regulate pornography even if one case calls the practice by a different name (adult establishments). Both cases identify problematic "adverse effects" or "harms," and some of those effects or harms are gender-based whether explicitly acknowledged or not. This "sociology approach" to analyzing the two different approaches to regulating pornography should throw into relief which narratives, understandings, or truths that law validates about pornography over others. As advocated in the preface, as an epistemic matter, the gap between the two cases and the understandings they validate should close. *Hudnut* provides the normative foundation for regulating the inegalitarian variant of pornography—its gender-based harms—while the zoning cases reflect the ways we actually regulate pornography by distancing the practice from the centrality of gender. Such a discussion exposes the underlying values and logic of free speech doctrine, zoning law, and definitions of pornography, hopefully opening those categorical choices to the possibility of rupture. Such a refinement of free speech categories would allow for a more accurate definition of the most problematic forms of sexually explicit speech and enable the Court to face up to the de facto findings of gender-based harms in the zoning and nude dancing cases, and thereby better balancing the First Amendment with the Fourteenth Amendment.

NOTES

1. *Miller v. California*, 413 U.S. 15 (U.S. 1973).
2. *Young v. American Mini-Theatres, Inc.*, 427 U.S. 50 (1976).
3. *Young*, 52.
4. A review of law review articles suggests some discrepancy about whether a majority of the Supreme Court characterized the ordinance as content-based. *Young* is a plurality decision. Mark Bernardin, "The Law and Politics of Dancing: Barnes v. Glen Theatre and the Regulation of Striptease Dance," *Hawaii Law Review* 14 (Fall 1992), 925-48. Bernardin argues that the majority of the Justices found Detroit's ordinance content-based. David L. Hudson, "The Secondary Effects Doctrine: The Evisceration of First Amendment Freedoms," *Washburn Law Journal* 37 (Fall 1997), 925-48. Hudson notes that the Court *analyzed* the ordinance as content-neutral. Andrea Oser, "Motivation Analysis in Light of Renton," *Columbia Law Review* 87 (March 1987), 344-67. Oser states that eight of the nine Justices thought the ordinance was content-based. Yet Justice Stevens's plurality opinion strikes a balance somewhere in between and indicates that the ordinance is based on content, as any proscribable category of speech is, but is not content-based in the sense that it explicitly targets the message.
5. Geoffrey R. Stone, "Content Regulation and the First Amendment," 25 *WM. & MARY L. REV.* 189 (1983) [hereinafter Content Regulation]; Geoffrey R. Stone, "Restrictions of Speech Because of its Content: The Peculiar Case of Subject-Matter Re-

strictions," 46 *U. CHI. L. REV.* 81 (1978) and Geoffrey R. Stone, "Content-Neutral Restrictions," 54 U. CHI. L. REV. 46 (1987) .

6. Erwin Chermerinsky, "Content-Neutrality as a Central Problem of Freedom of Speech: Problems in the Supreme Court's Application," 74 *S. Cal. L. Rev.* 49. (November 2000).

7. *Jacobson v. Massachusetts*, 197 U.S. 11 (1905).

8. *Young*, 78 (Powell, J., Concurring).

9. David L. Hudson, Jr., "The Secondary Effects Doctrine: The Evisceration of First Amendment Freedoms," 37 *Washburn Law Journal*. 55. (Fall, 1997).

10. Hudson, Jr., 37 Washburn L.J. 55. (Fall, 1997).

11. Hudson. A secondary effect on the neighborhood that "happen[s] to be associated with" a form of speech is, of course, critically different from "the direct impact of speech on its audience." *Boos v. Barry*, 485 U.S., at 320-321.

12. Hudson, Jr.

13. *City of Renton v. Playtime Theatres* , 475 U.S. 41 (1986).

14. *Renton*, 44.

15. Harvard Law Review, 1910. See Kimberly K. Smith, "Zoning Adult Entertainment: A Reassessment of Renton," *California Law Review* 79 (January 1991): 128. See Smith for reference to *Young's* secondary effects footnote.

16. *Renton* 47.

17. *Renton*.

18. *Tinker v. Des Moines Independent Community School District*, 393 U.S. 503 (1969).

19. Justice Rehnquist cites two other cases, which support his reasoning in *Renton*. Those two cases are *Procunier v. Martinez*, 416 U.S. 396 (1974) and *Greer v. Spock*, 424 U.S. 828 (1976). In both of these cases the Supreme Court tries to find a balancing standard of review to determine when regulations furthering legitimate government interests may be upheld even if they incidentally restrict speech.

20. Justice Rehnquist quoting Justice Powell in *Young. Renton*, 49.

21. Erwin Chermerinsky, "Content Neutrality as a Central Problem of Freedom of Speech: Problems in the Supreme Court's Application," *Southern California Law Review* 74 (November 2000), 61.

22. Cherminsky.

23. David L. Hudson, "The Secondary Effects Doctrine: The Evisceration of First Amendment Freedoms," *Washburn Law Journal* 37 (Fall 1997), 55-94, 66.

24. Lisa Malmer, "Nude Dancing and the First Amendment," *University of Cincinnati Law Review* 59 (1991), 1308.

25. *Renton*, 54.

26. *Barnes v. Glen Theatre, Inc.*, 501 U.S. 560 (1991). *City of Erie. v. Pap's A.M., tdba "Kandyland"* 529 U.S. 277 (2000) No. 98-1161. Hereafter referred to as *Pap's*.

27. *Pap's*.

28. *Young v. American Mini-Theatres*, 427 U.S. 50 (1976), *City of Renton v. Playtime Theatres*, 475 U.S. 41 (1986), and *Barnes v.Glen Theatre, Inc.*, 501 U.S. 560 (1991).

29. *Pap's*, 290.

30. *Pap's*, J. Scalia concurrence, 308.

31. *Pap's, 308.*

32. *Pap's, 308.*

33. Michael McBride, "*Pap's A.M. v. City of Erie*: The Wrong Route to the Right Decision," *Akron Law Review* 33 (2000), 307.

34. *Young*, 55.

35. *Renton*, 50.

36. Government may regulate adult establishments for content-based reasons if it provides evidence supporting a compelling state interest and if the regulations incidentally effect speech. Government must present evidence that it does have a compelling state interest and that such an interest outweighs free speech rights.

37. Erie's Public Nudity Ordinance in *Pap's*, 290.

38. *Pap's*, 291. *Renton* quoted in *Pap's*.

39. *United States v. O'Brien*, 391 U.S. 367 (1968).

40. McBride, 296.

41. McBride.

42. *Pap's*, part 293-94.

43. Akhil Reed Amar, "The Supreme Court, 1999 Term—Foreword: The Document and The Doctrine," *Harvard Law Review*, 114 (November 2000), 60 102n.

44. *Clark v. Community for Creative Non-Violence*, 468 U.S. 288 (1984).

45. *City of Los Angeles v. Alameda Books, Inc.* 535 U.S. 425 (2002).

46. According to the 1977 report, "robberies increased 3 times faster and prostitution 15 times faster in Hollywood than citywide (435)."

47. L.A. enacted the ordinance based on the 1977 report in 1978.

48. "The ordinance the city enacted, however, directed that 'the distance between any two adult entertainment businesses shall be measured in a straight line . . . from the closest exterior structural wall of each business.' Subsequent to enactment, the city realized that this method of calculating distances created a loophole permitting the concentration of multiple adult enterprises in a single structure." (J. O'Connor 432).

49. Respondents, *Alameda Books, Inc. and Highland books, Inc.*, rent and sell sexually oriented products in the same commercial space. "There are no physical distinctions between the different operations within each establishment and each establishment has only one entrance. Respondents concede they are openly operating in violation of the city's Code, as amended (J. O'Connor, 432)."

50. The Court of Appeals 9th Circuit.

51. The respondents sued for "declaratory and injunctive relief to prevent enforcement of the ordinance. At issue in this case is count I of the complaint, which alleges a facial violation of the First Amendment (J. O'Connor 432)." The Supreme Court in agreeing to hear the Alameda case seeks "to clarify the standard for determining whether an ordinance serves a substantial government interest under Renton, supra. (J. O'Connor, 433)."

52. *Alameda*, 439. J. Kennedy reiterates the point that municipalities must be given latitude to experiment with the elimination of secondary effects (p. 451).

53. *Alameda*, 48. J. O'Connor gives us a different understanding of Renton. She holds that Renton didn't ban adult theaters altogether and was merely a time, place and manner restriction. Additionally, she argued that the Court then considered whether the ordinance was content-neutral or content-based, finding the former because it addressed effects not content. Finally, she understands Renton to hold that the city must show a substantial government interest in regulating adult establishments while maintaining for reasonable alternative avenues of communication (J. O'Connor, 435). J. Kennedy: *Renton v. Playtime Theatres, Inc.*, 475 U.S. 41 (1986), described a similar ordinance as "content neutral," and I agree with the dissent that the designation is imprecise (*Alameda*, 444). J. Kennedy describes the Renton ordinance as a fiction on p. 448.

54. *American Booksellers, Inc. v. Hudnut*, 771 F. 2d 323 (7th Cir. 1985).

55. *Hudnut*, 324

56. *Hudnut*.

57. *Hudnut*, 325.

58. *Hudnut*.

59. *Brockett v. Spokane Arcades, Inc.* 472 U.S. 491 (1985). See discussion in *Hudnut*. Prurient refers to an unhealthy interest in sex or unhealthy sexual desires or proclivities.

60. *Miller v. California*, 413 U.S. 15 (1973). See a discussion of *Miller* in *Hudnut*.

61. Catharine A. MacKinnon, *Only Words* (Cambridge, MA: Harvard University Press, 2002). Catharine A. MacKinnon and Andrea Dworkin, *In Harm's Way: the Pornography Civil Rights Hearings* (Cambridge, MA: Harvard University Press, 1998). Catharine A. MacKinnon, "Pornography, Civil Rights, and Speech," *Harvard Civil Rights* 1 (1985), 21.

62. Ronald Dworkin, "Pornography and the New Puritans: Letters From Andrea Dworkin and Others," *The New York Times* (May 3, 1992), https://www.nytimes.com/1992/05/03/books/l-pornography-and-the-new-puritans-letters-from-andrea-dworkin-and-others-720092.html.

63. MacKinnon, *Only Words*.

64. Ariel Levy, *Female Chauvinist Pigs: Women and the Rise of Raunch Culture* (New York: Free Press, 2005).

65. Michel Foucault, *The History of Sexuality* (Vintage, 1990). The first part of the quote begins on p. 3 while the second part of the quote begins on p. 35.

66. Andrea Dworkin, *Intercourse* (New York Free Press, 1987).

67. *Hudnut*, 331.

68. *Hudnut*, 329.

69. *Hudnut*. 330.

70. Catharine A. MacKinnon, *Only Words* (Cambridge, MA: Harvard University Press, 2002).

71. *Hudnut*. 332.

72. Judge Easterbrook drawing from John Hart Ely, "Flag Desecration: A Case Study in the Roles of Categorization and Balancing in First Amendment Analysis," 88 *Harvard Law Review* 1482 (1975).

73. See Justice Scalia's opinion in *R.A.V. v. St. Paul*, 505 U.S. 377 (1992).

74. Anthony G. Amsterdam and Jerome Bruner, *Minding the Law: How Courts Rely on Storytelling and How Their Stories Change the Way We Understand the Law—and Ourselves* (Cambridge & London: Harvard University Press, 2000), 1.

75. Ludwig Wittgenstein quoted in *Foucault and His Interlocutors*, ed. Arnold I. Davidson (Chicago & London: Harvard University Press, 2000), 1.

76. Amsterdam and Bruner, 4.

77. This approach borrows from the hermeneutic tradition where we bring certain preoccupations to the interpretations of texts. Law does so too as Amsterdam and Bruner point out.

78. Pornography does produce a multiplicity of meanings, and anti-pornography feminists have sometimes neglected to be attentive to the potential range of meanings. At the same time, pro-sex defenders of pornography have also ignored the oppressive elements of inegalitarian pornography of the sort that reinforce gender inequality in uncritical celebration of the transgressive. See Hester, 2015.

79. Amsterdam and Bruner, 19-53.

80. Amsterdam and Bruner, 9.

81. Amsterdam and Bruner, 22-23.

82. Linda Alcoff, "How is Epistemology Political?," in *Radical Philosophy: Tradition, Counter-Tradition, Politics*, ed. Roger S. Gottlieb (Philadelphia: Temple University Press, 1993), 70-71. Also Amsterdam and Bruner, 26–37.

83. Satya P. Mohanty, *Literary Theory and the Claims of History: Postmodernism, Objectivity, Multicultural Politics* (Ithaca & London: Cornell University Press, 1997), 149.

84. *Brown v. Board of Education (I)*, 347 U.S. 483 (1954) and *Plessy v. Ferguson*, 163 U.S. 537 (1896).

85. This is Mohanty's argument in *Literary Theory and the Claims of History*. See also Linda Martin Alcoff, *Real Knowing: New Versions of the Coherence Theory* (Ithaca & London: Cornell University Press, 1996).

86. Linda Alcoff makes this distinction in, "How is Epistemology Political?" in *Radical Philosophy*.

87. Alcoff, *Real Knowing*, 25. Also Matsuda, "Public Response to Racist Speech: Considering the Victim's Story," in *Words That Wound*. Carol Smart, *Feminism and the Power of the Law* (London & New York: Routledge, 1989).

88. Matsuda, 35. Charles R. Lawrence III, "If He Hollers Let Him Go: Regulating Racist Speech on Campus," in *Words That Wound: Critical Race Theory, Assaultive Speech, and the First Amendment*, eds. Mari J. Matsuda and others (Boulder, San Francisco & Oxford: Westview Press, 1993), 69.

TWO

Language Games and the Zoning and Nude Dancing Cases

This chapter continues on an analytical path laid out in the preface. It lingers on the language used to describe pornographic practices in the zoning and nude dancing cases. The language in these cases is clearly different than the descriptions used in the *Hudnut* civil damage case. The language deployed in the zoning and nude dancing cases removes gendered descriptions whereas the civil damage ordinance in *Hudnut* highlights the place of gender. While this submersion of gender may seem like a banal insight, its significance is rooted in the very notion of Wittgenstein's language games. Ludwig Wittgenstein's work helps us to focus upon what words do within a context in order to determine meaning.[1] For Wittgenstein, language has no concrete meaning: meaning may only be derived within the context of a community's rules, practices, and way of life. Language is a testament, then, to the way we live: it is the constitution of our reality.[2] In what ways does the legal discourse in the zoning and nude dancing cases socially construct meaning around the practice of pornography? What does it make transparent and what does it hide? Unpacking the language games at play in the use of phrases such as "adult establishments," the description of nude dancing as "erotic," and the elaboration of the adverse effects of adult establishments as mainly harmful to property will help us to see what legal concepts and the discourse on pornography hopes to obscure—its gendered nature. The meanings hidden in the banality of the commonplace, unscrutinized assumptions should be highlighted and considered.

At this point, several important issues should be addressed about pornography and the claim that it remains a gendered practice. First, statistics tell us that women are increasingly viewing pornography. One of the main pornography websites, Pornhub, recently reported that as many as 29 percent of pornography accessed on their site in 2018 was retrieved by women. While acknowledging the significance of the 29 percent access rate, we should remember that Pornhub is not the only pornographic website available.[3] Other pornographic websites not only exist but cater to more violent, degrading, and misogynistic tastes. The statistics for those sites remain unassessed. The Pornhub statistics are limited in another way. Those statistics do not tell us the length of time spent on videos, whether viewers accessed the video for pleasure or curiousity, and whether the clicks represent repeated clicks rather than new viewers. Nonetheless, while the Pornhub statistic has limitations, we should note that 29 percent is certainly significant and poses challenges for the claim that pornography is gendered, particularly if women increasingly access pornography as entertainment.

Second, with the emergence of porn studies, scholars within that field have highlighted the evolving diversity of subgenres within porn emphasizing their liberating and transgressive dimensions.[4] Pornography, then, is not monolithic. Since the 1970s, the genre of pornography has grown, introducing more diverse representations of sexuality. Porn studies scholars often characterize the past debate in the 1970s and 1980s between pro-sex and anti-pornography feminists as contentious and polarizing, and specifically contend that anti-pornography feminists have a simplistic and reductive understanding of pornography and harm.[5] I want to acknowledge these claims from the pro-sex feminist side. As Helen Hester in *Beyond Explicit* asserts, a great deal of new material within pornography is politically engaged, "innovative and interesting."[6] Yet Hester, along with scholars such as Susanna Paasonen, also recognized that it is not only the anti-pornography side that has demonstrated polemicism in the debate about pornography.

While recognizing the evolving subgenres within pornography, some of which may indeed demonstrate real substantive, politically engaged challenges to heteronormative patriarchy, scholars such as Paasonen, Hester, and Lehman also maintain that not all pornographic material is radical, disruptive, progressive, and liberatory, as largely celebrated in porn studies.[7] Instead, such scholars hope to provide some balance to an overheated debate on both sides—the pro-sex and anti-porn side. While recognizing that increasing numbers of women watch pornography and that pornography as a genre is more diverse than in the past, this book attempts to address the specifically inegalitarian degrading and misogynistic variety as a problematic subcategory and emphasizes the hegemony of that inegalitarian variety in our culture. While the diversity and transgressiveness of some of the new porn available reflects a welcome change, it remains a small subgenre rather than the mainstay of the industry.

To be clear, several reasons may explain the perceived increase in women accessing a greater amount of pornography. As referenced above, the greater diversity of pornography available may cater specifically to female desires, broadening its appeal to previously untapped demographics. Ariel Levy's book *Female Chauvinist Pigs: Women and the Rise of Raunch Culture* raises a different explanation for the rise of female viewership of porn. According to Levy's argument, women are socialized in a culture saturated with the sexualization and objectification of women.[8] If one takes the notion of social construction seriously, then, as the sexual objectification of women becomes ubiquitous, so would an increasing identification with that hegemonic sexualized cultural ideal among both women and men. In fact, Levy's book chronicles the way in which younger women increasingly identify and take part in the objectification of other women without recognizing the adverse effects such objectification might mean for themselves. Nor does such a claim mean that men aren't objectified by pornography. Indeed they are, but different bodies have different histories with different consequences. Moreover, women may, in effect, internalize and come to desire those hegemonic depictions of inegalitarian sexuality.

Thus, we have two potentially counterveiling points explaining the increase in women's interest in porn—one potentially progressive and the other potentially retrogressive—yet none undermine the claim that the most problematic variety of pornography—the inegalitarian variant—remains gendered and harms women. To summarize, on the one hand, women may be accessing more porn because it has diversified and created scenarios of mutuality that especially appeal to women. On the other hand, there is the potentially countervailing point: the greater the cultural hegemony of inegalitarian porn, the more we are socialized by it and operate within its confines. Inegalitarian porn, in this view, shapes our desires, creating the very subjectivity upon which we may then be socially constructed.

In the pages that follow, the chapter will dissect the law's language and point to conflicting justifications upholding regulations on pornography in the zoning and nude dancing cases. Although the law in these cases upholds the regulation of pornography, the Supreme Court calls the practice by a different name: "adult entertainment." The key question animating the chapter is the following: what is the law willing and unwilling to say about pornography at this historical juncture? The chapter contends that the cases say too little about the centrality of gender to the practice of the inegalitarian variant of pornography. It is this insight which is central in the constitutionally invalidated civil rights approach to pornography in *American Booksellers v. Hudnut* (1985).

The critique that follows addresses three dimensions of the cases: (1) the definition of "adult establishments" in the zoning cases; (2) the description of nude dancing as "erotic"; and (3) the obfuscation of gender-based effects. The goal is to apply insights from critical and literary theory to "expose the particular gaps or unreflective dead spots" in the cases.[9]

This section scrutinizes implicit assumptions and analyzes the language describing the practice of pornography, the adverse effects of pornography, the place of gender in inegalitarian pornography, and the principles of free speech square with the empirical dimensions of the practice. Further, it analyzes whether they confirm or contradict broader cultural understandings about pornography.[10] The purpose is to expose contradictions previously unseen and subject these distinctions to rupture and revision.

DEFINING ADULT ESTABLISHMENTS

What is an "adult establishment" and what kind of entertainment takes place within one? Although obscenity law directly regulates speech, the Court has held that, like libel and fighting words, the obscene is a constitutionally proscribable category of expression.[11] The zoning approach to regulating pornography differs from the obscenity approach in that the latter's key concern is whether material patently offends the relevant community standards and has no scientific, literary, or political value; the former's key concern is in combating the troublesome side effects of pornography, which are purportedly separable and tangential to pornography's message.[12] However, in obscenity cases, the constitutionality of the material pivots directly on the notion of "offense."[13] *Young* and its progeny consistently avoid the language of "offense."[14] The divergent judicial approaches raise the question of whether the local ordinances at issue in the zoning and nude dancing cases regulate pornography at all. In fact, zoning regulations speak exclusively of "adult establishments" or adult "entertainment," not pornography.[15] Moreover, zoning ordinances address problem land uses and location concerns rather than the speech of the material sold or performed inside. Despite the sophistic legal distinctions put forth by the localities and affirmed by the Court, however, the reality remains that the law defines adult establishments by the pornographic content available inside. Yet porn comes with analytical and legal baggage, whereas adult entertainment has less problematic associations.

The amendments to Detroit's zoning ordinance in *Young* defined an "adult theater" as an establishment that presents "material distinguished or characterized by an emphasis on matter depicting, describing or relating to 'Specified Sexual Activities,' or 'Specified Anatomical Areas.'"[16] The amendment to the zoning ordinance further defined "Specified Anatomical Areas" as "1. Less than completely and opaquely covered: (a) human genitals, pubic regions; (b) buttock, and (c) female breast below a point immediately above the top of the areola; and 2. Human male genitals in a discernibly turgid state, even if completely and opaquely covered."[17] Likewise, the ordinance at issue in *Renton* defined adult theaters in much the same language.[18] An adult theater was defined as any "enclosed building used for presenting motion picture films, video cassettes, cable television, or any other such visual media, distinguished or characterized by an emphasis on matter depicting, describing or relating to 'specified sexual activities' or 'specified anatomical areas' . . . for observation by patrons therein." [19]

Is adult entertainment distinct from pornography or is the difference semantic? When law defines and categorizes, it makes meaning. [20] A necessary part of law requires us to interrogate the uses of definition and categorization as preparation for considered thought and action. [21] The definitions supplied in the zoning ordinances set forth what makes these establishments distinguishable from mainstream places of entertainment. [22] The distinctive element, of course, is the selling of pornography: adult establishments sell pornography. Yet elsewhere the Court affirmed a case which held pornography to be protected speech that can only be regulated when categorized as obscenity. [23] While the Court attempts to elide that, through zoning ordinances, law regulates pornography, it also unwittingly challenges claims about the inability of law to define pornography.

We all remember the famous remark by Justice Stewart about defining pornography, "I know it when I see it." [24] As a de facto matter, courts in the zoning cases have defined pornography with more specificity than Justice Stewart even if they have done so with misdirection. Those arguing that pornography is impossible to define, more specifically contend that definitions of pornography are overbroad, often including all sorts of entertainment or expression that should not properly be grouped with pornography. [25] According to this view, what constitutes pornography is, in the final analysis, subjective, varying with individual tastes. [26] With validity, regulation opponents fear that any definition will invariably encompass works with literary and educational significance. [27] Nevertheless, the zoning cases challenge those anti-regulation concerns since they define pornography without overbroadly encompassing every sexual depiction. [28] Nonetheless, the definitions of adult establishments set forth in the regulations at issue in *Young* and *Renton* have marked weaknesses. [29] For example, the definitions given in each ordinance place emphasis on body parts without clearly articulating criteria for distinguishing "adult films" from educational films about sex. [30]

As noted above, the concerns about defining pornography are not without basis. Yet, the imprecision with which the Court approaches the definition of pornography is no different than the imprecision with which it defines "tradition" in substantive due process jurisprudence or even the meaning of equal protection of the law. The Court has been able to formulate a working definition of other vague terms such as "viability" in *Roe v. Wade* and its progeny and "religion" in conscientious objector cases. [31] In all of those instances, the Court did not settle the definitions for all time. Such definitional imprecision is enmeshed with the sometimes messy inexactness of law; pornography is not more or less easily definable than fetal viability or religious belief.

Although the definition of adult establishments found in the zoning cases is a starting point for defining pornography, from the perspective of this book, one important flaw remains: the definition of pornography as articulated in the zoning cases obscures the gender disparity inherent in the most problematic forms of the practice, the very forms law seeks to regulate. Avoiding definitional overbreadth and focusing on the most troublesome forms of inegalitarian pornography rather than all forms of sexually explicit material may require acknowledging that, under current historical conditions, the gender hierarchy embedded in the inegalitarian heterosexual variant is particularly problematic.[32] Later chapters will address the current state of free speech doctrine which prohibits such a definition with respect to the specific content of pornography and the ability to regulate only the most problematic forms. Additionally, another later chapter will explore why we can point to the inegalitarian variant of pornography as other western nations committed to free speech principles have done, concluding that it is worthy of regulation in ways that gay pornography, for example, may not.[33]

If we are to "make the familiar strange again, to rescue the taken-for-granted and bring it back into mind," we must examine the language the Court uses to define pornography in the zoning cases.[34] The very term "adult establishment" redefines and re-describes the gendered practice of pornography in universal, non-sex-specific terms.[35] The term "adult" descriptively references the entertainment venue, whether a theater, bar, or store, thereby obscuring that, currently, pornography, even today, mainly appeals to a subcategory of adults: men.[36] We can identify that men disproportionately consume pornography by examining the economics of the industry. Producers and marketers understand who consumes that product without controversy even as porn producers have sought to broaden the genre's appeal with variety and the introduction of venues like adult cafes. The language of "adult entertainment" or "adult establishment" suggests equality, obfuscating the fact that most patrons of adult establishments are men, and women remain objects of the pornographic displays.

If we continue to utilize this "estranging method" where we "decontextualize the obvious and then recontextualize it in a new way," articulating new vantage points, we must also point to the language in the nude dancing cases.[37] The decisions in the zoning and nude dancing cases both perpetuate and obscure this gender inequality and its analytical significance.[38] For example, in *Erie*, the Court refers to "g-strings and pasties" to describe the coverings that female dancers must wear under Erie's ordinance and characterizes the message conveyed by nude dancers as erotic:

> Similarly, even if Erie's public nudity ban has some minimal effect on
> the erotic message by muting that portion of the expression that occurs
> when the last stitch is dropped, the dancers at Kandyland and other
> such establishments are free to perform wearing pasties and G-strings.
> Any effect on the overall expression is de minimis.[39]

The references themselves, isolated from historical context, are unre-
markable. However, by referring to "g-strings and pasties," the Supreme
Court places itself within an extensive tradition in philosophy and law
that refers to the female body without comparable references to the male
body.[40] Such references influence how law defines and regulates female
bodies, often serving as a rationale to apply general legal principles un-
equally.[41] Moreover, the reference to "g-strings and pasties" highlights
what the Court does not formally acknowledge in its decisions: that gender is relevant to understanding and assessing pornography's adverse
effects in the case. The bodies discussed in Erie, whether clothed, un-
clothed, or partially clothed, are female bodies.[42] The ordinance disregards the gender asymmetry in "adult establishments" by only referring
to female bodies.[43]

The adult entertainment establishments at issue in *Young* and *Renton*
arguably share the same gender disparity between male and female customers described above.[44] These important descriptive elements are not
included or weighed in the zoning cases even though they are analytically significant to the process of defining the practice of pornography and
assessing its effects. *Barnes* and *Erie* are different because the nude dancing establishments were male-owned and featured female dancers who
disrobed in front of predominantly male customers.[45] In these cases, the
gender asymmetry is clearer and less obscured than it is in the case of
adult establishments despite the Court's language games.

As a culture, we may debate why this gender disparity in pornography exists, if it's diminishing due to the increasing diversity of pornographic representations, and whether it will eventually disappear. Some
insist that the dispartity will always exist as it results from biological or
cultural differences between men and women. Nonetheless, the fact that
the gender asymmetry inherent in most problematic forms of pornography raises legitimate questions about pornography's gender-based effects. Though it may seem like a trivial insight, the fact of gender disparity matters enormously in the most predominant type of pornography,
the inegalitarian variant.[46] In my view, porn studies pays too little attention to this disparity. Surely, if transgressive and radical porn has the
potential to upend traditional, heterosexist patriarchy, then porn reflecting those oppressive power relations can certainly reinforce such inequality. This is the tension that lies at the core of porn studies claims about the
transgressive potential of porn.

The gender disparity in the inegalitarain variant matters because it affects why we regulate, how we weigh adverse effects, and the way we understand particularly troublesome variants of pornography, such as the types that fuse misogyny, sex, and violence. The difference in the way our culture understands male and female bodies and representations of male and female bodies influences the law's ability to assess pornography's adverse effects and to link those negative effects to a system of gender subordination and unequal citizenship.[47] An analysis of historical context and power is central to any balanced analytical approach. Unfortunately, this analytical approach is largely excluded from the legal discourse on pornography. It's an approach that Wittgenstein's concept of language games demand.

At this point in the book, we will not explore why pornography appeals to men more than women as measured by the pornography industry itself. What merits attention in this chapter, however, is that by defining adult establishments as something other than pornography and in gender neutral terms, the Court makes a pivotal categorizing and ultimately epistemic move. The baggage of pornography and its relationship to gender inequality, the First Amendment, unequal power, subordination, and sexual violence is distanced. The field or terrain of debate has shifted onto Tenth Amendment police power grounds where localities are simply attempting to deal with adverse effects and property devaluation rather than gender-based harms. These adverse effects are *secondary* rather than directly related to the speech content inside the establishments. Yet, we should be clear that the secondary effects doctrine elaborated in these cases encompasses the regulation of gender-based interactions like "[a] sidewalk encounter with bookstore patrons [that] too often led to sexually suggestive comments, unwelcome propositions, and furtive touches being thrown at neighborhood women."[48] We need only shift our vantage point, thereby challenging the Court's narrative and categorization to see that gender is central to understanding the practice of pornography even in the zoning and nude dancing cases.

The law in the zoning cases reflects our culture's competing understandings of and even ambivalence toward pornography. On the one hand, pornography represents our cultural efforts to throw off our puritanical chains in seeking greater liberty in making decisions about our sexuality, decisions that challenge traditional morality and orthodoxy. On the other hand, inegalitarian pornography subordinates and silences women.[49] The challenge to traditional sexual orthodoxy produces more liberatory understandings of homosexuality, sex for pleasure, and sex outside of marriage. These are precisely the concerns that the religious right, for example, ties to the proliferation of pornography. These concerns, however, are not the anxieties of anti-porn feminists. Instead, anti-pornography feminists celebrate that women can have more sex, yet seek to address the question of what kind of sex. For women, the challenge to traditional sexual mores that inegalitarian pornography both reflects and constructs enabled women to have sex outside of marriage without social condemnation. At the same time, inegalitarian pornography, despite its claims, has not necessarily expanded the sexual imaginary displacing the rather hegemonic conception of sexuality at play in our culture. Instead, it has reified female sexual objectification and fused sex and violence in hegemonic ways. While different genres of pornography may exist, they are not the forms that dominate the marketplace.[50]

In the case of the LGBTQ movement, the same challenges to traditional heterosexual mores produces a more progressive understanding of homosexuality. The challenge to the heterosexual norm creates conditions under which recognition, respect, and dignity is extended to the LGBTQ community. Yet the greater dignity and respect accorded to the LGBTQ community need not be philosophically nor politically allied with protecting inegalitarian pornography. Any assessment of pornography's liberatory potential must be measured by tracing power relations as they move through the political body. The fusion of sex and violence against women is incompatible with the liberatory impulses of the LGBTQ movement and the women's movement.

Within the porn studies movement, scholars have often emphasized queer pornography as a progressive challenge to the mainstream heterosexual variant. Helen Hester writes:

> This tendency toward valorization within porn studies partly manifests itself via an emphasis on queer theoretical standpoints and potentially dissident pornographies. As Paasonen notes, "Proporn . . . prosex authors who approach the genre from a more positive angle have chosen independent, queer, and artistic projects that challenge gender norms, porn cliches and the commodity logic of the porn industry. . . . By eschewing texts in favor of more transgressive fare, she argues, scholars are better able to position adult entertainment as the property of the "queer against the norm."[51]

Sometimes porn studies scholars effectively cherry pick these more progressive cultural challenges to the dominant heterosexual patriarchal understanding of sexuality embedded in the more mainstream inegalitarian pornographic fare to argue that the genre as a whole should be characterized by these radical transgressive features. Yet at other brief moments, porn studies momentarily recognizes the continued cultural dominance of mainstream inegalitarian heterosexual porn.

DEFINING PORNOGRAPHY AS EROTICA

The meaning of pornography or the message it sends is vigorously contested.[52] This contestation is elided in the zoning and nude dancing cases: the debate is submerged and shifted on to a Tenth Amendment terrain.

Understanding how erotic practices differ from pornographic practices is key to understanding and evaluating the claim that pornography produces gender-based effects. Throughout *Pap's*, the Court refers to the message of nude dancing as an erotic one distinguishable from the secondary effects of nude dancing:

> Even if the city thought that nude dancing at clubs like Kandyland constituted a particularly problematic instance of public nudity, the regulation is still properly evaluated as a content-neutral restriction because the interest in combating the secondary effects associated with those clubs is unrelated to the suppression of the erotic message conveyed by the nude dancing.[53]

Labeling nude dancing as erotic marks an unarticulated presupposition on the part of the Court, ignoring the debate about what language should be used to describe different forms of adult entertainment.[54] The choice to use the descriptor "erotic" rather than "pornographic" carries with it certain assumptions worth unpacking as these decisions about narrative and categorizations create meaning.[55] Throughout the *Pap's* decision, the Court makes a narrative choice to link the erotic with a nonreciprocal pornographic practice (nude dancing), whereby women display themselves for predominantly male audiences.[56] To opponents of pornography, it is precisely this sort of gender asymmetry within a commodified practice that should prevent the characterization or designation of it as erotic.[57] At a minimum, the Court never recognizes the ongoing debate about the very nature of inegalitarian pornography as gender-based subordination and exploitation nor considers how such assumptions may affect legal conclusions.

The Court overlooks the argument that, while pornography and erotica are both sexually explicit forms of cultural representation, their etiologies and meanings diverge. Some feminists point out that there are two types of sexually explicit descriptions: erotica and thanatica.[58] Pornography often reflects the creative perspective of thanatica, not erotica. Eros, the Greek root for erotica, connotes passionate and reciprocal love, whereas pornography combines thanatos, a destructive or death theme, and porne, which refers to a harlot, prostitute, or female captive.[59] Rosemarie Tong describes what distinguishes erotica from thanatica:

1. whereas erotic representations show sexual relationships between fully consenting, equal partners who identify emotionally with each other, thanatica representations show sexual relationships in which full consent, real equality, and emotional identification are absent;
2. and whereas erotica encourages both men and women to treat each other as full human persons, thanatica encourages men in particular to treat women as mere objects.[60]

Tong's comments mark a starting point from which to distinguish pornography and erotica. She suggests that pornography involves a certain psychic violence in which a lack of regard for the other (usually a female) is a defining element.[61]

The Kantian principle that no one should treat another as a means to an end or as a mere object used to satisfy one's desires without considering the desires and needs of the other leads to moral judgments about the qualitative difference between pornography and erotica.[62] Leslie Green, professor of law at York University in Toronto, rejects the pornography/ erotica distinction as idle, and argues that it does not mean that we may never use others instrumentally, but only that we must not think of them solely in terms of how they can benefit us.[63] He expands this notion, applying it to the sexual context:

> In ordinary sex we need others as objects in some of the most ordinary senses of the term: they are intentional objects of our desire, we want to see, smell, touch, and taste their bodies. This is not yet sexual objectification, however, for that involves subjecting them to our purposes without regard to their own.[64]

Green's comments about the nature of objectification raise important issues in a vein similar to the concerns that Martha Nussbaum addresses in an essay on objectification.[65] Nussbaum notes that objectification is a cluster concept, which under some circumstances reflects "necessary or even wonderful conditions of sexual life" and can be compatible with equality, respect, and consent.[66] While recognizing that objectification is potentially intrinsic to sexual gratification, Nussbaum is clear to make the case that "[u]nder some specifications, objectification . . . is always morally problematic."[67] Nussbaum understands that the kind of objectification that anti-pornography feminists challenge is problematic because "it cuts women off from full self-expression and self-determination—from, in effect, their humanity."[68] Nussbaum notes that philosopher Immanuel Kant grasped that objectification was central to sex and he understood that it posed challenges to the proscription not to treat another instrumentally. Yet Kant resolves this tension by recognizing an institutional context of marriage in which sexual objectification could be balanced against values of mutual respect, love, and deep regard.[69] Throughout Nussbaum's discussion of objectification, she emphasizes the importance of background conditions and context to assessing its impact.[70]

In an effort to more precisely comprehend the nature of objectification, Nussbaum presents seven features that form the cluster concept of objectification.[71]

1. Instrumentality. The objectifier treats the object as a tool of his or her purposes.
2. Denial of autonomy. The objectifier treats the object as lacking in autonomy and self-determination.

3. Inertness. The objectifier treats the object as lacking in agency, and perhaps also in activity.
4. Fungibility. The objectifier treats the object as interchangeable (a) with other objects of the same type; (b) with objects of other types.
5. Violability. The objectifier treats the object as lacking of boundary integrity, as something that is permissible to break up, smash, break into.
6. Ownership. The objectifier treats the object as something that is owned by another, can be bought, sold, etc.
7. Denial of Subjectivity. The objectifier treats the object as something whose experience and feelings (if any) need not be taken into account.[72]

Rae Langton adds three more features to Nussbaum's cluster. These features, she suggests, draw more from feminist thought than Kant.

1. Reduction to body: one treats it as identified with its body, or body parts.
2. Reduction to appearance: one treats it primarily in terms of how it looks, or how it appears to the senses.
3. Silencing: one treats it as silent, lacking capacity to speak.[73]

Langton wants to emphasize that denials of autonomy can also depend upon affirmations of autonomy. In the instance of sadistic rape, she notes, non-consent is actively sought in an effort to overcome a woman's choice, "mak[ing] her do what she chooses not to do."[74] Thus, one affirms autonomy in order to deny it.

While Green's criticisms of cramped understandings of objectification are important, his assessment of the pornography/erotica distinction misses the mark for two reasons. First, he is inattentive to the specific features of the objectification taking place in the inegalitarian variant of pornography. Following the work of Nussbaum and Langton, the inegalitarian hegemonic variety of pornography treats women instrumentally, denies their autonomy, views them as inert, perceives them as violable, denies their subjectivity, reduces them to their body, reduces them to their appearance, and silences them. These are the defining features in the hegemonic variety of pornography, which distinguish it from more benign forms of objectification. Second, Green does not give due consideration to the defining features of erotica.[75]

Nussbaum and Langton have articulated criteria to help us determine the problematic forms of objectification from the more banal forms. Sandra Lee Bartky notes that sexual objectification becomes a problem when one is perceived by others in a sexual light "independently of what women want: it is something done to us against our will," leaving the sexually objectified individual discomfited, humiliated, and performing badly in a competitive arena.[76] These distinctions help us better understand when a sexually explicit material displays elements that deny women's full humanity. Instead, Green implies that the objectification factor is an interpretive matter dependent upon subjective taste:

> Political philosophy cannot ride on the back of definition. While some suppose that there is an interesting distinction to be drawn between pornography and erotica, it is in fact idle. There is, of course, a usable distinction in ordinary language: erotica is less explicit and less visual than is pornography. But that is not what the objector has in mind, and her stipulative distinction misinterprets the interplay between our normative judgments and our classificatory systems in this area. People do not classify artifacts into "pornography" or "erotica" and on that basis form moral and political judgments about them. On the contrary, the judgments are engaged from the beginning, and "erotica" is often little more than a label for whatever sort of pornography is judged tolerable.[77]

Although judgment and interpretation are an integral part of distinguishing between pornography and erotica, we still must apply criteria to defend the assessment. Not any assessment will suffice. Put differently, the definition of pornography and its distinction from erotica is based on more than purely subjective taste. Pornographic material possesses certain characteristic elements that are absent from erotic material.[78] Interpretation requires that we marshal evidence and demonstrate that our understanding is a relevant one.[79] It is not an assertion of our personal opinions and, moreover, is subject to the requirements of public justification.[80] The critique that normative judgments inform our classification schemes does not vitiate the pornography/erotica distinction.[81]

If Green's critique stands, then the logical conclusion is that public meaning, upon which law depends, does not exist. While we can accept that values drive what we see as a relevant analytical fact, this does not ineluctably lead us to relativism or solipsism.[82] Amsterdam and Bruner describe the fact/value distinction differently but to the same end:

> Facts are themselves born of interpretation. No theory about a culture can, then, be verified by mere reference to the facts; rather, the theory will drive what counts as fact. . . . The knower does so by interpreting, by narrating, by making sense of what the knower encounters.[83]

This convergence between fact and value does not lead to relativism because we apply criteria to determine which observations are given the status of fact.[84] While those criteria are intersubjective and open to revision, they are not simply based on prejudice.[85]

Green's analysis of the pornography/erotica distinction also falters by misidentifying erotica. Green suggests erotica is "less visual" and "less explicit" than pornography.[86] This is not necessarily so. Erotica does, however, depict mutuality and consent in a way that is absent from pornography.[87] In the heterosexual inegalitarian pornography, men are rarely portrayed as violable objects.[88] The gender roles are rarely reversed.[89] Pornography often depicts unequal nudity, with men remaining more fully clothed and the women seldom enjoying the relative armor of clothing.[90] Women are also in the central focus of the camera lens for longer periods of time than are men.[91] Such gender asymmetry is just one measurable hallmark of pornography, and it suggests unequal power and lack of mutuality.[92] The nude dancing at issue in Erie exhibits these very same features: unequal power and lack of mutuality. Nude dancing reduces women to mere bodies by virtue of its focus on the nonreciprocal commodified exchange that takes place between female employees and male customers.[93]

Although the above discussion does not resolve the debate over the difference between pornography and erotica, or the more recent debate between egaliatrian porn and inegalitarian porn, it does challenge those who would throw up their hands when faced with the task of trying to establish criteria that would distinguish the two practices. Such a distinction is worthy of discussion both within and outside the law, even if it generates controversy. Moreover, it suggests that the language deployed by the Court and its assumptions should be open to greater discussion and analysis.

THE LANGUAGE OF SECONDARY EFFECTS AND THE SUBMERGENCE OF GENDER

Under the secondary effects doctrine, localities must provide evidence of the effects allegedly associated with adult establishments.[94] This is accomplished primarily through zoning studies.[95] A 1995 New York City report compiled information from studies both inside and outside the city, concluding that adult establishments produced fifteen different adverse effects

   a. crime, especially drug- and sex-related crimes;
   b. drug peddling in and in front of the premises;
   c. prostitution;
   d. noise in front of premises;
   e. parking problems;
   f. signage which is detrimental to property values and is unpleasant for children;
   g. reduction in property values;
   h. pornographic litter;
   i. greater incidence of sexual violence to women;
   j. harassment of women on street;
   k. dead zones which pedestrians and shoppers avoid;
   l. excessive nighttime activity;
   m. decline in neighborhood oriented businesses;

n. more difficult to rent office space in the area; and

o. sales tax revenues decline in the area surrounding the adult establishments.[96]

The effects cited in the New York City report are of the same variety advanced by other localities enacting zoning ordinances.

The reasons justifying regulation, like the reports, tend to be recycled. The *Renton* decision set this recycling dynamic in motion.[97] In *Renton*, the Court held that the city did not need to commission its own study to determine that adult establishments cause adverse secondary effects:

> The record in this case reveals that Renton relied heavily on the experience of, and studies produced by, the city of Seattle. In Seattle, as in Renton, the adult theater-zoning ordinance was aimed at preventing the secondary effects caused by the presence of even one such theater in a given neighborhood.[98]

The Court reaffirmed the principle that localities could rely on previous studies when revising zoning ordinances regulating adult theaters in *City of Los Angeles v. Alameda Books, Inc.* (2002).[99] The secondary effects doctrine permits cities to rely on land use studies from other areas regardless of differences in size, demographics, or city layouts. According to the Court, the lower court placed an unnecessary burden of proof on the City of Renton, which had no adult businesses, and instead relied on the experiences of Seattle to establish evidence of a relationship between adult establishments and secondary effects.[100]

The Court's decisions in the zoning and nude dancing cases highlight the general nature of the adverse effects.[101] Those decisions focus on property devaluation, community debasement, decreases in commercial activity, upsurges in sexual assaults, and increased prostitution.[102] When zoning or nude dancing cases mention sexual crimes, such as increases in rape rates, they do not acknowledge that women are overwhelmingly the targets of such crimes.[103] Among the secondary effects from the New York study listed above, several stand out as crimes that particularly target women: (a) an increase in sex related crimes, (c) prostitution, (i) greater incidence of sexual violence against women, and (j) harassment of women on the streets.[104] Further, other studies, such as a 1977 New York Department of City Planning study, documented that a far greater number of verified rape complaints were reported in areas of the city in which adult establishments were located.[105]

In addition, other cities besides New York have found correlations between increases in sexual crimes and proximity to adult establishments.[106] In Austin, Texas, sex crimes were 177 percent to 482 percent higher in four areas with adult businesses than in the overall city.[107]

The Court's failure to explicitly recognize the specifically gender-based effects of adult establishments deserves analysis. One explanation for the lack of a gender analysis may be that gender-based effects would qualify as primary effects, meaning that they are directly related to the content of the pornographic speech of adult entertainment. Under the secondary-effects doctrine, highlighting specifically gender-based effects would impermissibly move the focus from pornography's effects to pornography's viewpoint. As a result, the motivation for the regulation would be considered viewpoint-based rather than effects-based. Thus, effects such as increases in rape rates are not being analyzed from a gender perspective. Furthermore, the law fails to recognize the gender bias in certain kinds of problematic pornography.

The logic of secondary effects dictates that when regulating gender-based effects, localities must present them as general public safety issues rather than explicitly recognizing that the harm generated by adult businesses uniquely affects women. Unfortunately, the separation between content and effects is not as discrete as the Court suggests. It is the unique content of adult entertainment that produces these adverse effects, thereby unraveling the Court's distinctions. Moreover, the sophistic legal distinction between content and effects elides a more fundamental debate about the most serious injuries that the zoning studies recognized as correlating to proximity to adult establishments. Instead, the doctrine of secondary effects re-categorizes those serious gender based harms under a different, more general public safety label, thereby avoiding a frontal collision with the Supreme Court's free speech jurisprudence.

Critics have raised serious concerns about the reliability of the zoning studies, arguing that they lack scientific validity.[108] These studies often employ no minimum standard for methodological rigor.[109] The reliability of these studies becomes even more questionable when localities discuss the studies in generalized terms and use recycled studies from other cities.[110] The lack of demonstrated validity of these studies creates a problem for those concerned about gender-based harms because the studies discourage and lessen the fundamental debate about whether regulations on pornography are really effects-based or viewpoint-based. By characterizing these studies as scientifically valid and categorizing content-based restrictions under the content-neutral secondary-effects doctrine, the Court also avoids discussing whether pornography subordinates and injures women. The Court thereby avoids placing the force of its authority behind the idea that pornography harms women and settles for a far less controversial view: the content-neutral secondary-effects doctrine.[111]

Notwithstanding these critiques of the zoning studies, these zoning regulations are less problematic if alternate avenues of communication are open to adult establishments and if the regulations are placed within a larger theory of free speech. Cass Sunstein argues for a New Deal for free speech in which political speech is the most protected form of expression.[112] All other forms fall into a lower tier or category and may be subjected to various degrees of regulation.[113] Brandon Lemley argues that the secondary effects doctrine fits comfortably into Sunstein's Madisonian conception of free speech, one where political speech is the most highly valued.[114] While Lemley finds the civic republican underpinnings of Sunstein's New Deal for free speech troublesome and would prefer instead a more Holmesian free marketplace of ideas approach, he aptly describes the connection between secondary effects and a Republican understanding of free speech.[115] Under Sunstein's Republican understanding of free speech, adult entertainment is lower value speech and may face regulations if government has a "weighty" and legitimate purpose.[116]

What is among the most problematic aspects of the zoning and nude dancing cases is the failure of the Court to weigh the free speech issues against the adverse effects in an honest and principled way. The Court should "come clean" about the gendered nature of pornography, including pornography's particular impact on women. By recognizing the connection between adult establishments and gender-based effects, the Court could re-open the legal debate foreclosed by *American Booksellers* over pornography's subordination of women.[117] In that decision, the Seventh Circuit struck down a civil damages ordinance regulating pornography.[118] The language of the ordinance asserted that "pornography differentially harms women.[119] The differential harm cited by the ordinance consisted of unequal pay, sexual violence, including rape and exploitation on the streets, and insult and injury at home.[120] The Seventh Circuit struck down the ordinance as an impermissibly content-based restriction on speech, noting that the pernicious effects of pornography in fact demonstrate the power of speech.[121]

While the nature of the ordinance at issue in *American Booksellers* may differ from the zoning regulations at issue in the Supreme Court cases, they share remarkable similarities. Both case types recognize that pornography generates harmful effects. In the zoning and nude dancing cases, the Court places de facto content-based regulations on pornography without expressly saying that it is doing so. The Court does this by suppressing the gender inequality that the *American Booksellers* ordinance highlighted and by making a sophistic distinction between direct content-based effects and indirect content-neutral effects.

CONCLUSION

As some future anthropologist will one day note, our society regulated pornography, but it did so with cloaked, partial, and inconsistent reasoning. Because the law serves as a culturally important source for truth claims, its reasoning with respect to pornography regulation merits attention.

At this point in history, the most problematic forms of pornography perpetuate and reflect gender inequality.[122] Other nations with strong free speech traditions recognize the connection between inegalitarian speech and oppression by regulating it without inevitably chilling the highest form of speech: namely, dissident speech. While the law recognizes and regulates some of the problems associated with pornography, namely, those affecting general public safety or property values, it fails to recognize the specifically gender-based harms caused by pornography that affect women. The law has failed to place its imprimatur on a gendered understanding of pornography despite the ample support that zoning studies could provide for such a position.

NOTES

1. Words and gestures are conventionalized within a community. Wittgenstein, L.J.J. *Philosophical Investigations*. Edited by G. E. M Anscombe. Oxford: Blackwell and Mott, 1963. Section 243.

2. Linguistic games intertwine with forms of life. Wittgenstein, L.J.J. *Philosophical Investigations*. Edited by G.E.M Anscombe. Oxford: Blackwell and Mott, 1963.

3. https://www.pornhub.com/insights/2018-year-in-review#gender.

4. The following form some of the core arguments within the pro-sex and porn studies category. Kristin L. Cole, "Pornography, Censorship, and Public Sex: Exploring Feminist and Queer Perspectives of (Public) Pornography through the Case of Pornotopia." *Porn Studies* 1, no. 3 (2014), 227–41. https://doi.org/10.1080/23268743.2014.927708 . Lisa Duggan, *Sex Wars: Sexual Dissent and Political Culture*. Hoboken: Routledge, 2006. Ann Ferguson, "Sex War: The Debate between Radical and Libertarian Feminists." *Signs* 10, no. 1 (1984), 106-12. Albert Fredericks, "Adult Use Zoning: New York City's Journey on the Well-Traveled Road from Suppression to Regulation of Sexually Oriented Expression." *Buffalo Law Review* 46 (spring 1998): 433-66. Leslie Green, "Pornographies." *Journal of Political Philosophy* 8 (2000): 44. Susan Gubar, "Representing Pornography: Feminism, Criticism, and Depictions of Female Violation." *Critical Inquiry* 13, no. 4 (1987), 712–41. https://doi.org/10.1086/448418 . Jenna Jameson, and Neil Strauss. *How to Make Love like a Porn Star: A Cautionary Tale*. It Books, 2010. Berkely Kaite, *Pornography and Difference*. Bloomington & Indianapolis: Indiana University Press, 1995. Peter Lehman, *Pornography: Film and Culture*. New Brunswick, NJ: Rutgers University Press, 2006. Susanna Paasonen, *Carnal Resonance Affect and Online Pornography*. Cambridge: MIT Press, 2011. Shira Tarrant, *The Pornography Industry: What Everyone Needs to Know*. Oxford University Press, 2016. Lisa Duggan, Nan D. Hunter, and Carol S. Vance. "False Promises: Feminist Anti-Pornography Legislation." *New York Law School Law Review* 38, no. 133 (1993). Linda Williams, *Screening Sex / Linda Williams*. Durham: Duke University Press, 2008. Williams, Linda. *Hard Core: Power, Pleasure and "Frenzy of the Visible."* London: Pandora, 1990.

5. Helen Hester, *Beyond Explicit* . Albany, NY: State Univ Of New York Pr, 2015.

6. Hester, *Beyond Explicit*. Albany, NY: State University Of New York, 2015, 3.

7. Susanna Paasonen, *Carnal Resonance Affect and Online Pornography*. Cambridge: MIT Press, 2011. Helen Hester. *Beyond Explicit*. Albany, NY: State Univ Of New York, 2015. Peter Lehman, *Pornography: Film and Culture*. New Brunswick, NJ: Rutgers University Press, 2006.

8. Ariel Levy, *Female Chauvinist Pigs: Women and the Rise of Raunch Culture*. Black Inc., 2010.

9. Alan Hyde, *Bodies of Law*. Princeton University Press, 1997, supra note 7, at viii.

10. Anthony G. Amsterdam and Jerome Seymour Bruner, *Minding the Law*. Harvard University Press, 2000. The law is enveloped by culture and, in order to gain public acceptance, its categories must be seen as an extension of that culture. See Amsterdam & Bruner, p. 2. In support of this, Amsterdam and Bruner write: "The law, we are told, saves us from forgetfulness of our most basic obligations to each other and the state, from endless cycles of revenge, from the tyrannies of public powers and the blindness of private passions, from fecklessness and faction. Yet if law does any of these things at all well, it must do them by establishing continuities with the ways in which the people of a society conceive of it and of themselves, the ways in which they classify and comprehend, envision and dispute and puzzle out who they are and what they need and want, and why." Pp. 3-4. For this reason, Amsterdam and Bruner argue that checking the law's reasoning against other forms of thinking, imagination, or discourse is necessary.

11. See *Miller v. California*, 413 U.S. 15 (1973), 24 (holding that state regulation is permissible over a work that portrays sexual conduct in a patently offensive way, and has no other redeeming values); see also *New York Times v. Sullivan*, 376 U.S. 254 (1964), 283 (holding that First Amendment protection extends to all speech unless factual misrepresentations are made with actual malice); *Chaplinsky v. New Hampshire*, 315 U.S. 568 (1942), 572 (affirming the constitutionality of regulating fighting words based on the fact that any value derived from them is "outweighed by the social interest in order and morality").

12. See *Miller v. California*, 24.

13. See *Miller*. See supra note 59 and accompanying text.

14. See, e.g., *Young v. American Mini-Theatres*, 427 U.S. 50 (1976).

15. See *Young*, p. 53.

16. *Young*, p. 53.

17. *Young*, p. 53.

18. See City of Renton v. Playtime Theatres, Inc., 475 U.S. 41, 44 (1986).

19. *Renton*. (quoting ordinance language).

20. See Amsterdam and Bruner.

21. Amsterdam and Bruner, p. 19.

22. See Amsterdam and Bruner; see also *Young*, 427 U.S., p. 50 (defining a theater that presents "material distinguished or characterized by an emphasis on matter depicting . . . "Specified Sexual Activities' or "Specified Anatomical Areas'" as an adult establishment).

23. See 475 U.S. 1001 (1986) (summarily affirming *American Booksellers Ass'n v. Hudnut*, 771 F.2d 323 (1985)).

24. See, e.g., *Jacobellis v. Ohio*, 378 U.S. 184, p. 197 (1964) (Stewart, J., concurring). Justice Stewart famously remarked on the way to identify "hard-core pornography": "I know it when I see it."

25. See *Jacobellis* and accompanying discussion; see also Carlin Meyer, "Sex, Sin, and Women's Liberation: Against Porn-Suppression," 72 *Tex. L. Rev.* 1097, p. 1111 (1994).

26. See Lisa Duggan et al., "False Promises: Feminist Anti-Pornography Legislation," 38 *N.Y.L. Sch. L. Rev.* 133, 142 (1993).

27. Carlin Meyer, "Sex, Sin, and Women's Liberation: Against Porn-Suppression," *Texas Law Review* 72 (1994): p. 1111. See also pp. 1143-44.

28. Moreover, even in the case of *Jacobellis*, the Court held that the film in question, *The Lovers*, did not constitute obscenity despite the explicit character of one scene. *Jacobellis*, 378 U.S., p. 196.

29. See *Young v. American Mini-Theatres, Inc.*, 427 U.S. 50, p. 50 (1976); *City of Renton v. Playtime Theatres, Inc.*, 475 U.S 41, p. 44 (1986).

30. See *Young*, 427 U.S., p. 50; *Renton*, 475 U.S., p. 44.

31. See *Roe v. Wade*, 410 U.S. 113, 160 (1973) (defining viability as the point when a fetus is able to live outside the mother's womb, albeit with artificial life support, usually seven months into the pregnancy); *Welsh v. United States*, 398 U.S. 333, 344

(1970) (defining a conscientious objector as anyone "spurred by deeply held moral, ethical, or religious beliefs" who would have "no rest or peace if they allowed themselves to become a part of an instrument of war").

32. See Simon Hardy, *The Reader, The Author, The Woman and Her Lover: Soft-Core Pornography and Heterosexual Men*, pp. 164-65 (1998) (arguing that a stronger female voice is needed to transform heteroeroticism into a subject where men and women have equal voice). Does recognizing the centrality of gender to pornography make such definitions impermissibly viewpoint-based? If, empirically speaking, gender hierarchy is a key definitional component to pornography, then a prohibition on referencing gender would hardly seem viewpoint-neutral. Choosing to ignore historical context is also a non-neutral view. Moreover, free speech doctrine permits several viewpoint-based restrictions: the government prohibits pro-cigarette and pro-liquor ads but allows anti-smoking and anti-drinking ads; the government proscribes anti-union speakers in the period before union elections; securities law prohibits favorable views of a company proxy but allows unfavorable views. Viewpoint-based restrictions are not automatically unconstitutional. Cass R. Sunstein, "Words, Conduct, Caste," *University of Chicago Law Review* 60 (1993), 819.

33. See Martha Nussbaum's essay on "Objectification" in *Sex and Social Justice* where she analyzes the difference between objectifying a social equal versus objectifying a social unequal.

34. See generally Amsterdam and Bruner.

35. Helen Hester, *Beyond Explicit: Pornography and the Displacement of Sex*, 2014.

36. Even if we take the Pornhub statistic of women accessing 29 percent of the pornography on their website, such a statistic still reflects a gendered practice. If we follow the Pornhub statistic that means 61 percent of all accessed pornographic material is retrieved by men. We don't have statistics for the number of women who frequent adult entertainment venues.

37. See Amsterdam and Bruner.

38. See *Young v. American Mini-Theatres, Inc.*, 427 U.S 50 (1976); *City of Renton v. Playtime Theatres, Inc.*, 475 U.S. 41 (1986); *City of Erie v. Pap's A.M.*, 529 U.S. 277 (2000).

39. *Erie*, 529 U.S., p. 294.

40. See generally Lois McNay, *Foucault and Feminism: Power, Gender and the Self* (1993) (describing how this tradition is embedded in western enlightenment thinking).

41. See *Mueller v. Oregon*, 208 U.S. 412 (1908) (holding that a law limiting female laundry workers to a ten-hour workday was constitutional); *Geduldig v. Aiello*, 417 U.S. 484 (1974) (holding that California disability insurance excluding from coverage any work loss because of pregnancy does not violate the equal protection clause); see also Bordo, supra note 56, at 73 (1993) (noting that sometimes mechanistic conceptions of the body dominate, "from which all concern for the inner self have vanished"); Dan Danielsen, "Identity Strategies: Representing Pregnancy and Homosexuality," in *After Identity: A Reader in Law and Culture*, p. 44 (Dan Danielsen & Karen Engle eds., 1995) (noting that whether courts use definitions of pregnancy as a physical condition, removing gender from the analysis, or focus on female potential for pregnancy and not on pregnancy itself, we are left with an uncertain notion of the court's conception of the relationship between pregnancy as conduct versus as gender status; R. Darcy et. al, *Women, Elections, and Representations* pp. 18-24 (2d ed. 1994) (discussing the representations of women in a variety of political theories, including Plato's, Locke's, Machiavelli's and Mill's); Susan Bordo & Arlene Saxonhouse, "Aristotle: Defective Males, Hierarchy, and the Limits of Politics," in *Feminist Interpretations and Political Theory*, p. 34 (Mary Lyndon Shanley & Carole Pateman eds., 1991) (critiquing Aristotle's view that the female of a species is a defective male); Mary Lyndon Shanley & Carole Pateman, "Introduction," in id. at 5 (analyzing womanhood and manhood in political theory and analyzing the idea that women are subordinate to men); Patricia Hill Collins, *Fighting Words: Black Women and the Search for Justice*, p. 170 (1998) (noting that historical controlling of black women's reproduction and in turn sexuality has led to the a model that legitimates black women's sexuality only in relation to black men).

42. See *Erie*, 529 U.S. 277.

43. See *Erie*.

44. See *Young v. American Mini-Theatres, Inc.*, 427 U.S. 50 (1976); *City of Renton v. Playtime Theatres, Inc.*, 475 U.S. 41 (1986).

45. See *Erie*, 529 U.S. 277; *Barnes v. Glen Theatre, Inc.*, 501 U.S. 560 (1991).

46. Hardy, p. 49 ("But the fact remains that in no other genre is one sex focused on so exclusively for the sole edification of the other. As a genre mass-market (heterosexual) pornography remains overwhelmingly of women, but by men and for men. If for no other reason the genre demands particular attention for this singular lopsidedness.").

47. See Alan Hyde, *Bodies of Law*. Princeton University Press, 1997. See supra note 84 and accompanying text.

48. Georgina Hickey, "The Geography of Pornography: Neighborhood Feminism and the Battle Against 'Dirty' Bookstores" in *Minneapolis, Frontiers: A Journal of Women Studies*, Vol. 32, no. 1 (2011), pp. 124-151.

49. A claim made by anti-pornography feminists like Catharine MacKinnon and Rae Langton.

50. Shira Tarrant explains the changes in the pornography industry that place obstacles to make the kinds of money made in the 1970s and 1980s. Shira Tarrant, *The Pornography Industry: What Everyone Needs to Know*. Oxford University Press, 2016.

51. Helen Hester, *Beyond Explicit*. Albany, NY: State University Of New York Press, 2015, 3-4 quoting Paasonen, *Carnal Knowledge*, 42 and 247. Susanna Paasonen, *Carnal Resonance Affect and Online Pornography*. Cambridge: MIT Press, 2011.

52. See Amy Adler, "What's Left?: Hate Speech, Pornography, and the Problem for Artistic Expression," *84 Cal. L. Rev.* 1499, 1533 (1996).

53. *City of Erie v. Pap's A.M.*, 529 U.S. 277, 296 (2000) (emphasis added).

54. *City of Erie v. Pap's A.M.*, 529 U.S. 277, 296 (2000) (emphasis added).

55. Amsterdam and Bruner.

56. See *Erie*, 529 U.S. 277.

57. A commodified practice is one that has been subordinated to the logic of capitalism. In pornography, sexuality becomes a product to be bought and sold. As a commodity, sexuality loses its human and spiritual dimensions. See Donald G. Tannenbaum and David Schultz, *Inventors of Ideas: Introduction to Western Political Philosophy* (1998).

58. Rosemarie Tong, *Feminist Thought: A Comprehensive Introduction,* p. 113 (Westview Press 1989).

59. Tong; see also Steinem, pp. 35-36.

60. Tong, p. 113.

61. Tong.

62. Leslie Green, "Pornographies," 8 *J. Pol. Phil.* 44 (2000).

63. Green.

64. Green, p. 45.

65. Martha C. Nussbaum, *Sex and Social Justice*. New York & Oxford: Oxford University Press, 1999.

66. Martha Nussbaum, *Sex and Social Justice*, pp. 214-15.

67. Nussbaum, p. 214.

68. Nussbaum, p. 214.

69. Nussbaum, 225.

70. Rae Langton, "Autonomy Denial in Objectification" in *Sexual Solipsism* (2009). See also Sandra Lee Bartky in *Femininity and Domination*, p. 26.

71. Langton (2009), 225.

72. Nussbaum p. 218. Langton, pp. 225-26.

73. Langton, p. 228-229.

74. Langton, p. 234.

75. Langton, pp. 49-50.

76. Sandra Lee Bartky, p. 27.

77. Green, p. 45.

78. Hardy, p. 49 ("While the other genres are designed for a female or mixed audience, pornography is tailored for a male one. . . . Women's bodies are the central ingredients in pornography").

79. See Macedo, p. 10.

80. Macedo, pp. 10-11 (describing publicly justifiable arguments as those that are capable of being widely accepted and recognized as reasonable). The legitimacy of Supreme Court decisions in a constitutional democracy rests on this notion of public justification. According to this idea, the Court must provide publicly justifiable reasons for its decisions if they are to be respected.

81. Macedo.

82. See Hilary Putnam, *Reason, Truth, and History* 127-49 (1981). As the philosopher Hilary Putnam argues, there is no fact/value distinction; our values determine what we recognize as a relevant.

83. Amsterdam and Bruner, p. 221 (emphasis in original).

84. See Amsterdam and Bruner, p. 111.

85. Amsterdam and Bruner.

86. Green, p. 49.

87. Gloria Steinem, "Erotica vs. Pornography." In *Transforming a Rape Culture*, eds. Emilie Buchwald, Pamela Fletcher, and Martha Roth, pp. 31-46. Minneapolis: Milkweed Editions, 1993. See Steinem, pp. 36-37.

88. Steinem.

89. Steinem.

90. See Steinem, p. 33.

91. See Jensen and Dines.

92. Steinem, p. 33.

93. Such a claim does not ignore that men are objectified by pornography as well. Even MacKinnon's ordinance recognizes that men may face similar treatment as women in pornography if they are the object of violence and degradation. If where the context of pornography celebrates male dominance, men may still face objectification, but, in such a context, the meaning and effects of the objectification are different.

94. See Bryant Paul et al., "Government Regulation of 'Adult' Businesses Through Zoning and Anti-Nudity Ordinances: Debunking the Legal Myth of Negative Secondary Effects," 6 *Comm. L. & Pol'y* 355, p. 362-63 (2001).

95. See Bryant et al.

96. Affidavit of Richard "Bo" Dietl at 2-3, *Stringfellow's v. City of New York*, No. 113049/96 (N.Y. App. Div. Sept. 12, 1996).

97. *City of Renton v. Playtime Theatres, Inc.*, 475 U.S. 41, p. 51 (1986).

98. *Renton*, p. 50.

99. *City of Los Angeles v. Alameda Books, Inc.*, 535 U.S. 425 (2002).

100. *Alameda Books.*

101. See *Alameda Books.*

102. See *Alameda Books.*

103. See, e.g., *Young v. American Mini-Theatres, Inc.*, 427 U.S. 50, 55 (1976).

104. See *Young.*

105. See City of New York Department of City Planning, Adult Entertainment Study 10 (1994).

106. See City of New York Department of City Planning.

107. See City of New York Department of City Planning.

108. Paul Bryant, Bradley J. Shafer, and Daniel Linz, "Government Regulation of 'Adult' Businesses Through Zoning and Anti-Nudity Ordinances: Debunking the Legal Myth of Negative Secondary Effects," *Communication Law and Policy* 6, no. 2 (2001), pp. 355-391, https://doi.org/10.1207/s15326926clp0602_4 . See Paul et al. p. 366. The cases themselves do not characterize the studies as scientific; they just rely on the states' use of those studies.

109. See Paul et al.

110. See Paul et al.

111. See, e.g., *City of Renton v. Playtime Theatres, Inc.*, 475 U.S. 41 (1986).

112. Sunstein, *Democracy and the Problem of Free Speech* , p. 17, 122.

113. Sunstein, pp. 122-65.

114. Brandon K. Lemley, "Effectuating Censorship: Civic Republicanism and the Secondary Effects Doctrine," 35 *J. Marshall L. Rev.* 189 (2002); see also Sunstein, *Democracy and the Problem of Free Speech*, supra note 7, at 122.

115. Lemley, pp. 219-24.

116. Lemley, p. 220.

117. *American Booksellers Ass'n v. Hudnut*, 771 F.2d 323, 329 (7th Cir. 1985).

118. *Hudnut*, p. 327-328.

119. *Hudnut*, p. 329 (quoting ordinance language).

120. *Hudnut*.

121. *Hudnut*, pp. 327-28.

122. See generally Catherine MacKinnon, *Feminism Unmodified: Discourses on Life and Law* (1987).

II

The Legal Landscape that Acts to Exclude Knowledge Claims about Pornography

THREE

Categories and Epistemic Gatekeeping in Free Speech Jurisprudence

This chapter examines the categorical choices made by the Supreme Court in the zoning and nude dancing cases and by a federal appeals case in the *American Booksellers v. Hudnut* (1985) decision. By comparing and contrasting these categorical choices in both sets of cases, we can more closely examine the unscrutinized assumptions underlying them and better understand the effects these decisions have on our understanding of pornography. To be clear, these cases—the zoning and the civil damage ordinance cases—were never intended to be compared. Yet, determining similarity is a matter of one's choice of criteria: the determinative factor in categorizing is the axis of comparison chosen rather than nature or inevitably.[1] We make categories and, in doing so, they reveal our larger images of realities and our values.[2] This chapter emphasizes that despite differing categorizations, both sets of cases unequivocally recognize pornography's harm to the community. One set of cases transparently recognizes the gender-based harms from pornography while the other submerges those harms in a more general sea of community and property harms.

The chapter details the categorical decisions that law makes enabling it to simultaneously regulate pornography as a zoning matter and eloquently protect pornography as free speech. The introduction in chapter 1 already defended a comparison between the two sets of cases—the zoning cases and the civil damage ordinance—while yet another chapter looked closely at the differing linguistic descriptions of the practice of pornography, finding those differences a paradigm case of Ludwig Wittgenstein's notion of language games.

Even though this current chapter attempts to create a bright-line distinction between descriptive language and categories, the reality is that the two are entwined. The assumptions embedded in the free speech categories take on meaning within the context that language is used. Recognizing this reality leads to some overlap between the language and categories chapters. Nonetheless, the present chapter on free speech categories presses the analysis in a deeper and different direction than the previous linguistic chapter. The animating conclusion in the chapter is that both the content-neutrality principle and the secondary effects doctrine function as de facto gender-coded categories. In both instances, they function to disqualify gender-based understandings of a practice (the inegalitarian variety) that under current historical conditions is very gendered.

Several interrelated consequences follow from the initial decision to conceptualize the zoning and civil damage cases differently even though both regulate speech. In one instance, the law places the zoning cases into a category where policymakers use state police powers to regulate adult establishments. In the other, law strikes down the civil damage ordinance regulating pornography by placing it into the free speech category. The chapter will attempt to separate and analyze these interrelated strands for the purposes of identifying the problematic assumptions behind these distinctions. First, the alternate categorizations (zoning or speech) allow for the use of differing judicial tests to scrutinize the constitutionality of the regulations. As we will see, when the practice is understood as speech, the Court uses the stricter content-neutrality test to determine constitutionality. When the practice is understood as a problem land-use, the Court applies a less restrictive analysis under secondary effects doctrine. Second, the initial categorization into either zoning or free speech law entails implications for the definition of pornography. Zoning law avoids a constitutionally troublesome discussion of pornography as a gender-based practice while a civil-damage approach embraces it. Obscenity and commercial speech law offer yet more alternative definitions of pornography and different avenues for regulation. Those other regulatory approaches help us to better analyze our culture's accepted and rejected understandings/definitions of pornography and allow us to more closely examine the assumptions at play in the zoning and civil damage ordinances. Is pornography entertainment, discrimination, prurience, or simply a business? Each definition or understanding triggers a different legal category.

Third, the categorical choices lead to differing *descriptions* of the injuries from pornography whether in terms of "effects" or "harms." Is an ordinance emphasizing the property/community effects or more serious Fourteenth Amendment harms submerged within those general community effects? The choice to categorize these unwanted injuries as "effects" or "harms" tells us something about our values and social reality. Finally, and related to the previous point, the choices about categorizing these results as either "effects" or "harms" lead to differing standards to not only *describe* but to *prove* harm. The categorical choices influence what counts as evidence. In short, the standards used to prove harm in the zoning cases are far less stringent measures than in comparison to the civil damage case. It is no coincidence, the chapter asserts, that the federal court requires evidence of *causality* in the civil damage case, which presents those harms like sexual harassment as specifically gender-based.

SECONDARY EFFECTS DOCTRINE AND CONTENT-NEUTRALITY

An earlier chapter introduced the two different approaches to regulating pornography. The first approach discussed is one that attempts to zone establishments selling pornography. Sometimes the zoning regulations relocate the adult establishments to remote parts of a city or an industrial wasteland. As the reader recalls, the zoning approach to regulating pornography makes a distinction between businesses that sell pornography and the pornography itself. Zoning law tells us that we may delineate places that trade in pornography from the communicative message of books, magazines, movies, and acts such as nude dancing purveyed inside. Following the logic of zoning law, these businesses selling pornography are associated with certain problem effects. To be clear, these effects "happen to be associated" with adult establishments and are indirectly related to the speech content of the pornography sold inside. The use of the passive voice moves us away from the idea that the pornography sold inside the adult establishment *causes* these "effects." As noted in an earlier chapter, the Supreme Court labels this distinction "the secondary effects doctrine." To date, the Supreme Court has only ever applied the secondary effects doctrine to cases involving the regulation of pornography.

Under the secondary effects doctrine, the Court may not regulate adult establishments selling pornography for any reason related to the content of the pornographic material sold inside. To draw a connection between the content sold inside an adult establishment and effects would violate a central principle of modern free speech law, namely the content-neutrality principle. The next chapter will examine the rise and evolution of the content-neutrality principle. For now, it suffices to explain that the principle holds that government may not regulate speech based upon a like or dislike of its content. If a court determines that regulation is content-based rather than content-neutral, they will review the regulation at the level of strict scrutiny.

Historically, students of the Court characterize content-neutrality as outcome determinative, meaning that, once triggered, regulations typically fail First Amendment standards. Strict scrutiny entails a rigorous three-prong test. Courts consider whether government had a compelling state interest in passing the restriction under the first prong. The reason must be imperative or "compelling" rather than simply substantial or serious. The second prong requires that government narrowly tailor the law when attempting to achieve the stated objective. The final prong is sometimes collapsed into the second prong. It mandates that the regulation must use the least restrictive or burdensome means to achieve the compelling goal. Observers of the Court often quip that strict scrutiny is "strict in name, but fatal in practice." Few regulations survive strict scrutiny.

The secondary-effects doctrine utilized in the zoning cases effectively evades a direct confrontation with the core of modern free speech law, namely, the content-neutrality principle and strict scrutiny. The problem effects that zoning seeks to redress, according to its logic, are not the result of pornography's message per se. The effects zoning law attempts to confront include property devaluation, commercial dead zones, community debasement, decreases in commercial activity, upsurges in the number of sexual assaults and incidents of sexual harassment, and increased prostitution. The rationale underlying secondary-effects doctrine is that these effects are obliquely related to pornography's message. Instead, following the Court's logic, these secondary effects stem from problem land uses rather than speech.

Yet, when we examine the cases zoning pornography, we see that the Court struggles with its categorization of zoning regulations as only incidentally affecting speech. The confusion begins in part, because, although Justice Stevens in *Young* wants to decide the case on zoning grounds, he finds himself defending the decision on free speech grounds. He notes that while society will not tolerate the total suppression of erotic materials, few of us would be willing to send our loved ones to war defending our rights to view specified sexual activities.[3] This comment by Justice Stevens reveals a tension between the ideal of content-neutrality, its centrality to free speech doctrine, and the real effects produced by pornography—effects with which communities struggle.[4] Content-neutrality is a cardinal principle of free speech doctrine, holding that government may not regulate speech based on a dislike of the message. It is one developed in the aftermath of the communist speech decisions, some of the most egregious in American history. Justice Stevens's comment also suggests that not all speech is equally valued and accorded the most stringent level of protection.[5] Implicit in Justice Stevens's opinion is a hierarchy of speech classification for which non-obscene, sexually explicit material is of lesser importance and less troublesome to regulate.

In the *Young* plurality opinion, Justice Stevens attempts to strike a balance between the idealized and venerated place of free speech in our democracy and the doctrinal straightjacket of content-neutrality, especially if the Court strictly applies it. Clearly, the content-neutrality principle has played an important role in the protection of high value speech. Justice Stevens quotes Voltaire to emphasize the fundamental purpose of the First Amendment: "I disapprove of what you say, but I will defend to the death your right to say it."[6] Government, he argues, cannot regulate simply because a majority of citizens are offended or dislike a message, and that, as Justice Robert H. Jackson writes in *West Virginia State Board of Education v. Barnette*, "the freedom to differ is not limited to things that do not matter much."[7] The content-neutrality principle captures Jackson's sentiments: lots of speech offends yet should remain protected. In a democracy, holds the ideal, free speech is essential because public discussion, the right to express all viewpoints robustly and without fear of censorship, is vital for government to truly represent its citizens.

Yet Justice Stevens also considers the limitations of content-neutrality to upholding a commitment to free speech. Stevens admits that the Court cannot apply content-neutrality as an absolute principle and acknowledges that strict adherence to content neutrality would invalidate many cases that comprise free speech doctrine:

> [T]his statement, [an absolute commitment to content-neutrality,] and others to the same effect, read literally and without regard for the facts of the case in which it was made, would absolutely preclude any regulation of expressive activity predicated in whole or in part on the content of the communication. But we learned long ago that broad statements of principle, no matter how correct in the context in which they are made, are sometimes qualified by contrary decisions before the absolute limit of the stated principle is reached. When we review this Court's actual adjudications in the First Amendment area, we find this to have been the case with the stated principle that there may be no restriction on whatever expressive activity because of its content.[8]

He concedes that the Supreme Court sometimes deviates from the ideal of content-neutrality because the ideal is unworkable. Justice Stevens makes a similar argument in his more recent *R.A.V. v. St. Paul* decision where Justice Scalia's strong restatement of the doctrine could undermine sexual harassment law. In sexual harassment cases, law recognizes that pornography may be used in work places to create a hostile work environment. In that context, pornography is not protected free speech but rather a discriminatory act.

When do we deviate from the principle of content-neutrality and what criteria should we use? Justice Stevens's answer is partial, yet he touches upon a pivotal free speech issue: how do we define and apply the content neutrality principle? He explains that the Supreme Court regularly relies on content to distinguish proscribable categories of speech.[9] In the case of one such category, "fighting words," determining "what constitutes advocacy" and "what constitutes incitement" depends on the context and content of speech.[10] What one says matters just as much as how and when one speaks. In libel, courts depend on content to determine whether a writer published with malice and a reckless disregard for truth.[11] The next chapter will consider whether content-neutrality delivers on its promises: does it indeed function in a neutral manner with respect to assessing harm rather than the content of speech?

Justice Stevens contends that law's reliance on content is compatible with the requirements of content neutrality, which demands that government may not judge whether it favors or disfavors the content of speech.

> [A] common thread which ran through all the opinions was the assumption that the rule to be applied depended on the content of the communication. But that assumption did not contradict the underlying reason for the rule which is generally described as a prohibition of regulation based on the content of protected communication. The essence of that rule is the need for absolute neutrality by the government; its regulation of communication may not be affected by sympathy or hostility for the point of view being expressed by the communicator. Thus, although the content of a story must be examined to decide whether it involves a public figure or a public issue, the Court's application of the relevant rule may not depend on its favorable or unfavorable appraisal of that figure or that issue. [12]

The crucial question is whether Justice Stevens's distinction between the need to rely on content to apply the rule is separable from the reason for the rule (to avoid judgments about content). In *R.A.V.*, Justice Stevens notes that communities may dislike speech precisely because it harms. How can we distinguish between disfavor based upon an objective measure of harm versus bias masquerading as harm? An understanding of epistemology and of the value choices that categorizing inevitably entails may help us to delineate between harm and a simple dislike of speech.

The City of Detroit's findings that adult theaters devalue property, inhibit commerce, and debase communities are based on a tacit, if unexamined, assumption about the nature of pornography, one that facially violates the content-neutrality principle. [13] Leaving unexamined the question of why or how pornography produces these effects does not negate that Detroit makes an implicit judgment about the pornographic content which the Supreme Court accepts. The logic strongly suggests that the content inherently produces effects. Later, in the *Renton* decision, Justice William J. Brennan Jr. dissents, quoting a law review article, saying:

> as a practical matter, the speech suppressed by restrictions such as those involved [here] will almost invariably carry an implicit, if not explicit, message in favor of more relaxed sexual mores. Such restrictions, in other words, have a potent viewpoint-differential impact. . . . To treat such restrictions as viewpoint-neutral seems simply to ignore reality. [14]

This is the central paradox that runs throughout the zoning decisions and becomes more developed in *Renton*—that the pornographic content produces both primary and secondary effects. [15] Yet Detroit in *Young* even refers to the content of adult establishments to justify its ordinance. Detroit explicitly premises the ordinance on the assumption that pornography is inherently harmful, stating:

> In the development and execution of this Ordinance, it is recognized that there are some uses which, because of *their very nature*, are recognized as having *serious objectionable operational characteristics*, particularly when several of them are concentrated under certain circumstances thereby having a deleterious effect upon adjacent areas (Section 66 of Ordinance).[16]

The question is: why do adult establishments *by their very nature have serious objectionable operational characteristics?* What do these phrases mean? The answers to these questions are relevant to the Supreme Court's separation of content from effects in its analysis. These phrases, however obfuscating, negatively comment on pornography's content. Moreover, the phrases hint at a deeper common understanding about a practice historically hidden behind shaded windows and doors and located in remote or dangerous parts of cities, one simultaneously celebrated as free speech and regulated as a problem land use.

As noted earlier, the plurality opinion in *Young* relied more on the notion that non-obscene sexual speech is of lesser value than the idea that targeting secondary effects makes a content-specific regulation content-neutral.[17] As defined earlier, the Supreme Court describes secondary effects as those that are indirectly related to the message conveyed by adult establishments. *Young's* plurality opinion refers to secondary effects in a footnote, leaving the possibility for expanding the doctrine in *Renton*.[18]

The *Renton* decision produces a majority rather than a fractious plurality decision supporting the broadening application of the secondary-effects doctrine. While the Court reaffirms the application of the secondary effects doctrine to municipalities zoning adult establishments, it also muddies the conceptual debate about the content neutral status of the doctrine. Justice Rehnquist's majority decision clouds the issue by stating that the zoning regulations are permissible time, place, and manner restrictions and may be identified as content-neutral in targeting effects even if content-based in singling out the content producing those effects. He relies upon past cases such as *Tinker v. Des Moines School District* (1969) where the Court struck down a school ban on the wearing of arm bands as a protest against the Vietnam war. Despite striking down the speech regulations, the Court nevertheless went on to hold that content-based restrictions on expression may be permissible under certain extenuating circumstances. In those special circumstances, government regulators would have to provide factual evidence of those substantial effects on the community.

The doctrinal confusion continues in *Pap's*. In *Pap's*, the Court upholds a total ban on public nudity even though the decision explores whether

Erie really passed the ban as a pretext to target nude dancing. At a minimum, the nudity ban clearly had a disproportionate impact on the practice of nude dancing as opposed to nude sunbathing. As Justice Scalia notes, comments from legislators passing the ban indicated that the real purpose of the regulation was primarily to target nude dancing. The majority opinion upheld the ban on the basis that the restriction targeted the non-expressive elements of the nude dancing taking place in the Pap's establishment: the Erie regulation had only incidental effects on speech.

The *Pap's* decision further complicates matters by merging the incidental-burdens test with secondary effects. The incidental-effects doctrine emerges from *United States v. O'Brien* (1968). In that case, the Court upholds the conviction of an anti-war protestor, O'Brien, for burning his draft card. The Court found the anti-war message protected speech but the draft card burning proscribable conduct. The prohibition on draft card burning passed the content-neutrality criteria and strict scrutiny. In plain words, one may convey the message that they oppose the war, but do not burn your draft card.

Yet the tenuous reasoning over the conduct/speech distinction did not escape Justice Stevens in *Pap's*. The dispositive question becomes, does the conduct/speech distinction make sense in pornography cases or does it generate more conceptual tension? In Justice Stevens's dissenting opinion, he argues that the majority misapplies the incidental-burdens test, confusing the difference between secondary effects caused by speech and incidental burdens, a byproduct of regulating conduct. Justice Stevens explains the difference between secondary-effects doctrine and incidental burdens doctrine:

> When a State enacts a regulation, it might focus on the secondary effects of speech as its aim, or it might concentrate on nonspeech related concerns, having no thoughts at all with respect to how its regulation will affect speech—and only later, when the regulation is found to burden speech, justify the imposition as an unintended incidental consequence. Indeed, if Erie's concern with the effects of the message were unrelated to the message itself, it is strange that the only means used to combat those effects is the suppression of the message.[19]

Justice Stevens's point is that the premises in each doctrine differ. They have two different regulative perspectives or starting points. Under incidental burdens, the expressive conduct is understood first as conduct with communicative dimensions second. In secondary-effects doctrine, the expression is understood as protected speech that happens to produce adverse effects. In the case of secondary effects, government targets laws to combat effects, which only indirectly relate to content. Both doctrines address effects. One targets the conduct element used to express a message, and the other targets conduct/effects indirectly caused by speech. The distinctions, this chapter argues, miss the central importance of conduct in the analysis. In the end, conduct either with expressive dimensions or as a result of speech produces gender-based discrimination deserving of redress. The whole discussion rests upon a conceptual muddle in terms of speech and its relationship to action.

Yet Justice Stevens criticizes the opinion's application of both secondary effects and incidental burdens because the underlying premises of each doctrine conflict with one another. In his view, nude dancing cannot be both protected speech with effects and regulatable conduct with incidental burdens on speech. He writes:

> For these reasons, the Court's argument that "this case is similar to *O'Brien*," is quite wrong, as are its citations . . . neither of which involved secondary effects doctrine. The Court cannot have its cake and eat it too—either Erie's ordinance was not aimed at speech and the Court may attempt to justify the regulation under the incidental burdens test, or Erie has aimed its law at the secondary effects of speech, and the Court can try to justify the law under that doctrine. But it cannot conflate the two with the expectation that Erie's interest aimed at secondary effects will be rendered unrelated to speech by virtue of this doctrinal polyglot.[20]

As Justice Stevens points out, the Supreme Court's application of both doctrines creates greater conceptual confusion.

Many scholars have discredited the conduct/speech distinction. Sunstein comments on the inadequacy of conduct separated from speech in other First Amendment cases:

> When someone attempts to bribe a government official, perhaps he is "acting," or perhaps the regulation of criminal solicitation is "ancillary" or "incidental" to the regulation of conduct. But as stated, I think that this suggestion is unhelpful. Criminal solicitation and attempted bribes are speech, not action. They may lead to action; but by themselves they are simply words.[21]

In essence, the line between speech and conduct is difficult to draw, and many regulatable activities are verbal. Justice O'Connor's plurality opinion invokes incidental burdens, making too strong a distinction between conduct and speech without addressing the shortcomings of this distinction, especially in regard to pornography. In *O'Brien*, a relatively easy case, the conduct/speech distinction serves a purpose, but in more complicated cases it provides the least insight when most needed. Government's justification for regulating draft-card burning is "sufficiently strong and neutral."[22]

Justice O'Connor's comparison of *Pap's* to *Clark v. Community for Creative Non-Violence* (1984) illustrates the controversial point. In *Clark*, the Supreme Court upheld a regulation restricting camping in several national parks. The Supreme Court found the regulation content-neutral even though a group of demonstrators planned on camping as a way to protest homelessness. In *Pap's*, Justice O'Connor associated camping with nude dancing, arguing that nude dancing is regulatable conduct in the same way as camping. She writes:

> Assuming, arguendo, that sleeping can be expressive conduct, the Court concluded that the Government interest in conserving park property was unrelated to the demonstrators' message about homelessness. . . . Even though the regulation may have directly limited the expressive element involved in actually sleeping in the park, the regulation was nonetheless content neutral.[23]

But Justice O'Connor assumes arguendo precisely the issue that requires debate. Is camping analogous to nude dancing? What message does camping communicate? As with any activity, we may attach deeper symbolic meaning to camping. In this sense, camping may convey a message about a love for the outdoors or a philosophy of life. However, law draws a line between conduct such as murder (an activity that one may imbricate with larger symbolic meaning) and conduct such as nude dancing, which is suffused with expressive elements. In our culture, camping has little inherent expressive content, no more than playing baseball. That is, camping communicates no message without a self-conscious effort to connect it to a larger political philosophy such as the Green movement.

At a minimum, the Court's reasoning in the zoning and nude dancing cases generate an unresolved tension about their central premise. The operating premise of the zoning cases is that secondary adverse effects only tangentially touch upon free speech concerns. The focus is upon effects rather than the ideology of inegalitarian pornography. Justice Stevens seizes upon this tension between speech, secondary effects, and content-neutrality. Nothing in the original categorical choice to place the regulation of adult establishments into the zoning category diminishes the nagging ongoing tension about the speech dimensions of the case.

What does all of this analysis in the end tell us? First, the zoning cases spend significant time attempting to persuade readers that the ordinances simply zone land uses rather than regulate speech. The space taken to make such a point reveals the thinness of the rationales. Second, substantial consequences follow from that initial categorization of "zoning not speech," which the justices have struggled to justify. Those consequences are epistemic in nature. Once a regulation is primarily understood as one about zoning, gender's centrality to the practice of pornography is analytically buried. Concerns about property and commerce become foregrounded. While law may acknowledge adverse effects, it perpetuates a fiction that effects from adult entertainment aren't directly related to the content inside. Furthermore, law remains neutral about speech content that produces unwanted, serious, deleterious outcomes: increases in drugs, prostitution, and cat-calling; decreases in pedestrian traffic; and falling property values. Finally, zoning law cannot recognize as analytically significant problematic gender-based effects such as sexual harassment and even rape.

Both secondary effects and the content-neutrality principle within free speech doctrine operate as epistemic gatekeepers, determining what constitute reasonable claims about the problems stemming from pornography; or, to push this point further, these categorical distinctions call into question whether we are regulating pornography at all. Epistemically speaking, what constitutes an invalid knowledge claim about pornography? Invalid claims include that the Court is actually regulating adult establishments because of the pornography inside. That pornography inside the store is elsewhere considered protected speech under the First Amendment. Additionally, what cannot be said in the zoning cases is that pornography specifically produces some serious injuries for women and to analyze these injuries as Fourteenth Amendment concerns. To say otherwise is to violate the content-neutrality principle.

DEFINING PORNOGRAPHY AND
ITS CATEGORICAL IMPLICATIONS

The gender implications of the Court's categorizing choices extend to the differing definitions of pornography. How law defines pornography determines how we analyze regulations placed upon the practice. Is pornography adult entertainment, discrimination, obscenity, or commerce? In the zoning and nude dancing cases, we know that the pornography sold inside of the problem land-uses is referred to as "adult entertainment." As municipalities struggle with defining the practice, categorical choices, and ultimately epistemic choices, follow. Is pornography just another form of banal entertainment, prurient, or simply a profitable business? The answers to those questions require municipalities and courts to grapple with a definition of pornography and social meaning.

In the civil damage case, the pornography Indianapolis attempts to regulate is defined based upon the empirical and historical dimensions of the actual practice. The civil damage ordinance, in short, defines pornography as a gender-based practice, whereas the zoning cases avoid such a gender-centered definition. The last chapter spent some time discussing the language used to define pornography in each of the different kinds of cases. In this section, the emphasis is placed upon the categorical implications of those definitions: the zoning cases decenter gender, whereas the civil damage case places gender at the core of its understanding of inegalitarian pornography.

What are the implications of displacing gender in one instance and centering it in the other? The major categorical implication is that the zoning cases make the claim that they are not regulating speech, placing zoning regulations in the realm of the Tenth Amendment's police-powers doctrine. Under the police-powers doctrine, states have the power to regulate the health, morals and welfare of its people. The police-powers doctrine provides states with a broad plenary power to operate in the public's welfare. The Constitution provides no equivalent concomitant power to the federal government. Yet, when police-powers collide with a fundamental right such as free speech, the state must yield to the fundamental right. For zoning regulations on pornography to pass constitutional muster, they can either not be about speech, or their effects must be of a serious enough nature to overcome concerns about regulating based upon a dislike of the message.

When Indianapolis places gender at the center of its definition of regulatable pornography, it positions the civil damage ordinance in the cross hairs of First Amendment jurisprudence.

The civil damage ordinance defines pornography in the following manner:

"Pornography" under the ordinance is "the graphic sexually explicit subordination of women, whether in pictures or in words, that also includes one or more of the following:

1. Women are presented as sexual objects who enjoy pain or humiliation; or
2. Women are presented as sexual objects who experience sexual pleasure in being raped; or
3. Women are presented as sexual objects tied up or cut up or mutilated or bruised or physically hurt, or as dismembered or truncated or fragmented or severed into body parts; or
4. Women are presented as being penetrated by objects or animals; or
5. Women are presented in scenarios of degradation, injury abasement, torture, shown as filthy or inferior, bleeding, bruised, or hurt in a context that makes these conditions sexual; or
6. Women are presented as sexual objects for domination, conquest, violation, exploitation, possession, or use, or through postures or positions of servility or submission or display." [24]

While the ordinance allows for the substitution of "women" with "men," "children," or "transexuals" where appropriate, the definition focuses on the gendered nature of pornography. *Sexually explicit* is considered for purposes of the ordinance to include "simulated intercourse or the uncovered exhibition of the genitals, buttocks or anus." The definition highlights the core of pornography that MacKinnon and advocates contend undermine women's citizenship rights: the fusion of sex and violence. In the definition, women are objects acted upon to be abused, dehumanized, and brutalized. The definition is based upon the empirical reality of inegalitarian pornography that dominates the markets: the most violent and problematic forms of pornography objectify women, fusing sex and violence. While other forms of pornography exist, particularly variants that one might define as erotica, those are not subgenres that remain the most problematic in our culture. These other subgenres do not comprise the lion's share of downloads or compare to the cultural reach of inegalitarian pornography.

Importantly, as Judge Easterbrook notes in the *Hudnut* decision, the specificity of Indianapolis' definition and its emphasis on equality leads the federal court to conclude that the ordinance cannot be analyzed under obscenity law. Under obscenity law, the crucial concern is not about equality but instead about offense. Judge Easterbrook writes:

> To be "obscene" under *Miller v. California*, 413 U.S. 15, 37 L. Ed. 2d 419, 93 S. Ct. 2607 (1973), "a publication must, taken as a whole, appeal to the prurient interest, must contain patently offensive depictions or descriptions of specified sexual conduct, and on the whole have no serious literary, artistic, political, or scientific value." *Brockett v. Spokane Arcades, Inc.*, 472 U.S. 491, 105 S. Ct. 2794, 2800, 86 L. Ed. 2d 394 (1985). Offensiveness must be assessed under the standards of the community. Both offensiveness and an appeal to something other than "normal, healthy sexual desires" (*Brockett, supra,* 105 S. Ct. at 2799) are essential elements of "obscenity."[25]

As Judge Easterbrook highlights, in order for the ordinance to trigger an obscenity analysis, the challenged work must be considered as a whole to determine whether it has scientific, literary, artistic, or political value. The search for scientific, literary, artistic, or political value is often referred to as the "slap" test. Unlike ordinances that target a work on the basis of obscenity law, Indianapolis does not refer to pruience or offensiveness. The definitional core of prurience is the idea that a work excessively focuses on unhealthy sex. Judge Easterbrook frets that under the ordinance, we will be unable to distinguish *Debbie Does Dallas* from James Joyce's *Ulysses* or Homer's *Iliad*, which both treat women as submissive and objects for conquest and domination.

Inarguably, Judge Easterbrook is correct in asserting that the Western tradition is full of cultural products that depict women as objects without full humanity and as worthy of domination. MacKinnon defends the ordinance's definition by emphasizing that it is wholly unconcerned with an excessive emphasis on sex or explicitness. Instead, the ordinance focuses on the nexus of sex, violence, and gender subordination. The Indianapolis ordinance, whether fully embraced as a strategy or not, attempts to shift the legal terrain of free-speech theory. It introduces a new theory about speech and its connection to maintaining inequality, and it challenges the worn narratives about sex as either offensive or liberatory. Judge Easterbrook both accepts the accuracy of that new theory of speech and rejects it as incompatible with free-speech jurisprudence. The book will say more about this argument on the chapter concerning pornography's harm to women's citizenship rights.

Over time, regulations based upon offensiveness have had limited and decreasing potency in the law.[26] Generally speaking, courts have narrowed regulated categories of speech from *Chaplinsky*—which now stands only for regulating speech that provokes a fight rather than speech that causes emotional injury—to the *New York Times* libel case—which makes it difficult for public officials to sue for libel.[27] The community standards component of the obscenity law appears to contravene the content-neutrality principle as well. To determine whether obscenity violates community standards, courts would have to examine the content of the speech, an analysis prohibited under modern free speech principles.

Nonetheless, some have advocated a revival of obscenity law to address the most violent forms of pornography.[28] In fact, Canada uses such an approach to regulate inegalitarian pornography by retooling obscenity law to embrace gender-based harms as a reason to regulate. Advocates of such an approach believe that using obscenity law to combat the potentially problematic effects of violent pornography has several benefits. First, they contend, obscenity law does not just rest upon offensiveness to regulate. Obscenity law, it is also argued, leaves room to present harm-based evidence. Second, this harm-based evidence could be reviewed at a more intermediate level of scrutiny along the same lines as time, place, and manner restrictions, commercial speech, and/or the secondary-effects doctrine.[29] Huppin and Malamuth suggest that pornography is analogous to commercial speech in that it is less about communication and more about some other purpose: specifically, a masturbatory purpose. Analogously, in the case of commercial speech, the target is to sell a product rather than to communicate other fundamental free speech values like advancing truth or knowledge, facilitating democracy or self-government, and/or promoting individual autonomy and self-fulfillment through expression. Instead, Huppin and Malamuth argue, pornography is essentially masturbatory material. Frederick Schauer extends the "masturbatory" claim, arguing that pornography is a sexual surrogate rather than a discourse on sex. He contends that underneath *Roth, Miller,* and *Paris* is the notion that pornography is sex. The primary purpose of pornography, he says, is to induce sexual excitement. The typical piece of pornography shares more with sexual activity than a communicative process. As such, pornography regulation is an extension of regulating prostitution or adultery.

Pursuing pornography regulation through obscenity law would also diminish concerns about constitutionally defining pornography. If Schauer is correct that the main idea underlying obscenity law is that notion that pornography is sex, then we have a definition with an activity that is more a discursive practice than simply unsettling speech. Discursive practices produce discursive effects with material, ideological, and epistemic dimensions worthy of societal concern. They are closer to discriminatory practices than dissident speech.

Those who wish to revive obscenity law rather than move forward with a civil damage approach point to the experience of other nations in regulating violent pornography. In Canada, Great Britain, and Scotland, modest regulations on the most violent pornography have been put in place. In the case of *Regina v. Butler* (SCR 1992), the Canadian Supreme Court upheld restrictions on the most violent of pornography by redefining and reinvigorating obscenity law. Obscene materials are those where "a dominant characteristic . . . is the undue exploitation of sex, or of sex and any one or more of the following subjects, namely crime, horror, cruelty, and violence." The Canadian Supreme Court found that harm-based evidence could be based upon a combination of common reasoning, community standards, and evidence based upon expert opinion.[30]

In Great Britain, Parliament placed restrictions on the sale of extreme pornography in 2008. In the legislation, Parliament held that actual scenes or realistic depictions of explicit intercourse or oral sex with an animal, explicit sexual interference with a human corpse, explicit violence in a sexual context, and explicit serious sexual violence is regulatable. The law went into effect in 2009. Parliament acted based, in part, upon a 2007 report by the Ministry of Justice.[31] The report is entitled "The Evidence of Harm to Adults Relating to Exposure to Extreme Pornographic Material: A Rapid Assessment (REA)." The report found sufficient evidence to support the possibility of a relationship between extreme pornographic materials and the commission of sexually violent offenses. In some individuals, exposure to extreme pornography increased pro-rape attitudes and aggressive offenses.[32]

Scotland amended its Criminal Justice and Licensing Act of 2010, Section 42, to cover acts involving violent pornography. The Act covers materials whose only purpose is to produce sexual arousal and which realistically depicts acts that take or threaten a person's life, may result in a person's severe injury, rape or other non-consensual penetrative sexual activity, sexual activity involving a corpse, and sexual activity between an animal and a person.[33] The definition of pornography includes staged acts and applies irrespective of consent. The Scottish Parliament released a statement: "it is possible that such material may encourage or reinforce interest in violent and aberrant sexual activity to the detriment of society as a whole." The Scottish Parliament found that pornography is unlikely to "flip a switch" that creates sexually aggressive behavior unless a confluence of factors have created a propensity of pornography to do so.[34]

Canada, Great Britain, and Scotland were able to define pornography, updating their understanding and definitions of pornography to embrace evidence that pornography harms. Additionally, they concluded that pornography harmed by using a "confluence approach."[35] They defined that "confluence" approach as one where multiple factors converge to

produce the unwanted effects from pornography, and they advanced
such a method to assess harm and to define pornography without undermining a broad right to free speech, especially dissident speech. We will
address the matter of measuring harm in the next section.

In the case of the zoning laws regulating pornography, the definition
of pornography is at one remove. The ordinances at issue attempt to
define the locations that specialize in selling pornography yet inevitably,
even if indirectly, must also define what makes the adult establishment
unique—the pornography sold inside. As mentioned in the previous
chapter, in *Young v. American Mini-Theatres*, Detroit defines adult establishments as those businesses that sell materials that depict "'Specified
Sexual Activities,' or 'Specified Anatomical Areas.'"[36] Detroit went on to
more precisely define "Specified Anatomical Areas" as "(1) those less
than completely and opaquely covered: (a) human genitals, pubic regions; (b) buttock, and (c) female breast below a point immediately above
the top of the areola; and (2) Human male genitals in a discernibly turgid
state, even if completely and opaquely covered."[37] The City of Renton
defines adult establishments, which require a description of the pornography sold inside in a similar manner. In the nude dancing case, as the
previous chapter discusses, Erie's ban on nudity was general in nature
even though the legislative record indicated a concern with nude dancing
specifically.

Given these definitions of pornography from the zoning cases, two
important points emerge. First, even though the pornography that ordinances target as producing secondary effects is a highly gendered practice, both the obscenity and zoning definitions erase the analytic significance of gender. The hegemonic inegalitarian pornography under scrutiny in the ordinances, in its current historical iteration, is a gendered
practice, producing gendered harms. To elide the centrality of gender
when addressing regulations is to miss the profound gender inequality
embedded in the practice and the core harms to be addressed.

Second, despite the Supreme Court's efforts to rely on the notion that
adult establishments are simply problem land uses, given the merchan-
dise sold inside, they must define pornography. We see too that despite
Justice Stewart's famous quote about the difficulties in defining pornography ("I know it when I see it."), the Court is able to define pornography
in a workable, albeit imperfect, manner in the zoning cases, much like it
is able to define religion in the conscientious, objector cases. Moreover,
the experiences of other nations like Canada, Great Britain, and Scotland
demonstrate the conceit of Justice Stewart's quote. In particular, the political culture in the United States shares a great deal in common with
Canada. Specifically, like Canada, we are committed to pluralism, secu-
larism, federalism, and a common law tradition.[38] Canada both regulates
extreme forms of pornography and maintains a commitment to those
similar liberal values, especially free speech.

The initial categorization of pornography regulations matter a great deal. Those categorizations as part of either zoning or free speech law determine what law will acknowledge about pornography. Under the zoning definition of pornography, the significance of gender is erased. We regulate the establishments because they devalue property and encourage community debasement. Pornography is adult entertainment rather than prurient or discriminatory. When thoughtfully considered, the Court's acceptance of these descriptions in the zoning cases are quite astounding compared to the soaring language used to defend the very same practice in the free speech cases. Their logic concedes that pornography by its nature is more than simply speech: it produces, encourages, or creates conditions conducive to problem behavior. The curious question unanswered and unexplored is *why*? Anti-porn feminists suggest that the answer to the question has nothing to do with sexual explicitness per se. The Court's rationale in the zoning and nude dancing cases support the insights of feminists who argue that pornography subordinates without the baggage of asserting that the most profound harms from pornography harm women. To date, such a gender-based claim violates the First Amendment.

HARMS (COMMUNITY-BASED OR GENDER-BASED) AND EVIDENTIARY STANDARDS

Both the zoning and the civil damage cases seek to address injuries referred to respectively as "effects" or "harms." Elsewhere, the book analyzes the different language used by the cases to describe the injuries from pornography. As noted in the previous chapter, the zoning cases rely on the term "effects," whereas the civil damage case relies on the term "harm." For analytical purposes, the book argues that the different terms are largely based upon indefensible sophistic legal distinctions, ones that are primarily semantic in nature. While both terms target the problems or injuries from pornography, the zoning cases evade the centrality of gender to pornography and focus on harm to property and commerce.[39] In contrast, the civil damage ordinance defines pornography as a gender-based practice with gender-based injuries.

Under current historical conditions, pornography has been largely a male practice.[40] In a New York State adult establishment zoning case that relied on the Supreme Court's zoning precedents, men predominately patronized the adult establishment in question, and that establishment employed (or independently contracted) only women to display their bodies to mostly male customers.[41] We could examine the nude dancing case argued before the Supreme Court. In the Erie case, Pap's employed women to disrobe for men. If we review both the material sold inside and the marketing data of the adult entertainment business, we would see evidence of the gendered nature of pornography: largely men purchase pornography whether in print, films, or live entertainment. Yet the gendered nature of the practice slips away in the Court's secondary-effects doctrine analysis whereas the uneven gender balance remains centered in the civil damage case.

This focus on the gendered nature of inegalitarian pornography may seem like a trivial insight, but it matters enormously because it affects the way we understand particularly problematic variants of pornography, how we weigh harm, and why we regulate. Women, for example, may face particular dangers living in a neighborhood with adult entertainment, according to an Austin, Texas report finding that sexual crimes were more prevalent in areas with adult establishments than areas without them.[42] A 1977 New York Department of City Planning Report found rape complaints increased by 185 percent in the Times Square area, which contained the largest number of adult establishments in the city.[43]

Both the Court and the cities in the zoning and nude dancing cases nowhere emphasize that the zoning studies used to justify regulations also provide evidence of gender-based harms. Thus, the zoning cases effectively eliminate gender as an analytically relevant concept not only from the definition of pornography, but also from the list of its effects. Instead, these very gender-based harms stemming from a very gendered-based practice purposefully and sophistically remain submerged within a broad category of community-based effects. Moreover, under secondary-effects doctrine, the Court reasons that these effects are only indirectly related to the content sold inside of adult entertainment establishments.

The question remains whether the Court would classify gender-based harms, if localities recognize them as such, in the content-neutral, secondary effects category. The Court has not adequately defined what constitutes a primary effect. Nevertheless, if the rationale from *Hudnut* applies, it is likely that harm to women would fall into the primary effect category: a classification, as we know, with significant consequences. Under current legal categories, one could assume that viewing zoning pornography based on harm to women as a primary effect category would lead to a different speech classification. As discussed earlier, the proper analysis for determining the constitutionality of speech restrictions depends on whether speech is content-neutral or content-based. "The labeling of a speech restriction as content-based or content-neutral is usually outcome-determinative. If a speech restriction is content-based, it may very well be struck down; if a speech restriction is content-neutral, it is usually deemed constitutional."[44]

To review, we must remember that initial categorization triggers different levels of scrutiny and different evidentiary standards. Generally, the Court subjects content-neutral laws to a more relaxed, intermediate level of scrutiny.[45] Under intermediate scrutiny, the Court finds laws content-neutral if they further an important government interest; if they regulate for reasons other than the suppression of the message; if they incidentally burden speech no more than necessary to further that interest; and if they are narrowly tailored to further that interest, leaving open ample alternative avenues of communication.[46] In *Alameda Bookstore,* the Court reaffirmed the intermediate level of scrutiny approach to evaluating supposedly content-neutral zoning ordinances.[47] In contrast, the Court considers content-based laws presumptively unconstitutional, placing the burden on government to explain why its interests in regulating the speech are compelling and requiring government to demonstrate that the restrictions are narrowly tailored.[48] *Renton* avoids such a rigorous examination when the Court categorizes the ordinance as content-neutral. As a content-based ordinance, the *Hudnut* ordinance faces the highest level of review and fails to pass constitutional muster.[49]

The content-neutral, secondary-effects classification also influences evidentiary standards. In demonstrating government's interest in regulating pornography, localities must present evidence of adverse effects or harm. The evidentiary standards applied in *Hudnut* and *Renton* are vastly different. Under a more relaxed standard, the City of Renton easily established a *correlation* between adult theaters and adverse effects. Renton notes that "the record is replete with testimony regarding the effects of adult movie theater locations on residential neighborhoods."[50]

The Renton record quantified the perceptions of real estate developers and urban planners, documented the stories of crime victims, compiled crime statistics, and measured property values. The evidentiary standard becomes even more relaxed when Justice Rehnquist argues that the lower court "imposed on the city an unnecessarily rigid burden of proof."[51] He writes:

> the record in this case reveals that Renton relied heavily on the experience of, and studies produced by, the city of Seattle. In Seattle, as in Renton, the adult theater-zoning ordinance was aimed at preventing the secondary effects caused by the presence of even one such theater in a given neighborhood.[52]

Justice Rehnquist held that Renton did not need to commission its own study to determine that adult establishments cause adverse secondary effects. Instead, secondary-effects doctrine permits cities to rely on land-use studies from other areas regardless of differences in size, demographics, or city layouts. In *Alameda Bookstore,* the Court reaffirmed this evidentiary standard, allowing Los Angeles to rely on a 1977 study correlating adult establishments to increased crime rates and arguing that localities deserve latitude in addressing secondary effects.[53]

Contrast the evidentiary standards in *Renton* with those in *Hudnut.* In *Hudnut,* a federal court required more direct evidence of causality.[54] Proof of causality presumably required a more immediate temporal link between pornography and harm to women. This is not the same standard used in *Renton,* which applied a correlative measure to determine whether prostitution, for example, significantly increased after the emergence of adult entertainment establishments within a neighborhood.[55] The chapter that examines the claim that pornography undermines women's citizenship rights will more closely analyze this causality standard.

While the differing standards (correlation or causality) may appropriately fit the differing natures of the ordinances, one troubling element remains. The studies used to prove adverse effects are no more scientific nor less anecdotal than those used to link pornography with harm to women. Catharine MacKinnon and Andrea Dworkin published a collection of civil rights hearings on pornography.[56] In that collection, women testified about how exposure to pornography was inflicted on them, men testified about how they used pornography against women, and counselors testified about how pornography can be integral to sexual abuse. Much of that testimony could satisfy the need to establish a temporal link between pornography and harm to women and is stronger than the studies used in the zoning cases. The contrast underscores how supposedly content-neutral categories like secondary effects prejudicially select out gender-based claims. If effects like increases in rape rates are analyzed in a gendered context, the Court would presumably place them in the content-based category.

Not only do the zoning studies rely on quantifying the same sorts of information as that found in the civil rights testimony (they document crime stories and compile crime statistics), but courts also permit cities to admit zoning studies from other places in lieu of their own. These varying evidentiary standards have profound effects and determine what individuals can and cannot legitimately say about pornography. The choice to deploy one or the other of these categories (causality or correlation) is not only outcome-determinative, but is also gender-coded by preventing serious consideration of gender-based harm claims. Courts allow that pornography produces adverse effects on property and communities, but this acceptance falls short of recognizing gender-based harms.

In re-reading the zoning cases from the perspective of gender, the starkest difference between *Renton* and *Hudnut* is that the latter emphasizes pornography's specific harm to women and places those harms in a larger equality context. While land-use studies in the zoning cases indicate increases in rape complaints or sexual harassment, they remain either unmentioned or interpreted outside of a gender context. Recognizing the reality that a predominately male practice such as pornography generates some sex-related crimes and, connecting those crimes to gender-animus, the law at stake in *Hudnut* is placed in the content-based category. Under the comparison offered throughout the book, the content-neutral/content-based distinction precludes the possibility of redressing gender-based harms with gender-based remedies in the zoning cases and raises Fourteenth Amendment concerns.

It is the set of connections among gender-based harms, the Fourteenth Amendment, and pornography that scholars fear *Renton* encourages. Laurence Tribe comments, "the *Renton* view should be quickly renounced. Carried to its logical conclusion, such a doctrine could gravely erode the First Amendment's protections."[57] Tribe cautions that the secondary effects doctrine is too pliable and that courts may uphold a wide range of speech regulations under its tenets. David L. Hudson forewarns against the argument made above. He writes, "two categories of expression, indecent expression and discriminatory expression, are particularly ripe for abuse via the secondary effects doctrine because both are considered low-value types of speech that government officials tend to dislike."[58]

While disagreeing with the idea that discriminatory speech is unjustly vulnerable, the arguments raise several important points. The Court engages in a sleight of hand by analyzing content-based restrictions under content-neutral standards: the point that Justice Kennedy's concurrence and Justice Souter's dissent in *Alameda Bookstore* recognize.[59] The Court also engages in similarly evasive tactics when de-emphasizing the expressive dimensions of adult theaters and insisting that the ordinance targets effects only. Moreover, the secondary effects doctrine is unbounded and courts could apply the rationale to all kinds of cases. Nonetheless, the Court's findings that adult establishments produce effects that require government redress are correct. We should extend the Court's reasoning to embrace specifically gender-based effects from pornography.

CONCLUSION

A crucial perspective throughout the book is to consider how and why pornography exists in its current form. How does it thrive? What institutions, principles, values, ideologies, and structures must be in place to defend and even celebrate inegalitarian pornography? What conditions would need to change in order to understand pornography differently and perhaps for it to transform?

In answering these questions, an examination of law's categories within free speech doctrine become important. Law is an important site in the production of cultural knowledge and values. The principles of constitutional law and the rules of free speech doctrine influence what our culture says and knows about pornography. When we scrutinize the logic and assumptions of law's free speech categories, we find silently unanalyzed assumptions and value commitments. Once the hidden premises become analyzed for coherence, logic, and consistency, they become subject to rupture and change.

The premises of both secondary effects doctrine and content-neutrality are problematic even if the intentions are worthy. Both operate, the chapter asserts, as gender-coded categories, ignoring the most profound kinds of harm: harm to women. One approach allows in evidence of gender-based harms yet removes any analytical significance to the findings. Evidence of those gender-based harms is submerged by other community-based and property-based harms. The civil damage approach acknowledges the gender-based nature of the practice and its harms, yet the federal court finds such an understanding violative of content-neutrality. To argue that pornography produces gender-based harms requires causal evidence. Yet to find that adult establishments selling pornography produce community debasement requires correlational evidence.

Law recognizes the need to regulate pornography as a problem practice associated with all sorts of troubling effects. Yet, law seems to want to avoid a conclusion that the practice as currently constituted disproportionately affects women. As long as gender inequality isn't emphasized, the Supreme Court is willing to accept a correlation between the practice and increased rape rates. Once we understand the centrality of gender to the practice, a market-based reality, the content-neutrality principle, is violated.

A critic might rightly argue that zoning regulations appropriately use correlational standards because the adult establishments are concentrated in one area. The civil damage approach addresses pornography and its harms in a more diffuse manner. Without the concentration of pornography in one area, correlation becomes far more difficult to establish. We are left with an individual victim proving a direct connection between pornography and sexual violence.

The response to such an important critique is multilayered and answered by later chapters. Here, it must suffice to say that even if the critique is unanswerable, it negates none of the conclusions. Zoning regulations, for example, could recognize the elephant in the room—pornography produces gender-based harms—regulating with Fourteenth Amendment concerns in mind. Moreover, the effects from adult entertainment are not limited or contained by location. The citizenship-based harms that Judge Easterbrook describes—lower pay at work, insult and injury on the streets—follow women whether they go to these locations or decide never to view pornography even at home. Others who do consume pornography interact in the public realm, bringing the attitudes, ideologies, and beliefs with them. All we need to do is examine the "Me Too" movement. Yet to make such a link between the "Me Too" movement and pornography, the book will need to investigate harm and causality more closely.

NOTES

1. Anthony G. Amsterdam and Jerome Seymour Bruner, *Minding the Law* (Cambridge: Harvard University Press, 2000).

2. Amsterdam and Bruner.

3. Justice Stevens in *Young v. American Mini-Theatres*, 427 U.S. 50 (1976).

4. The same tension is present in the *Alameda Bookstore* decision. Justice Kennedy's concurrence notes that speech is powerful and requires protection from content-based regulation. See *Alameda Bookstore*, 535 U.S. at 445. At the same time, he recognizes that adverse effects from adult establishments are real and troublesome. He relies on the secondary effects distinction to bypass a direct connection between speech and effects. The effects of a zoning ordinance directed to the secondary effects of adult establishments are only indirectly related to speech content and are, therefore, regulable.

5. Note, "The Content Distinction in Free Speech Analysis After Renton," 102 *HARV. L. REV.* 1904, 1917, 75 (1989).

6. *Young*, 63.

7. *Young*, 63.

8. *Young* 65-66.

9. *Young*, 65-66.

10. See *Chaplinsky v. New Hampshire*, 315 U.S. 568 (1942) ("fighting words are likely to provoke the average person to retaliation, and thereby cause a breach of the peace. . . [and] by their very utterance inflict injury or tend to incite an immediate breach of peace.") See also *Oxford Companion to the Supreme Court of the United States* (Kermit Hall et. al. eds., 1992).

11. Any written material that "exposes one to public hatred, shame, obloquy, contumely odium, contempt, ridicule, aversion, ostracism, degradation, or disgrace, or to induce an evil opinion of one in the minds of right-thinking persons, and to deprive one of their confidence and friendly intercourse in society." *Kimmerle v. New York Evening Journal, Inc.*, 262 N.Y. 99 (1933). In *New York Times v. Sullivan*, 376 U.S. 254 (1964), the Supreme Court required two standards to prove libel: an awareness of falsity, and clear and convincing evidence of actual malice, which means a reckless disregard for the truth. See also *Oxford Companion to the Supreme Court*.

12. *Young* 67-68.

13. *Young*, 55.

14. *Renton*. (Brennan, J., dissenting) (citing Stone, "Restrictions of Speech Because of its Content: The Peculiar Case of Subject-Matter Restrictions," 46 *University of Chicago Law Review* 81, 111-12 (1978)).

15. Critics may argue that Justice Stevens is really making a point about viewpoint-neutrality rather than content-neutrality. Nonetheless, as Cass Sunstein notes, the line between restrictions based on harm and those based on content or viewpoint is thin. See Cass R. Sunstein, *Democracy and the Problem of Free Speech* (1995), 174. Two points are central to framing this concern over viewpoint-based restrictions. First, free speech doctrine permits several viewpoint-based restrictions: government prohibits pro-cigarette and pro-liquor ads but allows anti-smoking and anti-drinking ads; government proscribes anti-union speakers before elections about unionizing but encourages pro-union speakers; securities law prohibits favorable views of a company proxy but allows unfavorable views. See Cass R. Sunstein, "Words, Conduct, Caste," 60 *University of Chicago Law Review* 795, 819 (1993). Second, while we can never achieve a level of complete objectivity that would allow us to definitively differentiate between harm-based and viewpoint-based regulation, recognizing our fallibility and a need to refrain from regulating speech simply because we do not like it should not serve to evade questions about the discriminatory harms of pornography or hate speech. To avoid questions about gender-based or race-based harms is to attempt an end run around a question of justice. Government should not be in the business of censoring speech, but it should be in the business of protecting individuals from injurious speech, especially those in historically oppressed groups. To protect individuals in historically oppressed

groups from particular forms of pernicious speech would extend to minorities and women a long-standing tradition in Anglo-American law that regulates (but does not altogether proscribe) harmful speech. See Catharine A. MacKinnon, *Only Words* (1993), 92-93. Restrictions on pornography and hate speech would fall within that tradition while incorporating the experiences of minorities and women.

16. *Young,* 55.

17. See *Content Distinction,* 1909.

18. *Young* 71.

19. *Pap's,* (Stevens, J. Dissenting). See https://www.law.cornell.edu/supct/html/98-1161.ZD.html

20. *Pap's.*

21. Cass R. Sunstein, *Democracy and the Problem of Free Speech* (New York & London: The Free Press, 1993), 125.

22. Cass R. Sunstein, "Words, Conduct, Caste," *University of Chicago Law Review* 60 (Summer 1993): 836.

23. *Pap's,* See https://www.law.cornell.edu/supct/html/98-1161.ZD.html

24. *Hudnut,* 324.

25. *Hudnut.*

26. Huppin, M., & Malamuth, N. (2012). "Adult Entertainment: The Obscenity Co-nundrum, Contingent Harms, and Constitutional Consistency." *Stanford Law & Policy Review.* Retrieved from 23 Stan. L. & Pol'y Rev 31. Retrieved from www.lexisnexis.com/hottopics/lnacademic.

27. Huppin et al.

28. Huppin et al.

29. Huppin et al.

30. Huppin et al.

31. Huppin et al.

32. Huppin et al.

33. Huppin et al.

34. Huppin et al.

35. Huppin et al.

36. *Young,* 53.

37. *Young,* 53 note 4.

38. Brett Boye, "Obscenity and Community Standards." *Yale Journal of International Law* 33 (2008), 299.

39. See Clay Calvert, "Free Speech and Content-Neutrality: Inconsistent Applications of An Increasingly Malleable Doctrine," 29 *McGeorge Law Review* (1997) 69.

40. See Pornhub https://www.pornhub.com/insights/2018-year-in-review.

41. *Stringfellow's of New York, LTD. v. City of New York,* 653 N.Y.S. 2d 801 (1996). A New York state court heard *Stringfellow's* even though it concerned constitutional issues like free speech and police powers. A federal district court remanded the case to the state court because on the issue of free speech, New York's constitution provided greater protection than the federal constitution. *Hickerson v. City of New York,* 932 F. Supp. 550, 555 (S.D.N.Y. 1996). "New York has a long history and tradition of fostering freedom of expression, often tolerating and supporting works which in other states would be found offensive to the community." *Islip v. Caviglia,* 73 N.Y.2d 544, 556 (1989). If *Stringfellow's* could not win its free speech case in the state court, they were even more unlikely to win in federal court.

42. Joseph P. Rose, chair of New York City Planning Commission. Affidavit, A-481. New York Supreme Court, Appellate Division, index number 103568/96, 103569/96 ("the Rose Affidavit") ("during a two-year period in the early 1970s, sales tax revenues in the area declined by 43 percent compared to an 11 percent increase citywide. Crime data for 1975 indicated that Midtown police posts in which one or more adult uses were located had 69.5 percent more verified complaints of criminal activity than any other Midtown posts. Complaints for felonious assault were 142 percent higher, grand larceny complaints were 89 percent higher and *rape complaints were 185 percent higher*

[emphasis added]"). See also Joseph P. Rose, Adult Entertainment Study, (New York: Department of City Planning, 1994) DCP# 94-08.

43. Rose Affidavit, A-490. See *Renton*, 475 U.S., 47; *Alameda Bookstore*, 535 U.S., 440.

44. David L. Hudson, "The Secondary-Effects Doctrine: 'The Evisceration of First Amendment Freedoms.'" *Washburn Law Journal* 37 (fall 1997): 55-94, 58-59.

45. See Calvert, 69.

46. Clay Calvert, "Free Speech and Content-Neutrality: Inconsistent Applications of An Increasingly Malleable Doctrine," *McGeorge Law Review* 29 (1997). *Calvert.*; Content Distinction, 1904; see also *Renton*, 475 U.S., 47-48.

47. *Alameda* 535 U.S., 440.

48. *Content Distinction*, 1905.

49. See *American Booksellers, Inc. v. Hudnut*, 771 F.2d 323, 332-34 (7th Cir. 1985).

50. *Renton v. Playtime Theatres*, 475 U.S. 41, 51 (1986) (citing *Northend Cinema, Inc. v. Seattle*, 585 P.2d 1153 (1978)).

51. *Renton*, 475 U.S., 50.

52. *Renton*.

53. *City of Los Angeles v. Alameda Books, Inc.*, 535 U.S. 425, 430 (2002) (O'Connor, J., plurality opinion).

54. *Hudnut*, 771 F.2d, 333-34.

55. *Renton*, 475 U.S., 51.

56. Catharine A. MacKinnon & Andrea Dworkin, eds., *In Harm's Way: The Pornography Civil Rights Hearings* (1987).

57. Hudson, 68.

58. Hudson.

59. *Alameda*, 535 U.S., 444-45, 457.

FOUR

A Critique of the
Content-Neutrality Principle

The chapter traces and problematizes the ascendancy of content-neutrality and the emergence of viewpoint-neutrality as the core of free speech doctrine. Content-neutrality prohibits government from regulating speech not just on the basis of a category of speech (like racist speech) but also on the basis of regulating a specific viewpoint within that category (racist speech directed at African Americans but not whites). The chapter scrutinizes the Supreme Court's decision in *Brandenburg v. Ohio* (1969) where the majority opinion equated the discriminatory expression of the Ku Klux Klan to communist speech without deliberating about the different conceptual issues raised by the racial dimensions of the case.[1] This ahistorical and acontextual approach to free speech conflates Klan speech (a species of hate speech) with communist speech (purely dissident speech), ignoring crucial analytical concerns about oppression, inequality, and power. As a result, contrary to the connotations of the content-neutrality principle, the doctrine is non-neutral in application.

In an age when the Pentagon monitors dissenters and employers fire employees for their political beliefs, a clear conceptual distinction between dissident speech and hate speech is crucial.[2] At the same time that the threat of government regulation of dissent has increased, the harm from hate speech and pornography has not dissipated. Without a clear conceptual line delineating dissent from hate speech, law offers a false dichotomy: it either augments the power of government to silence all critique (the bad speech as well as the good) or defends the harmful speech of those seeking to marginalize historically oppressed groups through inaction (as greater speech benefits all). In both instances, any examination of how power and oppression operates falls away from the free speech analysis. This chapter maps where the conflation between racist and dissident speech occurs.

The chapter is limited in scope. It seeks to establish and is organized around three main points. First, modern free speech doctrine is shaped in response to the communist speech cases. Second, the core of modern free speech doctrine has its nascent articulation in *Brandenburg*, a case that problematically blurs the line between dissident and racist hate speech. Third, *R.A.V. v. St. Paul* (1992) radically restates and reinforces the content and viewpoint-neutrality doctrine at the center of free speech.[3] The chapter does not address critics, for example, who argue that hate speech is distinctly different than pornography.[4] A retort to those advocating the conceptual distinctness of the two practices is defended later in the book. In this chapter, hate speech and pornography are understood as similar, or more specifically, homologous practices.

Other scholars have made the above three lines of argument separately. This chapter integrates them as part of a larger project to re-read free speech doctrine in such a way that balances free speech concerns with that of the Fourteenth Amendment. The chapter employs the method of a "symptomatic reading," applying it to several key Supreme Court free speech decisions.[5] The method comes from the critical theory tradition in which a reader approaches the text (in this case free speech decisions) with certain questions in mind that the text never intended to answer given the historical times. In this case, hate speech as a legal category develops long after the *Brandenburg* decision. As a result, it would have been difficult for the Court of the *Brandenburg* era to consider the very question this chapter poses: did the Court inappropriately conflate hate speech with dissident speech in the decision? Nonetheless, the purpose of posing the question and reading the text against a backdrop of the reader's own historical times and ideological commitments permits us to uncloak the assumptions and biases of modern day free speech doctrine.[6] As critical theory teaches us, all knowledge is dependent upon historical, economic, and social forces. The law and precedent are no exception. When biases are left hidden or unscrutinized, they can lead to repression, especially when such assumptions skew knowledge claims about race, class, gender, and sexuality.[7] The goal in re-reading several key Supreme Court free speech decisions is to reveal the presuppositions embedded in "objective" knowledge claims or "neutral" modes of analysis and to bring about a change in our understanding of modern-day free speech doctrine, one that incorporates the experiences of historically oppressed groups.

Put differently, a symptomatic reading begins with theoretical commitments or guilt. The reader approaches the text from a particular horizon and reads the text repeatedly.[8] Out of this repetition, the reader generates a "problematic," which manifests itself in the absence of an unposed question. The unposed question is one that is unthinkable within the terms and conceptual boundaries of the text but is posed by the reader after successive readings.[9] To engage in a symptomatic reading, looking for gaps in the text, asking questions that the text prevents given its conceptual boundaries, is to expose the relationship between politics, ideology, and writing.[10] Symptomatic readings disrupt ideologies and attempt to shift the problematic or terrain of the debate.[11] Symptomatic readings always have an unfinished character and are repeated across time by individuals with different histories, different politics, and different ideologies.

THE COMMUNIST MENANCE: UNION ORGANIZING AND SUBVERSIVE SPEECH

When contemplating restrictions on hate speech or pornography, critics often raise the specter of the communist speech cases, which caution about the temptation to regulate "distasteful speech." As one scholar, Nicholas Wolfson, writes:

> Censorship of racist speech may someday lead to the chilling of socialists or libertarians or Marxists or critical legal scholars.[12]

But it is precisely this slippery slope argument that deserves closer scrutiny. Are hate speech codes and pornography ordinances similar to the sedition laws that prohibited communist speech? Is it possible to disagree with the outcomes in the communist speech cases, to uphold the principles embodied in the eloquent dissents of Justices Oliver Wendell Holmes, Hugo Black, and William O. Douglas, while rejecting the way in which modern-day free speech jurisprudence conflates dissident speech with hate speech? To understand the centrality of the content-neutrality principle to modern-day free speech jurisprudence, an overview of the communist speech cases is necessary. Modern-day free speech jurisprudence is shaped as a reaction to those cases.

The communist speech cases, which are widely understood as wrongly decided, shape the content-neutrality principle. David Yassky writes:

> The *Schenk-Debs-Gitlow* line of cases has baffled First Amendment scholars. Virtually all commentators agree that the cases were wrongly decided—Robert Bork being the salient exception. Still, the problem remains explaining just how the Court managed to so completely ignore the seemingly clear constitutional prohibition against censorship. The implicit assumption in contemporary free speech scholarship is that the Court simply and unaccountably forgot about the First Amendment.[13]

These cases clearly represent the nadir of free speech law. The cases occur during the World War I and World War II era and they include, among others, *Schenk v. United States* (1919), *Debs v. United States* (1919), *Frohwerk v. United States* (1919), *Abrams v. United States* (1919), *Gitlow v. New York* (1925), *Whitney v. California* (1927), and *Dennis v. United States* (1951).[14] These cases, particularly the dissents, contain the nascent jurisprudence of the modern First Amendment. The dissents represent the centrality of free speech in a democratic society. Nonetheless, these dissents are later invoked in complicated cases involving hate speech, and pornography, to which they do not neatly apply.

The modern interpretation of the First Amendment, in which the absolutist interpretation is ascendant, began its speech-protective form in the early 1900s.[15] In the communist speech cases, the Supreme Court upheld sedition laws that convicted communist advocates of inciting speech. The individual cases were almost indistinguishable from one another, and they effectively penalized those rejecting the political orthodoxy of the time.[16] As dissidents, Schenk, Frohwerk, Debs, et cetera, expressed an affinity for communism. Because the factual details of the cases are remarkably similar, they lead one to suspect, in Justice Scalia's words, that "the suppression of ideas is afoot."[17] *Schenk, Frohwerk, Abrams*, and *Gitlow* all involved printed pamphlets that favored communism and criticized World War I in varying degrees.[18]

The communist speech cases begin with *Schenk*, which introduces the issue of when government may regulate speech that incites listeners to unlawfully overthrow government. Justice Holmes holds that government may regulate speech only when a "clear and present danger" exists.[19] He finds that Schenk's speech constituted that kind of serious seditious threat. Justice Holmes writes:

> The question in every case is whether the words used in such circumstances and are of such a nature to create a clear and present danger that will bring about the substantive evils that Congress has a right to prevent. It is a question of proximity and degree.[20]

Justice Holmes's opinion prefigures two elements that are part of the ongoing free speech debate and are especially relevant to pornography and hate speech cases. Those elements include the roles of content and context in evaluating speech and the relationship between conduct and speech.

Justice Holmes emphasized the need for weighing content and context in speech cases. In the "Holmesian calculus," content analysis could not be separated from contextual analysis.[21] With a content analysis, the Supreme Court considers word choice, meaning, intent, and circumstance. The Supreme Court weighs the immediacy and gravity of prescribed objectives in the speech, the composition of the audience, the place, and the eruptive potential surrounding the speech.[22] In *Schenk*, the Supreme Court assessed the content of the speech (a pamphlet criticizing consignment) combined with contextual factors—a draft-age audience, a costly war, labor unrest, and the Bolshevik revolution—to conclude that

Schenk's speech created a clear and present danger. The Court determined that the background conditions were sufficient for speech to move from talk to action.

Such a rich content and contextual analysis is imperfect, and it sometimes leads to undemocratic conclusions. Even those advocating a contextual approach would admit that it is hardly formulaic and may easily regulate too much speech. The same approach leads Justice Holmes to a different conclusion in a very similar case (*Abrams*) wherein he begins to critique his own clear and present danger test.[23] This is why, in part, later free speech cases such as *R.A.V. v. St. Paul* deemphasize the role of context in evaluating speech. Such a context-based approach allows for too much subjectivity on the part of justices. Thus, one must concede that those opposed to regulating hate speech or pornography have a valid concern.

The final significant aspect of Justice Holmes's opinion is the relationship between speech and conduct. The debate over the relationship between speech and conduct is a complicated one. Justice Holmes suggests that speech's effectiveness in influencing conduct is less important as a constitutional question, provided that the overall tendency and intent of the speech is to provoke unrest. Thus, Justice Holmes is not looking for absolute causality between speech and conduct. He clearly understates the need to correlate speech's influence on conduct, but this is the very issue he redresses in *Abrams*.[24]

In *Abrams*, Justice Holmes begins to recalibrate the clear and present danger test to become more speech protective. He supplements the clear and present danger test with an immediacy requirement, which precludes the regulation of speech unless threatened by an illegal act.[25]

Although Justice Holmes fine tunes the clear and present danger test, he never alters the underlying premise, which is to prevent violence. Aviva Wertheimer writes:

> His [Justice Holmes] dissent in Abrams marked the initial shift from a restrictive construction of the "clear and present danger" test to a more libertarian position in which the test was used more often to protect speech than restrict it.[26]

By the 1940s, Justice Holmes's *Abrams* dissent became law, and he rigidified the distinction between words with an overall tendency to incite violence and words causing imminent violence.[27] Justice Holmes's new variation of the clear and present danger test emphasized and singled out speech that caused or would inevitably cause violent reactions if unstopped. His distinction becomes solidified in *Chaplinsky v. New Hampshire* (1942) and foreshadows the modern-day importance of distinguishing conduct from speech.[28]

Justice Holmes's shift to a more speech-protective position warrants a return to his *Abrams* dissent. In the *Abrams* dissent, he critiques and revises the clear and present danger test because it proscribes too much speech. But, he also does more than simply throw into question the clear and present danger test:

> It is only the present danger of immediate evil or an intent to bring it about that warrants Congress in setting a limit to the expression of opinion where private rights are not concerned. [29]

Justice Holmes begins to elaborate a larger free speech theory: one wary of the state's power to silence opposition, one that welcomes the competition of many different viewpoints, and one that moves toward content neutrality.

> If you have no doubt of your premises or your power and want a certain result with all your heart you naturally express your wishes in law and sweep away all opposition. . . . But when men have realized that time has upset many fighting faiths, they may come to believe even more than they believe the very foundations of their own conduct that the ultimate good desired is better reached by free trade in ideas— that the best test of truth is the power of the thought to get itself accepted in the competition of the market, and that truth is the only ground upon which their wishes safely can be carried out. That at any rate is the theory of our Constitution. [30]

Upon a quick reading, it is difficult for anyone to disagree with the sentiments in this passage. Democratic institutions are dialogical. They rely on discourse rather than force to persuade fellow citizens. The more one holds an idea to scrutiny and defends it, the more certain we are of its value or its unimportance.

Justice Douglas in *Dennis* echoes this position and adds that all viewpoints, even distasteful ones, are important to scrutinizing our assumptions and testing the truth of speech. Justice Douglas writes:

> Free speech has occupied an exalted position because of the high service it has given our society. Its protection is essential to the very existence of democracy. The airing of ideas releases pressure which otherwise might become destructive. When ideas compete in the market for acceptance, full and free discussion exposes the false and they gain few adherents. Full and free discussion even of ideas we hate encourages the testing of our own prejudices and preconceptions. Full and free discussion keeps a society from becoming stagnant and unprepared for the stresses and strains that work to tear all civilizations apart. [31]

Justices Holmes's and Douglas's passages form the core values of democratic government. They represent the best of a tradition that requires one to reflect on one's beliefs, defend them, and persuade or be persuaded.

Moreover, reflection and reasoned debate are the conditions for peaceful political change. The right to express all viewpoints, Justice Douglas argues, even benefits minority groups such as African Americans or women fighting for equality. Justice Douglas writes:

> Full and free discussion has indeed been the first article of our faith.
> We have founded our political system on it. It has been the safeguard
> of every religious, political, philosophical, economic, and racial group
> amongst us.[32]

He defends this interpretation of free speech using the language of faith, metaphorically placing a commitment to free speech beyond critical revision. Our commitment to free speech, which Justice Douglas interprets in a libertarian way, is an article of faith—a premise we must accept as truth. While one may agree that free speech is the foundation of democratic government, one may disagree with Justice Douglas's libertarian understanding of free speech.

Justices Holmes's and Douglas's elaboration of free speech and its role in democracy raise several issues that remain relevant to modern-day legal and philosophical debates about hate speech and pornography. Both Justice Holmes and Douglas conflate two different kinds of speech. The strongest version or interpretation of the Holmes/Douglas libertarian position eliminates justifications for almost every proscribable category of speech in modern-day constitutional law and leaves courts without guidelines for determining when to apply traditionally proscribable categories of speech such as fighting words. The history that Justice Holmes and Douglas present about the First Amendment is inaccurate too. As is well documented, the founders, in passing the Alien and Sedition Act, proscribed quite a bit of political speech, which explains why modern-day free speech jurisprudence cannot rely upon originalism to justify outcomes like that in *R.A.V. v. St. Paul*.[33] Moreover, while the core of their free speech theory articulates the centrality of free speech to democracy, their concept of how we arrive at the truth and their use of the market metaphor is faulty.

The Court ought not to confuse the speech of minorities and women seeking political change with hate speech. The speech of Martin Luther King Jr. constitutes dissident speech, which is "directed at the powerful institutions that govern our lives."[34] Hate speech targets the "least powerful segments" in our political community.[35] Mari Matsuda argues that the conflation of dissident speech with hate speech suggests that we have no criteria for distinguishing injurious speech from other kinds of speech.[36] Under that logic, we ineluctably find ourselves protecting all speech, even libel and fighting words, which are traditionally proscribable areas of speech.

Moreover, free markets sometimes malfunction, creating what economists euphemistically call dislocations. The free marketplace of ideas is subject to similar distortions. Racism or sexism frequently affect the ability of the speaker's ideas to compete; prejudice consciously or unconsciously devalues ideas because they come from a member of the discredited group (women, African Americans, gays and lesbians, etc.). Racism or sexism can also affect the speaker's ability to speak. This is the more pernicious effect of racism or sexism because the speaker may internalize racist, sexist, or homophobic beliefs. In describing the effects of segregation in the *Brown v. Board of Education* decision, Lawrence writes:

> Psychic injury is no less an injury than being struck in the face, and it often is far more severe. *Brown* speaks directly to the psychic injury inflicted by racist speech in noting that the symbolic message of segregation affected the "hearts and minds" of Negro children "in a way unlikely ever to be undone."[37]

As a result, some viewpoints compete on an unequal footing or never make it to the marketplace.

The free marketplace of ideas presumes that rationality or reason is the invisible hand under which the market operates, yet racism, sexism, or homophobia constitute irrational judgments about individuals based on their immutable characteristics. *Black's Law Dictionary* defines discrimination as the disparate treatment of similarly situated individuals based on arbitrary or unreasonable distinctions such as race or sex. Sexism, racism, and homophobia short-circuit rationality or reason, the one cognitive process necessary for developing criteria for and reaching a consensus about the truth in the so-called marketplace. Rationality or reason is also a crucial cognitive process for the operation of self-government. In democracies, we rely on good, publicly justifiable reasons to exercise legitimate authority.

The marketplace metaphor is too often reflexively invoked as a defense of absolutism to the extent that it has become First Amendment dogma. Such absolutist dogma sidelines equally legitimate and compelling interpretations of free speech. Sunstein writes:

> The most striking development in free speech law is that marketplace thinking has become so dominant, and the competing views so dormant, that it's difficult to even identify those competing views.[38]

This is problematic for Sunstein and other scholars, including myself, because the object of free speech is not the object of the marketplace. The end of the political sphere, which is justice, is different from the end of the economic sphere, which is maximizing profit and satisfying consumers. Free competition in the marketplace usually produces efficient economies and satisfies consumer wants, but laissez-faire competition among all kinds of speech, even the most violent, may not produce results conducive to self-government. A constitutional democracy relies on speech and reason to resolve political dilemmas justly. Therefore, the dialogical nature of democracy necessitates that some forms of speech, which provoke violence or corrode reasoned discussion, breaking down deliberation, deserve scrutiny. Speech serves a political end in that self-government depends upon our ability to reason and exchange ideas, deliberate, and debate. A concept of free speech that permits assaultive racist language into the marketplace of ideas, even eloquently defends it, misses the foundational purpose of free speech in a democracy. It allows into the marketplace a form of expression that corrodes the invisible hand upon which the market depends: namely, reason.

The cases during the communist-threat era posed a question about the proper role of government in censoring the speech of those rejecting political orthodoxy and even advocating revolution. The decisions largely missed the mark, but modern free speech doctrine becomes importantly shaped by those mistakes. The dissents, in particular, begin to articulate a nascent libertarian interpretation of free speech, one wary of government's power to regulate speech, one that invokes the marketplace metaphor, and one that leaves the speech of the Ku Klux Klan indistinguishable from the speech of union organizers. The emerging conception of free speech in those dissents does not sufficiently anticipate the important theoretical differences between dissident speech and hate speech, which surface in future free speech cases.

HOW AND WHY DISSIDENT SPEECH
AND KLAN SPEECH BECAME CONFLATED

Beginning in 1969 with *Brandenburg v. Ohio*, the Supreme Court takes a decisive turn in its interpretation of the First Amendment by narrowing proscriptions on speech. This interpretive turn begins with *Brandenburg* when the Supreme Court refines the inciting-speech standard, reintroducing the standard of imminent harm first advocated by Justice Holmes.[39] This standard makes it more difficult for government to regulate dissident speech, preventing future outcomes such as those in the communist-speech cases.

But, while *Brandenburg* and the communist-speech cases both involve questions about subversive advocacy, they differ in at least one substantial way. *Brandenburg* concerns the racist speech of the Ku Klux Klan, whereas the previous subversive speech cases involved communist speech. Should law approach both kinds of speech in the same way, treating racist speech as equivalent to communist speech? Is the Supreme Court's premise that it must protect Nazi speech to protect communist speech sufficiently nuanced? Does the Court's unwillingness to consider vastly different harms prohibited by the Fourteenth Amendment signal their version of non-neutrality?

The content-neutrality principle articulated in *Brandenburg* is the core of free speech doctrine and becomes applied to successive cases such as *National Socialist Party v. Skokie, Illinois,* and later to hate speech and pornography cases.[40] In *Skokie,* the Supreme Court allows neo-Nazi organizations to march down the streets of a town with a significant population of holocaust survivors. The content-neutrality principle as articulated in *Brandenburg* and *Skokie* holds that government may not abridge speech because of its content, even if the content is verbally assaultive or has an emotionally painful impact.[41] Sunstein describes this content-neutrality approach as placing all speech, from that of Martin Luther King Jr. to George Wallace, on the same footing.[42] The Supreme Court's choice of *Brandenburg* to establish the same footing principle was not likely coincidental. As Professor David Rabban writes:

> In an attempt to demonstrate the political neutrality of its free speech principles, the liberal Supreme Court might have deliberately chosen *Brandenburg*, a case that overturned the conviction of a Ku Klux Klan leader, as the vehicle for its most protective interpretation of the First Amendment.[43]

Rabban argues that by choosing speech widely acknowledged as pernicious, the Supreme Court could presumably illustrate that distasteful speech at the periphery ensures protection for vital political speech at the core of the 1st amendment. This strong libertarian commitment to content neutrality dominates modern day free speech jurisprudence.

At issue in *Brandenburg* is whether Ohio may prosecute a Klan leader for making several threatening comments about African Americans and Jews. The Supreme Court finds that the First Amendment protects Brandenburg's speech. It reaches this decision through a comparison to the communist speech cases. Justice Douglas quotes a famous communist speech dissent, applying its reasoning to the Klan's speech:

> Every idea is an incitement. It offers itself for belief, and, if believed, it is acted on unless some other belief outweighs it or some failure of energy stifles the movement at its birth. The only difference between the expression of an opinion and an incitement in the narrower sense is the speaker's enthusiasm for the result. Eloquence may set fire to reason. But whatever may be thought of the redundant discourse before us, it had no chance of starting a present conflagration. If, in the long run, the beliefs expressed in proletarian dictatorship are destined to be accepted by the dominant forces of the community, the only meaning of free speech is that they should be given their chance and have their way.[44]

Justice Douglas's logic holds that, to protect one sort of speech, it's necessary to protect the other.[45] With this quote as excerpted from the communist speech case and applied to the *Brandenburg* case, Justice Douglas conceptually and discursively conflates dissident speech with communist speech.

The implications of content neutrality as articulated in *Brandenburg* become attenuated in *National Socialist Party v. Skokie*. In *Skokie*, the Supreme Court upheld the right of a neo-Nazi group to demonstrate in a town where many concentration camp survivors relocated. The town passed an ordinance prohibiting the distribution of materials inciting hatred towards groups because of race, national origin or religion. The question before the Supreme Court was whether the ordinance violated the National Socialist Party's First Amendment rights. This case is a difficult one. We detest few groups more universally than Nazis and "few evoke our sympathy more fully than concentration camp survivors."[46] The Supreme Court found that Skokie's ordinance did violate the First Amendment.

Did both *Brandenburg* and *Skokie* conflate hate speech with dissident speech, ignoring analytical concerns about oppression, inequality, and power? The Constitution is neither silent nor neutral in regard to race, and, under the Fourteenth Amendment, the Klan cannot simply have its way should the "dominate forces of the community" accept their ideas. Critical race theorists point to the unique and regretful role of race in our history and politics:

> [R]ace—like gender and a few other characteristics—is different; our entire history and culture bespeak this difference. Thus, judges easily could differentiate speech that subordinates blacks, for example, from that which disparages factory owners.[47]

Matsuda makes the point more strongly, writing:

> I believe racist speech is best treated as a *sui generis* category, presenting an idea so historically untenable, so dangerous, and so tied to the perpetuation of violence and degradation of the very classes of human beings who are least equipped to respond that it is properly treated as outside the realm of protected discourse.[48]

Matsuda offers three broad guidelines to determine whether speech falls into a regulatable category due to its racist content. She bases the guidelines on workable laws in other countries, which consider if the speech discriminates; connects to violence; and conveys hatred, persecution, or inferiority.[49]

Under Matsuda's framework, communist speech—the "poster boy" example of speech regulations gone awry—is neither undemocratic nor exclusive. While some may object to the primary goal of socialism, the equal distribution of resources, its tenets do not call for the supremacy of one group over another based on their unchangeable features. Matsuda writes:

> We have fought wars and spilled blood to establish the universal acceptance of this principle. The universality of the principle, in a world bereft of agreement on many things, is a mark of collective human progress.[50]

It is, then, the premise of racial superiority that nations have universally rejected as pernicious and arbitrary, not the premise of economic equality. Moreover, the Fourteenth Amendment provides clear directives to eliminate racial caste in the United States.

The articulation of content-neutrality in *Brandenburg* and *Skokie* summons the image of an ideal rule functioning in an ideal society: an absence of history and context that follows from application of the content-neutrality principle allows the Court to elide racial and gender inequities in their free speech calculus. While every idea may hold a potential for incitement, the more relevant point is that some speech has a greater potential and likelihood for incitement than others, especially given historical context. The probability of Klan violence against the African-American community does not turn on the Klan's eloquence; it turns on their racial anger and resentment. Yet, an ahistorical and acontextual approach discounts the past and, in doing so, underestimates harm. It finds irrelevant the Klan's long, clear history of racial violence such as lynching. The failure to take into account these historical forces, which affect the present, miscalculates the potential for injury and violence. Without a historical framework, law may easily disregard the link between racist speech and physical violence against African Americans.[51] As one scholar wrote about the Klan's speech in *Brandenburg*:

> The rambling, prejudiced speech at issue in the *Brandenburg* case alluded to the possibility that "there might have to be some revenge taken" against ethnic minorities. It would not have taken a psychologist to see the danger that this Klan-type advocacy might have incited action.[52]

A precondition of hate crimes is that the offenders consider the victims as inherently inferior and worthy of abuse. Verbal abuse often precedes physical violence.

For yet another reason, it is not neutral to discount history and context. Not only does it underestimate the harm from such speech, it privileges a violent reaction which is a culturally specific response to assaultive speech. Avia Wertheimer establishes that preventing violence has always been a foundational concern of free speech doctrine. She traces this underlying concern from the early sedition cases through the communist speech cases, and, finally, links it to the fighting words doctrine.[53] In the case of incitement, the Court focuses on whether the Klan will inspire whites to commit racial violence or will provoke African Americans. Without reference to context and history, the Court easily concludes that the Klan speech will not incite violence. In the case of fighting words, law asks what words would make a "reasonable man" respond with his fists.[54] Historically, who qualifies as reasonable or who is the model for reasonableness? Can this model of reasonability be abstracted from race and gender? Put more starkly, when law invokes the term "reasonable person" is the image that of an African American (man or woman) or a white woman? In the history of Western civilization,

African Americans and women were excluded from citizenship and the protection of law based upon their purported lack of reasoning abilities. When law invokes the reasonable man standard, this is ostensible shorthand for the description of a white male citizen. Re-interpreted from this perspective, the fighting words doctrine asks what words would make a white heterosexual male respond violently?

Moreover, the violent response to a face-to-face insult consists of a very gendered and culturally specific response to "verbally assaultive speech" with an "emotionally painful impact." Matsuda rightly notes that the "bring men to blows" standard is narrowly male-centered and underinclusive.[55] Charles Lawrence writes:

> The fighting words doctrine presupposes an encounter between two persons of relatively equal power who have been acculturated to respond to face-to-face insults with violence: The fighting words doctrine is a paradigm based on a white male point of view. It captures the "macho" quality of male discourse. . . . In most situations, minorities correctly perceive that a violent response to fighting words will result in a risk to their own life and limb. This risk forces targets to remain silent and submissive. This response is most obvious when women submit to sexually assaultive speech or when the racist name caller is in a more powerful position—the boss on the job or a member of a violent racist group.[56]

Lawrence metaphorically pulls the rug out from under the neutrality argument. Women, for example, typically leave a verbally assaultive situation rather than escalate conflict to the point of violence.[57] Lawrence's argument applies to *Brandenburg* as well in that African Americans are unlikely to violently react under similar threatening circumstances. Yet, the failure to react violently among women, African Americans, or gays and lesbians in no way diminishes the underlying injury. In a society where white, heterosexual men are privileged, they are able to respond to such emotionally assaultive words with violence. Law protects both the kinds of speech that such a group finds harmful as well as their reaction to that speech. Other minority groups without the strength in numbers or the differential physical power are forced to refrain from violence. Furthermore, law views the sorts of regulations that protect minority groups from such assaultive speech as content-based and unconstitutional.

Under Matsuda and Lawrence's analyses, fighting words is not premised upon a content-neutral assessment of speech. The fighting words "bring men to blows" standard requires rather than transcends the need to refer to content and context. The question "What words would make a reasonable man respond with his fists?" necessitates that law place words against a background of historical and factual patterns. Embedded in those historical and factual patterns are hidden assumptions based on the experiences of heterosexual, white men. The Court universalizes those assumptions even though they represent a particular group's experiences. The content-neutrality principle and the rules it articulates such as fighting words masquerade as neutral and enable the assumptions behind the principle to remain silently unanalyzed.[58] In a highly pluralistic society, those political assumptions deserve a closer look. Law should broaden its model of harm and recognize that the reaction of women and minorities to harmful speech, even if nonviolent, is significant and worthy of protection.

Compare the content-neutral approach taken in *Brandenburg* and *Skokie* with the approach in *Beauharnais v. Illinois* (1952).[59] In *Beauharnais*, the Supreme Court held that pamphlets deriding African Americans as a race constituted group libel. Beauharnais, a member of a white supremacy group, distributed pamphlets on the streets of Chicago advocating segregation.[60] The Supreme Court wrote:

> It is not within our competence to confirm or deny claims of social scientists as to the dependence of the individual on the position of his racial or religious group in the community. It would, however, be arrant dogmatism, quite outside the scope of our authority in passing on the powers of a State, for us to deny that the Illinois legislature may warrantably believe that a man's job and his educational opportunities and the dignity accorded him may depend as much on the reputation of the racial and religious group to which he willy-nilly belongs, as his own merits. This being so, we are precluded from saying that speech concededly punishable when immediately directed at the individuals cannot be outlawed if directed at groups with whose position and esteem in society the affiliated individual may be inextricably involved.[61]

The Court found that the false assertions in the pamphlet influenced the social, economic, and political position of African Americans as a group, and they found reasonable the fear that racial violence would ensue. In other words, the hate speech produced ideological, material, and epistemic effects on the lives of the targeted group.

This opinion is important in several respects. It acknowledges the racist libel in question as a class-based, group harm. The Court posits the individual as part of a historically oppressed group, an aspect that distinguishes *Beauharnais* from succeeding free speech cases.[62] Secondly, *Beauharnais* prefigures *Brown v. Board of Education*. The Court in *Beauharnais* connects speech to discriminatory effects, a link implicit in *Brown* but overlooked until Charles Lawrence's reinterpretation of that historic decision. In Lawrence's view, both cases concern group defamation. Lawrence writes that *Brown* identifies

> the inseparability of discriminatory speech and action in the case of segregation, where the injury is inflicted by the meaning of segregation. *Brown* reflects the understanding that racism is a form of subordination that achieves its purposes through group defamation.[63]

Although scholars widely argue *Beauharnais* no longer stands as good law in the aftermath of cases such as *New York Times v. Sullivan*, which become more speech protective, Lawrence argues *Brown* remains useful, carrying forward the link between speech and discrimination implicit in *Beauharnais*. [64]

Thirdly, the Court applies a content- and context-based approach in *Beauharnais*. The Court recognizes the lingering structural inequalities from a history of racial discrimination and connects that history to racially motivated violence.

> Illinois did not have to look beyond her own borders or await the tragic experience of the last three decades to conclude that willful purveyors of falsehood concerning racial and religious groups promote strife and tend powerfully to obstruct the manifold adjustments required for free, ordered life in a metropolitan, polyglot community. From the murder of the abolitionist Lovejoy in 1837 to the Cicero riots of 1951, Illinois has been the scene of exacerbated tension between races, often flaring into violence and destruction. [65]

The Court found Illinois' regulation reasonable after weighing specific contextual factors such as a history of racial oppression, racial violence throughout the nation, and detrimental economic effects from racial defamation. Later free speech cases throw into question this contextual approach with the consequence of limiting law's ability to weigh the harm associated with speech targeting historically oppressed groups. In fact, *R.A.V. v. St. Paul* becomes the strongest statement of content neutrality, undercutting the content- and context-based approach applied in *Beauharnais*. The approach in *R.A.V.* leads to a closer focus on the question of whether content-neutrality is really neutral.

In sum, assessing *Brandenburg's* meaning is complicated. On the one hand, *Brandenburg* protects greater dissident expression, providing a foundation for decisions such as *Cohen v. California*. That case protected a student's use of the phrase "Fuck the Draft," which he imprinted on his jacket to protest the Vietnam War. The *Brandenburg* decision also sets the foundation for later cases such as *New York Times v. Sullivan*, which continue the trend of tolerating more non-orthodox political views. On the other hand, *Brandenburg* treats all speech equally, making no distinctions between injurious racist expression and speech opposing the Vietnam War. *Brandenburg* seems to allow a power analysis to drop out of its assessment of harm.

This failure to distinguish between different kinds of speech leaves the particular harms from discriminatory speech invisible. Without addressing the shortcomings of content-neutrality (its failure to provide pragmatic criteria to distinguish between dissident speech and hate speech) the Court perpetuates inequality, ignoring the charge of the Fourteenth Amendment. One need not look far to find warrant for this claim.

The Supreme Court applies content neutrality to strike down laws prohibiting burning crosses on the lawns of African-American families and applies the same principle to protect the right of newspapers to publish the names of rape victims.[66] The Court's current application of content neutrality disparately impacts minorities and women, ignoring discriminatory injuries and disproportionate effects in a way that should make us question its actual neutrality.

The Court makes decisions regarding cross-burning or publishing rape victims' names as if the Fourteenth Amendment did not exist.[67] Yet, upon a holistic documentarian reading of the Constitution, democratic principles animate the First Amendment. Amar writes "No amendment stands alone as a discrete legal regime" and should be read with an eye toward how later, progressively more democratic and inclusive amendments modify the previous ones.[68] The Court should not interpret the First Amendment in isolation from the Fourteenth Amendment, recognizing that some speech, under certain conditions, has a relationship to gender and racial subordination.

So, while *Brandenburg* strikes down sedition laws, which most agree proscribe too much core political speech, and begins a speech-protective era, it also problematically treats all speech the same. Thus, in the specifics of the *Brandenburg* case, democratic and undemocratic aspects emerge that prevent it from becoming neatly categorized as a progressive decision, one that expands liberty. Those countervailing aspects raise some distinct concerns about how justly the Supreme Court applies free speech principles.

Moreover, the political timing of *Brandenburg* is dubious. The ascendancy of content neutrality coincides with the rising political power of minorities and women. When minorities and women gain enough political power to petition government to protect rather than oppress them, *Brandenburg* articulates the "same footing" rationale, which courts augment over time.[69] This rationale departs from Anglo-American law, which always recognized that some speech injures due to content and context.[70]

Some critical race theorists make this point about political timing and the rise of a new speech protective era more strongly. Delgado and Yun write:

> In former times, society was much more structured. Citizens knew their places. Women and blacks understood that they were not equals of white men—the Constitution formally excluded them—and coercive social and legal power reminded them if they were ever tempted to step out of line. . . . Today, however, the formal mechanisms that maintained status and caste are gone or repealed. All that is left is speech and the social construction of reality. Hate speech has replaced formal slavery, Jim Crow laws, female subjugation, and Japanese internment as a means to keep outsider groups in line.[71]

In Richard Delgado and David Yun's view, the new speech-protective era maintains inequality and is one of the primary mechanisms of discrimination in a political culture that has outlawed previously institutionalized forms of discrimination. They characterize this new era as *suspect* rather than *coincidental.*

R.A.V. V. ST. PAUL (1992): A RADICAL INTERPRETATION OF CONTENT-NEUTRALITY

One of the strongest modern-day articulations of the content-neutrality principle is found in *R.A.V. v. St. Paul* (1992). Justice Scalia authored the 5-4 decision, finding content-based a St. Paul, Minnesota ordinance prohibiting a subset of fighting words. The St. Paul ordinance proscribed the display of a symbol, which one knows or has reason to know, "arouses anger, alarm or resentment in others, on the basis of race, color, creed, religion or gender." Robert Viktora violated the ordinance by burning a cross on the lawn of a neighboring African-American family. Specifically, then, the Court struck down the ordinance because it treated Viktora's race-based hate speech differently from all other forms of fighting words.

Three other justices concurred in result only, offering different reasons for their conclusions. According to the concurrences, St. Paul drafted an overly broad ordinance in that it both "failed to identify which injuries would sustain a conviction"[72] and proscribed conduct causing "only hurt feelings, offense, or resentment."[73] For the concurring justices, the ordinance overreached by regulating both harmful conduct and uncivil but constitutional conduct. Moreover, St. Paul overextended its ordinance by criminalizing hate speech rather than providing more appropriate civil and tort-based remedies.[74]

For the purposes of this chapter, Justice Scalia's opinion merits the greatest attention in that it radically restates the principle of content-neutrality. At the same time, concurrences like the one written by Justice Stevens lay bare the cracks in the edifice of the content- and viewpoint-neutrality doctrine. Prior to *R.A.V.*, the Court never applied the content-neutrality principle to strike down a regulation directed at already criminalized speech.[75] The decision reinforces the finding in *American Booksellers v. Hudnut*, which strongly commits to the principles of content and viewpoint neutrality.[76] In describing the extent of the *R.A.V.* decision, now Justice Elena Kagan writes:

> What *R.A.V.* shows, then, is the depth, not the tenuousness, of the Court's commitment to a viewpoint neutrality principle. And what *R.A.V.* did, in applying that principle to a case of non-facial discrimination in an unprotected sphere, was to render that principle even stronger.[77]

The decision points to the need to scrutinize and rethink our assumptions about the neutrality of current free speech principles. What is the relationship between examining content to determine whether speech falls into a proscribable category and unconstitutionally assessing speech on the basis of content?

Justice Scalia's opinion hinges on whether the Court understands cross burning as uniquely harmful, deserving special attention. Amar writes:

> The issues lurking beneath *R.A.V.* are far more difficult than are those that *Johnson* [flag burning case] presented. May government treat racial hate speech differently from other forms of hate-filled expression? Within the category of racial hate speech, can government treat words such as—and I apologize in advance—"nigger" differently from words such as "racist," "redneck," "honky," or "cracker"? Although not posing and answering these questions in so many words, the R.A.V. majority strongly implied that nothing in the First Amendment authorizes such differential treatment.[78]

The logic of Justice Scalia's position is that the Court cannot differentiate between racist speech directed at whites and the racist speech directed at historically oppressed minorities. To distinguish the former from the latter is to privilege one viewpoint over the other. Justice Scalia writes:

> St. Paul has no such authority to license one side of a debate to fight freestyle, while requiring the other to follow the Marquis of Queensbury rules.[79]

In Justice Scalia's reading, St. Paul drafted an underinclusive ordinance, regulating not all viewpoints but only those disfavored by the city. Justice Scalia's opinion and his rendering of the content- and viewpoint-neutrality principle is the free speech equivalent of colorblindness. In the speech version of colorblindness, the word "honky" is just as assaultive as the word "nigger."

Justice Scalia's concerns harken back to those articulated in the dissents of Justices Holmes, Brandeis, and Douglas in the communist speech cases. Those dissents do not directly address issues such as content-neutrality, but they prefigure that doctrine. The underlying motivation is the same in both sets of cases. Given that free speech is so fundamental to the stability of democracy, we run a risk when placing government as the arbiter of good and bad speech. Not only is there the potential for government to misuse and outstrip its powers in regulating speech, but Justice Scalia's opinion raises yet another serious concern; the difference between harm-based and viewpoint-based arguments can verge of the semantic. Justice Elena Kagan make this point about pornography regulation, which shares similarities to hate speech.

Justice Kagan, who is sympathetic to pornography regulation but who also is concerned with upholding content- and viewpoint-neutral principles, writes:

> so long as a legislature reasonably decides, as surely it could do with respect to pornography, that speech causes harm, then regulation responding to that harm (however framed) might be considered neutral, rather than an effort to disfavor certain viewpoints. But this approach, too, makes any distinction between viewpoint-based regulation and harm-based regulation collapse upon itself. Using this analysis, almost all viewpoint-based regulation can be described as harm-based, responding neutrally not to ideas as such, but to their practical consequences.[80]

Her critique directly counters Justice Stevens's concurring opinion in which he asserts that the St. Paul ordinance regulates based on harm, not content. Justice Stevens writes:

> Threatening someone because of her race or religious beliefs may cause particularly severe trauma or touch off a riot, and threatening a high public official may cause substantial social disruption; such threats may be punished more severely than threats against someone based on, say, his support of a particular athletic team. There are legitimate, reasonable, and neutral justifications for such special rules.[81]

In Justice Stevens's view, the ordinance favors neither side, but instead focuses on the unique mode and harm of the symbolic speech.

The crucial issue in this debate is an epistemological one. Who sets the standards and the measures for what determines an actionable harm versus simply hurt feelings? How do proponents of hate speech regulations prove harm to courts and what kinds of evidence of harm will courts find acceptable? In short, then, opponents of the harm-based distinction have a point. Without indicating when harm-based reasons become an appropriate substitute for viewpoint-based reasons, we reduce the First Amendment to a formal rule of legislative drafting.[82] Government could easily recast all viewpoint-based regulations into harm-based regulations. Criteria are needed to distinguish what constitutes a harm-based from a viewpoint-based justification. Justice Kagan seems to throw up her hands in trying to determine such distinctions. Yet, philosophically speaking, an unwillingness to epistemically distinguish harm-based justifications from viewpoint-based justifications for speech regulations is nihilistic. Law is fundamentally about making reasonable distinctions. Philosophically, the difficult job is in determining the criteria.

Justice Kagan highlights alternative content- and viewpoint-neutral approaches to regulating pornography. Government could pass viewpoint neutral laws prohibiting the use of fraud, force, or trickery to induce performances in pornography.[83] Or, government could apply prostitution, pimping, and pandering laws, all of which target conduct rather than expression.[84] The same sorts of content and viewpoint neutral approaches were available to St. Paul to prosecute R.A.V. St. Paul could have prosecuted the conduct rather than the expressive element of burning a cross on the lawn of an African-American family.

However, such a strategy elides the crucial issue in this disagreement over whether harm-based justifications amount to de facto content- or viewpoint-based justifications. The crucial issue is whether law may regulate speech that generates effects that are prohibited by the Fourteenth Amendment. If these gender- or race-based harms genuinely exist, as women and minorities say they do, then law fails to weigh their harm claims with the same seriousness that it weighs fighting words. The content- and viewpoint-neutrality principle, then, functions in a de facto racially and gendered coded way.

Despite Justice Scalia's argument to the contrary, law cannot avoid examining the racial content of cross burning in its free speech analysis. Justice Scalia contends that St. Paul engages in "wordplay" by suggesting that ordinances regulating racist insults are harm-based rather than content-based. He writes:

> What makes the anger, fear, sense of dishonor, etc. produced by violation of this ordinance distinct from the anger, fear, sense of dishonor, etc., produced by other words is nothing other than the fact that it is caused by a distinctive idea, conveyed by a distinctive message.[85]

While Justice Scalia makes an important point, he also excludes an important contextual element. Distinctive ideas and distinctive messages flow from distinctive histories. The symbolism of a burning cross on an African-American family's lawn is lost without reference to history, context, and content. If one pushes Justice Scalia's argument to an extreme, every kind of injurious speech has a viewpoint. For example, segregation was once considered a protected viewpoint. Moreover, at some point, one may fairly say that government disfavors a particular kind of speech precisely because it harms.

Justice Stevens offers a differing view of free speech analysis. He writes:

> Our decisions demonstrate that content-based distinctions, far from being presumptively invalid, are an inevitable and indispensable aspect of a coherent understanding of the First Amendment.[86]

He continues:

> In the broadest terms, our entire First Amendment jurisprudence creates a regime based on the content of speech. The scope of the First Amendment is determined by the content of expressive activity.[87]

Justice Stevens's words are reminiscent of his plurality opinion in *Young v. American Mini Theatres*. Content, context, and history form the backdrop against which the Court evaluates harm. The message of racial supremacy, the placement of the burning cross on an African-American family's lawn, and our long history of Klan violence targeting African-Americans are necessary elements in evaluating whether such expressive conduct qualifies as fighting words. Those elements would also serve to distinguish race-based insults from other kinds of viewpoint-based speech. The chapter argues that law can distinguish between harm-based and viewpoint-based ordinances and should not treat them as identical.

This view-from-nowhere perspective elaborated by Justice Scalia and entailed by the content- and viewpoint-neutrality doctrine is untenable. The decision to ignore a history of systematic racial violence and oppression when interpreting the meaning and assessing the harm from a cross-burning on an African-American family's home is hardly politically or ideologically neutral. Such reasoning functions as a speech version of the colorblindness principle, an approach that misconstrues the guiding theory of the Fourteenth Amendment. The Fourteenth Amendment charges us with the responsibility to eliminate racial castes, not to ignore the analytical significance of race in a nation that used race as a central means of maintaining inequality between whites and blacks. When colorblind policies are applied to unequal conditions—conditions where whites utilized race for centuries to maintain the inequality of African Americans—they perpetuate and reinforce inequality. Similarly, Justice Scalia's articulation of the content- and viewpoint-neutrality ignores unequal racial power, a history of racial oppression, and lingering racial inequality.

CONCLUSION

This chapter traces the ascendancy of content-neutrality and the emergence of viewpoint-neutrality as the core of free speech doctrine. It attempts to problematize law's understanding of the content- and viewpoint-neutrality principles. The principle of content neutrality is a preeminent concern in free speech doctrine, because, in the past, government censored speech at great cost to those holding unpopular political perspectives. If past is prologue, history forewarns us about using the state to silence disagreement. Some of the Supreme Court's most infamous cases permitted the censorship of communist speech and held that communist expression incited civil unrest.

Yet, with the expansion of free speech rights beginning with *Brandenburg,* the Supreme Court ignores the particular harms in discriminatory racist and sexist expression. Successive Supreme Courts compared discriminatory racist expression to communist speech without deliberating about the different conceptual questions raised by the racial or sexual aspects of these cases. In short, the Court conflated dissident speech with hate speech and pornography. In *R.A.V. v. St. Paul* (1992), the Court articulates one of the strongest versions of content neutrality and its primary place in free speech doctrine, ensuring that no principled distinction can be made by the Court distinguishing between dissident speech and hate speech.[88]

The chapter asserts that our inability to recognize the difference outlined above has much to do with the larger interpretive commitments underlying free speech categories.[89] Those commitments hold law to a particular conception of neutrality, one that cannot recognize or address the unequal power, dominance, and exploitation under which some historically excluded groups continue to exist.

Under the strong version of neutrality, the Court fails to recognize that a particular historically excluded group, like African Americans, is differentially harmed by a race-based practice. Nor can it recognize that race-based injuries require distinct race-based remedies. In the case of free speech and the content-neutrality principle, acknowledging the racist dimensions of hate speech is to impermissibly invoke content. The move toward an ahistorical and acontextual understanding of content neutrality, as Justice Stevens points out, is not only incoherent, but also a departure from free speech precedent.[90] In the past, the Court relied on content and context to assess whether speech fell under a proscribable category as discussed in the section about communist speech.

By examining this strong version of content neutrality, the chapter critiques the Court's hidden assumptions underlying its conception of neutrality as well as its narrowly white and male-centered model of harm.[91] Those assumptions have severe political consequences for women and minorities. The hidden assumptions in free speech categories affect women and minorities by discounting their reactions to injurious speech and by diminishing the seriousness of their injuries.

Although the chapter analyzes the Court's conception of neutrality, it does not argue that the motivation to protect dissident speech is ill-conceived. On the contrary, the desire to protect dissident speech is a preeminent concern. The problem with free speech doctrine is that it confuses the need to protect dissident speech with the desire to protect hate speech or inegalitarian pornography. The Constitution's commitments to equality, freedom, and fairness provide a foothold to challenge unjust and harmful practices such as hate speech. Sometimes the Court applies the wrong conception of free speech to particular cases, but the contradictions produced by such cases nag our politics until redressed.[92] The chapter advocates that the Court broaden the assumptions underlying free speech categories and its model of harm, balancing the First with Fourteenth Amendment concerns. In a plural society, law's assumptions should reflect the experiences of all its citizens, not just a few under the false guise of a universal model of harm.

NOTES

1. *Brandenburg v. Ohio*, 395 US 444 (1969).

2. Geoffrey Stone, *Perilous Times* (New York: W.W. Norton & Company, Inc., 2004), Lee C. Bollinger & Geoffrey R. Stone, ed., *Eternally Vigilent: Free Speech in the Modern Era* (Chicago and London: University of Chicago Press, 2002), Mark A. Graber, *Transforming Free Speech: The Ambiguous Legacy of Civil Libertarianism* (Los Angeles: University of California Press, 1992).

3. *R.A.V. V. St. Paul*, 505 US 377 (1992).

4. Judith Butler, *Excitable Speech: A Politics of the Performative* (New York and London: Routledge, 1997).

5. Ellen Rooney, "Better Read Than Dead: Althusser and the Fetish of Ideology," *Yale French Studies* 88 (1995). See also Louis Althusser and Etienne Balibar, *Reading Capital*, trans. Ben Brewster, 1997 ed. (New York and London: Verso).

6. Rooney, "Better Read Than Dead: Althusser and the Fetish of Ideology." See also Alan Hyde, *Bodies of Law* (Princeton: Princeton University Press, 1997).

7. Rooney, "Better Read Than Dead: Althusser and the Fetish of Ideology." See also Louis Althusser, *For Marx*, trans. Ben Brewster, 1996 ed. (New York and London: Verso).

8. Rooney, "Better Read Than Dead: Althusser and the Fetish of Ideology."

9. Rooney.

10. Lynn Mills Eckert, "Language Games: Regulating Adult Establishments and the Obfuscation of Gender," *Southern California Review of Law and Social Justice* 15 (2006).

11. Alan Hyde, *Bodies of Law* (Princeton: Princeton University Press, 1997).

12. Nicholas Wolfson, "Free Speech Theory and Hateful Words," *University of Cinncinnati Law Review* 60 (1991).

13. David Yassky, "Eras of the First Amendment," *Columbia Law Review* 91 (1991).

14. *Schenk V. United States*, 249 US 204 (1919), *Debs V. United States*, US (1919), *Frohwerk V. United States*, 249 US 209 (1919), *Abrams V. United States*, 250 US 616 (1919), *Gitlow V. New York*, 268 US 252 (1925), *Whitney V. California*, 274 US 357 (1927), *Dennis V. United States*, 341 US 494 (1951).

15. Cass R. Sunstein, *Democracy and the Problem of Free Speech* (New York: The Free Press, 1995).

16. Sunstein, 2.

17. Justice Scalia in *R.A.V. V. St. Paul*, 390.

18. The only aberration in these cases is the *Whitney* decision. In that case, the Supreme Court upheld Charlotte Whitney's conviction for violating California's Syndicalism Act. Ms. Whitney chaired a committee that drafted a party platform for the Communist Party. She testified that her views differed from those in the platform but that as the chair she dutifully ratified it. The unusual aspect of this case is that Justice Holmes concurred with the majority opinion in one of the most repressive decisions of the era. In every other case succeeding *Schenk*, Justice Holmes dissents. Some scholars note that Justice Holmes concurred in the judgment because the principal constitutional issues were improperly raised in a trial court and were unreviewable on appeal. See Howard Owen Hunter, "Problems in Search of Principles: The First Amendment in the Supreme Court from 1791–1930," *Emory Law Journal* 35 (1986). In any case, Justice Holmes distinguishes Ms. Whitney's expression from the communist speech in previous cases by framing Ms. Whitney's expression as a preparatory step necessary for the overthrow of government.

19. The historical context in which the Court handed down the decision is instructive. During times of political, economic, and social upheaval, courts tend to overreact, protecting too much speech rather than too little. In the early 1900s, Congress and the states enacted sedition laws aimed to silence dissent during a politically unstable time. In 1917, the Bolshevik Revolution began in Russia and the United States entered the war against Germany and Austria-Hungary. That same year, Congress passed the Espionage Act of 1917, making unlawful efforts to interfere with military recruitment

or to encourage dissent within the military. A year later, in 1918, Congress enacted a sedition law, which prohibited disloyal speech about the military, government, and/or the flag.

20. *Schenk v. United States*, 52.

21. Howard Owen Hunter, "Problems in Search of Principles: The First Amendment in the Supreme Court From 1791-1930." *Emory Law Journal* 35 (1980): 59-137, 103-104.

22. Hunter.

23. David Rabban contends that Justice Holmes really articulated another version of the "bad tendency test" in *Schenk*, but that Zechariah Chafee Jr. misconstrued the phrase "clear and present danger" to supplant the bad tendency test. According to Rabban, Justices Holmes and Brandeis used this misconstruence to their advantage in later decisions. See David Rabban, "Free Speech in Progressive Social Thought," *Texas Law Review* 74 (1996), 1019. See also Rabban, "The Emergence of the Modern First Amendment Doctrine," *University of Chicago Law Review* 50 (1983).

24. In later free speech doctrine, courts deploy a causal standard in pornography cases like *American Booksellers Association V. Hudnut*, 771 F2d. 323 (1985) yet deploy a correlation standard in the nude dancing cases like *City of Renton V. Playtime Theatres Inc*, 475 US 41 (1986).

25. Rabban, "The Emergence of the Modern First Amendment Doctrine," 1309.

26. Aviva O. Wertheimer, "The First Amendment Distinction between Conduct and Content: A Conceptual Framework for Understanding Fighting Words Jurisprudence," *Fordham Law Review* 63, no. December (1994).

27. Wertheimer.

28. Wertheimer, *Chaplinsky v. New Hampshire*, 315 US 568 (1942).

29. Justice Holmes in *Abrams v. United States*, 629.

30. Justice Holmes in *Abrams*, 630.

31. *Dennis v. United States*, 584 (Douglas, J. Dissenting).

32. *Dennis*.

33. Sunstein, *Democracy and the Problem of Free Speech*, xii-xvi.

34. Mari J. Matsuda Charles R. Lawrence III, Richard Delgado, Kimberle Williams Crenshaw, "Introduction," in *Words That Wound: Critical Race Theory, Assaultive Speech, and the First Amendment*, ed. Charles R. Lawrence III Mari J. Matsuda, Richard Delgado, Kimberle Williams Crenshaw (Boulder Westview Press, 1993), 10.

35. Matsuda et al.

36. Mari J. Matsuda, "Public Response to Racist Speech: Considering the Victim's Story," in *Words That Wound: Critical Race Theory, Assaultive Speech, and the First Amendment*, ed. Charles R. Lawrence III Mari J. Matsuda, Richard Delgado, Kimberle Williams Crenshaw (Boulder, San Francisco & Oxford: Westview Press, 1993), 32.

37. Charles R. Lawrence III, "If He Hollers Let Him Go: Regulating Racist Speech on Campus," in *Words That Wound: Critical Race Theory, Assaultive Speech and the First Amendment* (Boulder, San Francisco & Oxford: Westview Press, 1993), 74.

38. Sunstein, *Democracy and the Problem of Free Speech*, 4.

39. Most scholars consider the "clear and present danger plus imminence test" controlling in modern day free speech doctrine

40. *Nationalist Socialist Party V. Skokie, Illinois*, 432 US 43 (1977).

41. Donald Alexander Downs, *Nazis in Skokie: Freedom, Community and the First Amendment* (Notre Dame: University of Notre Dame Press, 1985), 2.

42. Sunstein, *Democracy and the Problem of Free Speech*, 5

43. Rabban, "Free Speech in Progressive Social Thought," 953

44. Justice Douglas in *Brandenburg* quoting Justice Holmes in *Gitlow, Brandenburg V. Ohio*, 436-37 (Douglas, J. Concurring).

45. Richard Delgado and David Yun, "The Speech We Hate: First Amendment Totalism, the ACLU, and the Principle of Dialogic Politics," *Arizona State Law Journal* 27 (1995), 1285.

46. Edward L. Rubin, "Review of Nazis in Skokie: Freedom, Community, and the First Amendment by Donald Alexander Downs," *California Law Review* 74 (1986), 234.

47. Richard Delgado and Jean Sefancic, *Must We Defend Nazis? Hate Speech, Pornography, and the New First Amendment* (New York and London: New York University Press, 1997), 68.

48. Matsuda, "Public Response to Racist Speech: Considering the Victim's Story," 35.

49. Matsuda, 31, 36.

50. Matsuda, 37.

51. See Wertheimer, "The First Amendment Distinction between Conduct and Content: A Conceptual Framework for Understanding Fighting Words Jurisprudence," Sefancic, *Must We Defend Nazis? Hate Speech, Pornography, and the New First Amendment*, and Kent Greenawalt, *Fighting Words: Individuals, Communities, and Liberties of Speech* (Princeton: Princeton University Press, 1995).

52. David Crump, "Camouflaged Incitement: Freedom of Speech, Communicative Torts, and the Borderland of the Brandenburg Test," *Georgia Law Review* 29 (1994), 4.

53. The Court defines fighting words as "those by which their very utterance inflict injury or tend to incite an immediate breach of peace" (Wertheimer, "The First Amendment Distinction between Conduct and Content: A Conceptual Framework for Understanding Fighting Words Jurisprudence," citing *Chaplinsky v. New Hampshire*).

54. Matsuda, "Public Response to Racist Speech: Considering the Victim's Story," 35.

55. Matsuda.

56. Charles R. Lawrence, "If He Hollers Let Him Go: Regulating Racist Speech on Campus," 69.

57. Matsuda, "Public Response to Racist Speech: Considering the Victim's Story," 35. The point in using Lawrence's quote is not to draw a direct comparison to pornography, but to indicate that the categories we accept as neutral are, in actuality, viewpoint based in some manner. We accept the male reaction to fighting words as universal, but consider minorities' and women's perspectives about harmful speech as viewpoint based.

58. Linda Alcoff, "How Is Epistemology Political?," in *Radical Philosophy: Tradition, Counter-Tradition, Politics*, ed. Roger S. Gottlieb (Philadelphia: Temple University Press, 1993), 76.

59. *Beauharnais v. Illinois*, 343 US 250 (1952) and *National Socialist Party of America v. Village of Skokie*, 432 U.S. 43 (1977).

60. Beauharnais wrote: "One million self respecting white people in Chicago unite. . . . If persuasion and the need to prevent the white race from becoming mongrelized by the negro will not unite us, then the agressions . . . rapes, robberies, knives, guns, and marijuana of the negro, surely will." *Beauharnais v. Illinois*, 252.

61. *Beauharnais*, 733-34.

62. Catharine MacKinnon, *Only Words* (Cambridge: Harvard University Press 1993), 81-83.

63. Charles R. Lawrence, "If He Hollers Let Him Go: Regulating Racist Speech on Campus," 75.

64. See Sefancic, *Must We Defend Nazis? Hate Speech, Pornography, and the New First Amendment*, 62. The Court has never explicitly overruled *Beauharnais* but decisions like *New York Times v. Sullivan*, 376 US 254 (1964).and *R.A.V. v. St. Paul*, 505 U.S. 377 (1992) effectively undermine it.

65. *Beauharnais v. Illinois*, 731-32.

66. Sunstein, *Democracy and the Problem of Free Speech*, 163.

67. MacKinnon, *Only Words*, 71-110.

68. Akhil Reed Amar, "The Supreme Court 1999 Term Forward: The Document and the Doctrine," *Harvard Law Review* 114, no. November (2000), 29.

69. Susan Bordo, *Unbearable Weight: Feminism, Western Culture, and the Body* (Los Angeles and London: University of California Press, 1993), 215-243, makes a similar

claim about the rise of poststructuralism's gender skepticism, which undermines the ability to see any continuity of experience among women.

70. See Sunstein, *Democracy and the Problem of Free Speech*, Wertheimer, "The First Amendment Distinction between Conduct and Content: A Conceptual Framework for Understanding Fighting Words Jurisprudence," Charles R. Lawrence, "If He Hollers Let Him Go: Regulating Racist Speech on Campus," MacKinnon, *Only Words*.

71. Richard Delgado and David Yun, "The Speech We Hate: First Amendment Totalism, the ACLU, and the Principle of Dialogic Politics," 1298.

72. Kent Greenawalt, *Fighting Words: Individuals, Communities, and Liberties of Speech*, 56.

73. *R.A.V.*, 112 S. Ct. at 2541 in Greenawalt, 56. See also Brennan Neville, "Anti-Pornography Legislation as Content Discrimination under *R.A.V.*," *Kansas Journal of Law & Public Policy* 121 (1995), 121-130.

74. Delgado and Sefancic, *Must We Defend Nazis? Hate Speech, Pornography, and the New First Amendment*, 4.

75. See Wertheimer, "The First Amendment Distinction between Conduct and Content: A Conceptual Framework for Understanding Fighting Words Jurisprudence," 873-902.

76. Elena Kagan, "Pornography and Hate Speech Regulation after *R.A.V.*," *University of Chicago Law Review* 60 (1993), 877.

77. Kagan.

78. Amar, "The Supreme Court 1999 Term Forward: The Document and the Doctrine," 125-26.

79. *R.A.V. v. St. Paul*, 392.

80. Kagan, "Pornography and Hate Speech Regulation after *R.A.V.*," 880.

81. *R.A.V. v. St. Paul.*, 416 (Stevens, J. Concurring).

82. Kagan, "Pornography and Hate Speech Regulation after *R.A.V.*," 881-82.

83. Kagan, 887.

84. Kagan.

85. *R.A.V. v. St. Paul*, 392.

86. *R.A.V.* 420 (Stevens, J. Concurring).

87. *R.A.V.*

88. *R.A.V.*

89. Satya P. Mohanty, *Literary Theory and the Claims of History: Postmodernism, Objectivity, Multicultural Politics* (Ithaca and London: Cornell University Press, 1997), Carol Smart, *Feminism and the Power of Law* (London and New York: Routledge, 1989), Robin West, *Progressive Constitutionalism: Reconstructing the Fourteenth Amendment* (Durham and London: Duke University Press, 1994).

90. *R.A.V. v. St. Paul*, 420 (Stevens, J. Concurring).

91. Matsuda, "Public Response to Racist Speech: Considering the Victim's Story," 35. Also see Charles R. Lawrence, "If He Hollers Let Him Go: Regulating Racist Speech on Campus," 69.

92. Stephen Macedo, *Liberal Virtues* (New York: Oxford University Press, 1990), 116.

FIVE

Pornography Harms: Where Speech Act Theory, Causality, and the Performative Fall Short

This chapter attempts to introduce and analyze three different conceptual frameworks that evaluate the anti-pornography feminist claim that pornography constitutes discrimination, thereby undermining women's citizenship rights. Two of the models attempt to bolster the claim that pornography constitutes discrimination, while the other argues that pornography as a speech act ought not be regulated and cannot be properly thought of as constituting discrimination. The first model uses speech act theory to explain the subordinating and silencing argument advanced by Catherine MacKinnon. The probobalistic causal model advocated by Anne Eaton provides an alternative to speech-act theory to explain the claim that pornography harms women. Along the way, the chapter also confronts Judith Butler's critique of the speech-act model. That critique based upon the notion of the performative quality of speech asserts that pornography cannot constitute discrimination as described by Rae Langton and that any form of government regulation upends the opportunity to resignify harmful speech like pornography in liberatory ways.

The chapter explains why these critiques fail in an effort to set up the idea that law must embrace a new conceptual understanding of the way speech harms. In addressing speech act theory, we find a complicated conceptual framework, which never clearly articulates the mechanism by which pornography subordinates and silences women.[1] In Judith Butler's critique of speech act theory, we find an altogether different problem. She diminishes the harm from pornography and presents an unrealistic theory for social change. In the case of Anne Eaton's attempt to introduce a complex model of causality based on the framework used by epidemiologists, it falters too. As the next chapter will argue, speech does not act in a causal manner. In the words of Foucault, causality is a mystification of the way in which speech "does things."

A BRIEF SUMMARY OF
THE "PORNOGRAPHY AS SPEECH ACT" ARGUMENT

J. L. Austin, who writes in the analytical philosophical tradition, argued that speech does not just describe the world: it also "does things" in the world. By locating the discussion of pornography in the context of speech act theory, we "place[s] language within the realm of social activity rather than mere expression: speech and action aren't opposed but rather speech is action."[2] The name that Austin gave for explaining what speech does in the world is speech act theory. Austin identified three different dimensions of speech: locution (an asserted proposition), illocution (an action constituted by the utterance), and perlocution (the effect of the utterance on the audience).[3] In the case of pornography, anti-pornography feminists like Langton are mostly concerned with the illocutionary force of the speech—what pornography as speech does. Within the category of illocutionary speech, we find that Langton focuses on a subcategory, namely, exercitive speech, or the sort of authoritative speech that denies or confers powers.[4] Langton's argument attempts to show that pornography is a subordinating illocutionary act, using the analogy between speech in an apartheid context and pornography.[5]

In an exercitive speech act, a decision is made to act with the very articulation of the utterance. For example, when a pastor pronounces a couple, "husband and wife," the utterance is an exercitive act. For an exercitive speech act to succeed, several conditions must be met. We sometimes call these criteria "permissibility or felicity conditions." First, the speaker must intend to engage in an exercitive speech act. Second, the speaker must be able to effectively convey that exercitive intent. Third, the listener must understand the exercitive intent. Finally, the speaker must have the authority to carry out the exercitive intent. As noted above, Langton cites the example of a minister pronouncing a couple man and wife as the quintessential exercitive act. The minister intends to marry the couple and effectively conveys that intent when uttering, "I pronounce you man and wife." The listeners understand the exercitive intent and the pastor has the authority to declare the couple man and wife introducing them as such to the community. The utterance of "I pronounce you man and wife" functions to marry the couple, fulfilling the pastor's intent through his authority. The act of pronouncing the couple man and wife is also dependent upon the audience's acceptance of the pastor's intent. For Langton, pornography is analogous to that exercitive act example of the minister declaring a marriage.

Langton provides another example of an illocutionary exercitive speech act in the context of an apartheid regime. Langton writes:

> Consider this utterance: "Blacks are not permitted to vote." Imagine that it is uttered by a legislator in Pretoria [during the time of apartheid] in the context of enacting legislation that underpins apartheid. It is a locutionary act: by "blacks" it refers to blacks. It is a perlocutionary act: it will have the effect, among others, that blacks stay away from polling booths. But it is, first and foremost, an illocutionary act: it *makes it the case* that blacks are not permitted to vote. It—plausibly—subordinates blacks.[6]

If we are to count the utterance above as subordinating, the speaker must have the authority to create the status while speaking. Langton argues that in much the same way as the racist apartheid speech above, pornography too has exercitive, illocutionary force. Pornography, then, makes it the case that women are subordinated: its force is constitutive of reality.[7] Here, we distinguish between pornography's perlocutionary force, its effects, such as lower pay at work and violence on the streets (to paraphrase Judge Easterbrook in *American Booksellers v. Hudnut* [1985]).[8] Langton recognizes that to the extent that these effects are verifiable, then we can identify this perlocutionary act as subordinating as well. Yet, this is different from the illocutionary claim that pornography in and of itself ranks women as inferior. Langton's argument hinges on whether pornography fulfills the felicity or permissibility conditions of authority.[9]

In setting the four criteria that exercitive speech must meet—the permissibility or felicity conditions—Langton attempts to philosophically defend the notion that pornography subordinates and silences.[10] Again, if Langton is to succeed in providing philosophical rigor to MacKinnon's claims that pornography harms through speech act theory, pornography must meet the criteria defining exercitive speech. While Langton agrees that pornography falls short of the paradigmatic ideal of apartheid speech, she contends that pornographic speech sets permissibility conditions for heterosexual sex by degrading, demeaning, subordinating, and silencing women. Moreover, pornographers, she suggests, occupy a place of admiration and respect in our culture, a point open to empirical verification.[11]

Kate McGowan challenges Langton's argument that pornography is an exercitive act. Pornography, McGowan contends, meets none of those permissibility conditions mentioned above.[12] McGowan notes that pornographers don't have the power or authority to set the parameters for heterosexual sex.[13] Moreover, some of the producers of pornography may not intend to silence or subordinate women. Even if some *do* intend to subordinate and silence, listeners may not understand the intent. Moreover, Daniel Jacobson argues that the right to free speech does not depend upon its effectiveness at silencing.[14] Therefore, we have some complexities undermining the claim that pornography is an illocutionary exercitive speech act that subordinates based upon concerns about whether pornographers really have the authority and the intent "to make it so." Furthermore, it is unclear that listeners will understand the subordinating goal of pornographers—maybe some will, but others will not.

McGowan attempts to save the "pornography as speech act" argument by introducing the idea of the conversational exercitive, a concept borrowed from David Lewis.[15] A conversational exercitive is one that relaxes Austinian rules by acknowledging that in conversations all participants unselfconsciously set permissibility conditions rather than a clear authority. Furthermore, no parties (the speaker or listeners) are required to self-consciously convey exercitive content nor understand it. Instead, participants are part of a fluid context, where any one of them could set the permissibility conditions for exercitive speech success. In the context of pornography, then, pornographic speech is ongoing and sets permissibility conditions for heterosexual sex without an authority figure and without a clear intent that listeners will recognize. Unfortunately, McGowan's concept of conversational exercitive speech, while relaxing required criteria for success, still cannot tell us whether pornography sets the very permissibility conditions that subordinate and silence women. We are left with a vague understanding of the precise mechanisms of discrimination.

Speech-act theory, then, leads us to a conceptually murky ending. It can only take us so far conceptually in explaining both how pornography is discrimination (illocutionary force) and how pornography injures through lower pay at work or injuries on the streets (perlocutionary effects).[16] Philosopher Lisa Schwarzman notes that the distinction between illocutionary and perlocutionary speech is tricky and unstable. Often, in my view, the distinction causes more conceptual confusion than clarity. More important than the distinction itself is that, functionally speaking, pornography undermines women's citizenship status. Whether it does so just through speaking (under certain felicity conditions) or through the effects on others is less of a central concern and can be regulated on both grounds.[17]

Generally, speech act theory suffers from misconceptualizing pornography as a discrete act occurring at a discrete time with a locatable authoritative voice.[18] Three immediate concerns arise from such an atomistic framework. First, theorists have difficulty locating the authoritative or "sovereign" speaker in the case of pornography.[19] We must ask whether the authoritative speaker is the owner of a pornographic outlet, the people who produce porn, the actors, or the boyfriend who imposes pornography on a quiescent partner?[20] Second, we are left to consider what qualifies as a speech act? Perhaps it is one particular pornographic movie or all the pornography in circulation at a particular moment.[21] Third, pornography conveys its message in a far more complicated way than speech act advocates theorize.[22] Instead of the discrimination occurring at the moment of an utterance, the practice of pornography is one that communicates through "bodily movements, gestures, comportment, posture, movement, facial expression, dress, adornment, and so on."[23] Yet speech act theory fixates on a single authoritative source with a specific intention at a particular moment in time. Such a conceptual focus cannot fully explain the culturally and socially oppressive force of pornography, one rooted in cumulative and hegemonic acts.[24]

Foucault's understanding of both discourse and its relationship to power removes us from this speech act conundrum. Discourse is a body of knowledge about a particular subject that circulates throughout the social body. Discourse regulates and shapes desire in ways that are not necessarily discretely expressed or concentrated. It is everything written, spoken, and communicated about a subject, and it contains its own premises, rules, and logic. No sovereign or authoritative voice is necessary for the discourse to produce discriminatory effects.[25] The force of the discourse, its power, rests upon its ability to establish a dominance about cultural meaning and sexual practice. It is conceptualized neither as a solitary act nor as requiring a concentrated authoritative voice.[26] With an understanding of discourse, the intent of individual pornographers and the degree of authority they have to convey a message are irrelevant to the adverse effects produced. The effects such as silencing and subordinating occur irrespective of authority and intent.

JUDITH BUTLER'S CRITIQUE OF PORNOGRAPHY AND HATE SPEECH AS A SPEECH ACT

Judith Butler believes that proponents of hate speech and pornography regulation wrongly assume that those engaged in such speech have the power and authority to cause harm. Butler challenges this notion that the speaker of hate speech or pornography has the authority, or "sovereignty," to ensure that harm follows the utterance, insisting that a gap exists between the speaker's words and its effects. Within that gap, a potential exists for the victim of the assaultive speech to "restage" and "resignifiy" the speech, recouping and redirecting it to liberatory and transformative ends. One can take the intended epithet "queer" or "dyke" and resignify the meaning of the word from a pejorative to a liberatory meaning. Hate speech and pornography regulations, Butler cautions, upend or short-circuit that opportunity for resignification. In her view, the possibility that speech may have a different meaning than the one intended by the speaker is what makes political and social change possible. Thus, in the potential for reconfiguring meaning, speech has a performative quality. Government regulations subvert the performative.

A number of issues undermine Butler's claims about sovereignty and the lack of effaciousness of hate speech and pornography. As argued by Lisa Schwarzman, Butler presents an inaccurate understanding of illocutionary acts.[27] Illocutionary acts are those utterances that perform as we speak something and their effaciousness depends upon the contextual social conventions being met in order to succeed. We refer to this context as felicity conditions. Perlocutionary acts concern the consequences brought about by speech. Butler links the possibility that felicity conditions are mostly linked with perlocutionary acts rather than illocutionary acts, thereby misconceiving the former.[28] According to Schwarzman, this Austinian distinction between perlocution and illocution is "tricky" and unstable. Instead of recognizing the instablity in the distinction, Butler mistakenly links "the word as the injury" to transitivity and diminishes the role of context in ensuring that felicity conditions are met. Butler claims that "[i]mplicit in this distinction [between per-locutionary and illocutionary acts] is the notion that illocutionary speech acts produce effects without any lapse of time—that the saying itself—the doing—are occurring simultaneously."[29] She refers to this simultaneous phenomena—"to say is to do" at the same moment—as transitivity. For Butler, then, hate speech and porn regulation advocates assume that those sorts of utterances are efficacious, unilateral and transitive. Both Levin and Schwarzman challenge Butler's understanding of hate speech and porn regulation advocates' arguments.[30] Butler's characterization of their arguments, then, rests upon a misconceptualization of illocutionary speech acts and the significance of context in ensuring efficacy.

Neither Austin, MacKinnon, nor Matsuda, for example, argue that words harm by themselves.[31] Austin specifically speaks of not just the words or utterances but the entire speech act, which requires consideration of context, power, and social convention for efficacy. The proponents of hate speech and porn regulations do not assert that the words themselves alone, devoid of context, injure. Mari Matsuda writes that words themselves are not the injury but rather the way in which the words are uttered and the context in which they are spoken matter. Schwarzman writes: "According to Austin's account, a performative utterance is never reducible to the words themselves; the words must be said in a particular context, or accompanied by other actions, and it is essential that they secure 'uptake.'"[32]

The crucial question, then, becomes, how is uptake secured? In a word, uptake is secured by the context. Yet Butler spends little time analyzing the context in which uptake either fails or succeeds. As Schwarzman notes, securing uptake is no simple matter and requires the kind of lingering analysis that Butler avoids. Moreover, context would have an effect upon the authority or "sovereignty" of the speaker. Such sovereignty or authority, depending upon context, could be broader than simply locating power in "government" alone. As Schwarzman asserts, the questions about whether social conventions or context empower an authority may be complex. Pornography injures because of the context as does hate speech. Uptake may not always occur, but is neither as random nor as unpredictable as Butler suggests.[33] Social structures make speech injuries more or less likely. When uptake fails, it is largely due to a group's lack of social power more than other reasons.

Yet Butler believes that any attempt to "pin down" context is problematic.[34] Such an effort to locate and describe context gives it a static quality, suggesting that rituals and conventions are not subject to change: they are permanent and enduring. Butler insists that context is always subject to rupture, reinterpretation, reinvention, and change. Butler's assumptions about the instability of context negate the possibility of public meaning because context is too fluid. While social conditions may not last for eternity, they are often more stubbornly stable than Butler acknowledges. Nor does resignification simply occur when an individual has the idea to recoup an utterance for their own reinterpretation. Instead, as Scharzman notes, social movements require arduous organizing and endless strategizing to challenge and dislodge the very social structures that rigidify hierarchy and make resignification difficult. Resignification succeeds only when social movements dislodge those social structures: social movements through law, policies, and protest create the very preconditions that make resignification possible. In short, resignification alone as a strategy of political change is ethereal: it relies on language without a recognition that the social structures shaping context aren't easily altered.[35] While Butler is correct in arguing that social structures are impermanent, they are, nonetheless, moored. Furthermore, language isn't detached from the material conditions that give it meaning. Those material conditions and structures do not simply disappear when a group decides to restage and resignify a term like "dyke." The meaning of the word changes and the injury diminishes when changing material and social conditions lead to a more favorable context. Butler has yet to provide an example where simply resignifying language leads to real liberatory social change in the political and material conditions of minorities.

While Butler believes in the transformative possibilities of language and society, she does not adequately explain how and when those transformative possibilities can take place. As Schwarzman argues, an inevitable tension exists in Butler's larger body of works. In *Gender Trouble*, Butler explains that inevitable failures arise in the way that speech works, which can lead to social change. Yet the description of the performative and its relationship to political change in *Gender Trouble* is at odds with the message from *Excitable Speech*, where resignifying appears easier, speedier and more efficacious.[36] Even in the case of gender, the social structures that moor unequal power and material inequality are more stubborn than Butler's theory of social and political change acknowledges. As strategy, the efficaciousness of restaging and resignification is more a sign of the success of social movements than a cause.

THE CAUSAL ARGUMENT

An alternative approach to understanding pornography's harm to women is offered by Anne Eaton in "A Sensible Antiporn Feminism." [37] Eaton develops what she titles a sensible Antiporn Feminist (APF) hypothesis about harm, which defends a philosophically sensible and scientifically respectable conception of causation. [38] In the article, she argues that pornography's harm to women is the cumulative effect of multiple, complex factors of which inegalitarian porn is one among many in a composite causal chain. Eaton contends that anti-porn feminists should adopt an epidemiological model of causation to describe how pornography harms rather than a simplistic deterministic model. The harm from pornography, she finds, is neither necessary nor sufficient for its putative injuries but rather raises the chances of harm depending on the context. Pornography, it seems, operates as a feedback loop. Pornography is both the result of gender inequality and facilitates and accelerates this inequality in a cumulative manner. Rae Langton summarizes Eaton's argument in the following way:

> Eaton's aim is to identify a 'sensible anti-porn feminism,' as her title has it: one that (i) restricts a causal hypothesis to 'inegalitarian' pornography; (ii) is more precise about the nature of the causal relation, being probabilistic rather than deterministic, cumulative rather than isolated, and with two distinct stages, involving consumers, and then other parties; (iii) is alert to both the strengths and the weaknesses of the empirical evidence; and finally (iv) is more pluralistic about the possible remedies, legal and otherwise, that may be appropriate if the harm hypothesis is vindicated. [39]

Unlike MacKinnon, Langton, and McGowan, Eaton does not attempt to make the case that pornography not only causes harm but constitutes discrimination. [40]

Among the first terms she clarifies in the article is the definition of pornography itself. Borrowing from Larry May, she notes that anti-porn feminists are most concerned with ineqalitarian pornography rather than all pornography. Inegalitarian pornography consists of sexually explicit representations that as a whole eroticize relations characterized by gender inequity. [41] By relations, Eaton and May point to various acts, scenarios and postures. [42] Generally, anti-pornography feminists connect inegalitarian pornography to two different kinds of harm. The first set of harms stem from the production of pornography where, in order to make the pornography women must be brutalized, raped, and coerced. The second set of harms flows from exposure to pornography, which anti-pornography feminists contend shapes the conduct and attitudes of the audience. This second description of harm is labeled the harm hypothesis, and it is the thesis that Eaton clarifies and strengthens throughout the article. It is also the claim with which this chapter is concerned: these attitudes shape conduct in ways that undermine women's citizenship rights.

Eaton rejects a deterministic model of causality in describing pornography's harms as related to exposure from pornography. In that deterministic model of causality, *a* causes *b*. Instead, she suggests, pornography should be evaluated under a probabilistic model of causality.

> The heart of the view [probabilistic causality] is this; x is a cause of y if and only if (i) x occurs earlier than y and (ii) the probability of the occurrence of y is greater, given the occurrence of x, then the probability of the occurrence of y given not x. That is x bears positive statistical relevance to y in the sense that the occurrence of x makes the occurrence of y more likely.[43]

A probabilistic understanding of causation admits that causes may be more or less effective. One measures effectiveness of a cause by how much it raises the probability of the effects. Pornography, according to Eaton, is one key factor that raises the probability of harms rather than the element singly responsible for them.[44] Moreover, Eaton argues that this probabilistic understanding of causality is one consistent with tort law.

> Seeing pornography as one salient ingredient in a larger causal pie is not only in line with our best science but also fits with current legal practice in the realm of tort law . . . tort law adheres not to a single-cause model of injury but to a recipe model of causality, where two or more defendants can be held jointly and severally liable for a single injury—a practice referred to as the joint and several liability of concurrent tortfeasors.[45]

Eaton cites Don Adams in an article entitled "Can Pornography Cause Rape," which uses the logic of tort law to apply to the notion that pornography causes harm to women.[46]

Adams's describes an actual tort case where a business is held liable for a robbery committed by someone unaffiliated with the corporation because the company had failed to change a blown light bulb for several weeks. The court held that the company's failure to change the lightbulb negligently contributed to conditions that made the mugging more likely. Adam's argument is enticing in making an analogy between the evidentiary standards in tort law and the methods we should use to assess pornography's harm. Yet, the chapter will argue that causality, in either its more simplistic or complex forms, is a conceptually problematic way to understand the epistemology of harm.

Langton has two powerful responses to Eaton's thesis and probabilistic causal approach to determining harm. Both criticisms suggest that the harms of pornography are unlike the harms of disease and these insights about the different harms have broader implications for the epistemology of harm itself.[47] The first argument is that, unlike disease, pornography masks its own harm.

> Suppose a cigarette company marketed a kind of cigarette that caused cancer, but also caused many people to stop noticing the symptoms of cancer, in others and (more rarely) in themselves, and prevented people caring about symptoms if they did notice them. MacKinnon's causal claim about pornography has an epistemological dimension, not noted by Eaton, but relevant to questions about the complications and difficulties about evidence: the more pornography succeeds in turning the world into a pornographic place, the less it looks as though pornography is doing any harm.[48]

In short, if one accepts that a causal approach is the appropriate way to measure harm from pornography, one faces a dilemma at the level of epistemology. Pornography affects our ability to recognize, identify, and appropriately and proportionately redress harm.[49] This is a point that Judge Easterbrook makes in *American Booksellers v. Hudnut* (1985), even as he defends pornography as protected free speech.

Second, Eaton's epidemiological model leaves little room for the significance of testimony, often characterized as merely anecdotal without causal rigor. Pornography is a social practice and relies upon interactions with other humans. Testimony, interviews, and other qualitative methods give us insight into how others experience pornography. Langton notes that testimony may have limits, but it can also provide important insights. Langton writes:

> Perhaps someone can know, say, that watching a particular horror movie gave him nightmares . . . perhaps someone can know that watching pornography made him want more pornography, and more extreme pornography; and that he began to find certain material arousing that he never expected to find arousing, including sexual scenes with children, animals, and torture. Someone can know that commitment to moral and political principles didn't stop such images becoming a turn-on. Someone can know that masturbating to pornography for many hours in the week left him less interested in sex with his partner. Someone can know that porn led him to demand things of his partner that he would never have thought of, or led him in the end to sexual alienation, or ennui.[50]

The insights above are abstracted from the testimony and interviews of real men and women. For individuals, the debate about the epistemology of pornography's harms are far less abstract. They need not prove causality to conclude that pornography produces harmful effects that have reduced the quality of their lives.[51]

If we take Langton's critiques seriously, a causal standard, even a probobalistic one weighing and weighting multiple factors, becomes epistemically immunized from recognizing harm while simultaneously ignoring evidence of victims' experience with and perpetrators use of pornography. Those are serious vulnerabilities that make the standard of causality unattainable.

Causality is unattainable for yet another set of reasons, some of which are similar to the critiques applied to speech-act theory. First, the standard of causality is both unreachable and inappropriate in the humanities. If we reach back to Hume's critique of causality, he reminds us that causality is really based upon inductive reasoning.[52] We expect that what happened before will happen again provided that the same conditions adhere. Therefore, we infer repetition without ever explaining cause. In the case of the hard sciences, where we expect predictability, causality remains elusive. The best "the hard sciences" can do is falsify rather than prove cause. Even in instances such as cigarette smoking, science is unable to establish that smoking *causes* lung cancer. Yet we would not allow the inability to prove causality, in this instance, to interfere with public health. Instead, we rely upon a correlational standard. Surely, given the greater complexities and uncertainties surrounding human agency in the social sciences, we can see that the causal standard is not only unachievable but effectively prevents serious evaluation of otherwise reasonable claims. Under such a high standard, libelous claims, tort claims, seditious claims, and, in fact, all currently regulatable categories of speech fail to reach causal certainty.

Second, the use of causality in the context of law, like the singular focus on a speech act, fixates on one movie, magazine, or performance, at a particular time, as a cause. Yet the force of pornography comes not from a singular piece at a specific moment in time but rather from its cultural dominance as a subordinating discourse: its ability to shape meaning, desire, and actions. To trace cause back to a particular moment in time, to a particular pornographic product broadly or narrowly defined, misses the mechanism by which pornography harms and "does things." The mechanism of pornography conditions on the ideological, material and epistemological levels—all of which will be discussed in a following section.

Third, the actual studies which attempt to prove or disprove pornography's harm pose serious weaknesses. Shira Tarrant's most recent book, *The Pornography Industry: What Everyone Needs to Know*, demonstrates why relying on causal or correlational studies to prove harm is really an epistemological problem.[53] Like Eaton, Tarrant spends some time reviewing the studies on whether pornography harms. Tarrant attempts to write a book that provides an unbiased view about the pornography industry.[54] In reviewing the data about pornography's potential harms, she writes:

the argument that pornography causes rape excludes questions about the possibility of sexual pleasure through pornography and conflates causation with possible correlation. Recent studies about how people respond to pornography reveal a variety of effects, but none of those conclusively find that pornography causes rape.[55]

Yet Tarrant fails to seriously engage the epistemological limitations of causality and social scientific research more generally, and she ignores the way in which pornography may be both pleasurable and discriminatory. The problem with hinging the justifications for regulating inegalitarian pornography on causality are manifold. Although scholars like Anne Eaton present us with a more complex and nuanced model of probabilistic causality, they miss the point. Causality in the complex human world is a mystification and it amounts to a kind of formalism.[56]

From the outset, the empirical studies cannot avoid bias. These porn studies require us to define the very terms we measure. They rely upon the starting definitions and assumptions of the researchers. How do those researchers, for example, define pornography? How do they define inegalitarian, subordinate, demeaning or objectifying? How do they define and conceptualize what constitutes violence?

To be clear, a critical approach to understanding the empirical studies debate about pornography's harm is not to suggest that knowledge is only a factor of power—that truth and objectivity do not exist. In the case of those empirical studies, we have researchers on both sides with biases and prejudgments. Yet bias is not inherently bad: we need bias in order to organize knowledge. Feminists, and all of those fighting for justice, rely upon concepts of truth and objectivity to make claims about the wrongness of inequality and oppression. Yet, we also need to problematize concepts of truth and objectivity without eliminating them. History is replete with instances of discriminatory, oppressive, and brutal acts of oppression justified by "objective truth"—only later to be proven false and littered with bias.[57]

Scholars such as Hilary Putnam and Linda Alcoff contend that for humans the problem with truth is not that it does not exist but rather that we have trouble accessing it free from our own experiences and biases.[58] Pre-judgments, in the human world, are how we come to know. As a result, we have no God's-eye-view-from-nowhere, no transcendent observation post from which to view truth and engage in objective searching. These pre-judgments, which are indispensable to getting as close to the truth as humanly possible also make our truth claims fallible. To the extent that we accept our fallibility—the notion that we sometimes get the truth wrong—we are better able to scrutinize and correct our prejudgments and biases, enabling us to zero in on the truth. When new "facts," observations, or experiences become available, we must incorporate them in an effort to achieve a fuller picture of the truth. The move to incorporate new observations, facts, and experiences explains why multi-culturalism, bringing in marginalized voices, is compatible with truth, objectivity, and epistemology. The more perspectives we incorporate, tested against criteria set by the diverse experiences in the community, the better picture of truth that we gain.

In the case of those empirical studies on pornography, we must be aware that not everyone experiences pornography in the same way (whether oppressive or liberatory). Those studies depend upon subjective definitions of the very terms to be "objectively" measured, and, the measurer's values determine the relevant analytical facts in any measurement. In the end, the interpretive dilemma is unavoidable in social scientific studies. Moreover, both sides debate where power lies, influencing this debate about pornography's harms: does power reside with the forces of regulation or the forces of the adult industry? Historically, law has failed to see the world from the perspective of women or non-whites. Others have argued persuasively that the normative standard for citizenship has been based upon the experiences of a white, heterosexual man. This is why Ronald Dworkin is able to argue that the real victims of proposed pornography regulation are the poor men who buy it: women are the ones with the power hold on the men who need it.[59] As a result, we should not be surprised that liberal law hides those very specific and privileged or dominant life experiences of their normative model (the white, heterosexual man) in the universal.

By speaking of those specific, dominant life experiences as if they were universal, law obscures the privileged social location of the model citizen behind a cloak of neutrality. Fighting words, for example, is hardly a neutral legal category, but is instead premised on the experience of white, heterosexual men's response to emotionally abusive language. As Mari Matsuda and Charles Lawrence have pointed out, minorities and women rarely respond to such assaultive language with a violent response.[60] Historically, such a violent response to abusive and harassing speech would have led to greater violence against them. Yet, white heterosexual men insulted by abusive language fight back and find law protecting and justifying their violent actions.

In summary, these complex, abstract epistemic debates should be applied to our discussion of empirical studies about pornography's harms. We must read and understand their meaning with a measure of caution and epistemological sophistication. The fact/value distinction is not a bright line demarcation: what we see as an analytically relevant fact is informed by our values. Tarrant ignores the epistemic complexities when she labels only anti-porn scholars as activist, failing to recognize that even those "objective" studies proving no causal link between pornography and harm entail bias. The problem is twofold: causality is not the appropriate standard and none of these studies is accurately understood as objective. Given the very nature of the human subjects being studied in the social sciences, no one should presume that any study lacks prejudgments worthy of scrutiny.

In the end, all empirical debates in the social sciences are grounded in hermeneutics, or put more plainly, in meaning. We can measure, but the very variables we use demand definitions, which are inevitably imbued with our own biases. Moreover, the interpretation of measurement results represent interpretive problems. All social scientific empirical findings require interpretation, an indispensable value-laden activity required to determine meaning. In fact, to see harm, which is described momentarily in places like *Hudnut* when Judge Easterbrook connects pornography to real-world material harms, is to require an epistemic shift in determining under what circumstances speech harms and is worthy of regulation. Moreover, we should consider whether our willingness to make an epistemic shift that recognizes harm is affected by the social location of the victim and the epistemological gatekeeper.

One can point again to Ronald Dworkin's essay in the *New York Review of Books* entitled "Pornography and the New Puritans."[61] In that essay, as noted above, men are the victims of their need for pornography, not women who are the object of the pornography. Moreover, Professor Dworkin remains a hallowed legal scholar with a gatekeeping role in reproducing legal knowledge. Is it possible that the social location of Professor Dworkin made him less likely to understand the phenomenological effects of pornography on women? Is it possible that the harm from his failure to take a hermeneutic leap to view the world from the perspective of those with less social power were multiplied by his role as an epistemic gatekeeper?

CONCLUSION

The chapter attempts to analyze the conceptualization of pornography as a speech act, finding that it does not ultimately capture the harm in pornography. To silence and subordinate, pornography need not be authoritative, nor traced to a single source. Moreover, pornography's subordinating message is conveyed through more than speech: it entails gestures, movements, comportment, and facial expressions. A complex understanding of causality does not provide clarity on the manner that pornography silences and subordinates either. Causality, in the social sciences, is effectively non-existent. Even in the hard sciences, without the unpredictability of human subjects, falsification is the closest one comes to proving causality. The notion of discursive effects better explains the claim that inegalitarian pornography harms by undermining women's citizenship rights. If we are to understand what anti-porn advocates mean when they argue that pornography silences and subordinates women, we must turn to a different concept to explain harm. The next chapter will develop the concept of discursive effects to better understand the harm from pornography.

NOTES

1. Nancy Bauer, *How to Do Things with Pornography*. Cambridge: Harvard University Press, 2015.

2. Joan Mason-Grant, *Pornography Embodied: from Speech to Sexual Practice*. Rowman & Littlefield, 2004, 70.

3. See Rae Langton, *Sexual Solipsism Philosophical Essays on Pornography and Objectification*. Oxford Univ. Press, 2013. See Also Cynthia A. Stark, and Florida State University Department of Philosophy. "Is Pornography an Action?: The Causal vs. the Conceptual View of Pornography's Harm." *Social Theory and Practice*, vol. 23, no. 2, 1997, pp. 277–306, doi:10.5840/soctheorpract199723213.

4. Mason-Grant, 71.

5. Mason-Grant, 70.

6. Mason-Grant quoting Langton, 72.

7. Mason-Grant, 74.

8. *American Booksellers v. Hudnut* 771 F.2d. 323 (7th Cir.1985).

9. Mason-Grant, 75.

10. Mason-Grant, p. 72.

11. Mason-Grant, 76.

12. Mary Kate Mcgowan, "Oppressive Speech." *Australasian Journal of Philosophy* 87, no. 3 (2009): 389–407. https://doi.org/10.1080/00048400802370334.

13. Schwarzman challenges this understanding of authority, arguing that Austin emphasizes an a "total speech situation" in which context, social convention, and structure of social power must be considered to determine the efficaciousness of uptake or felicity conditions. Lisa H. Schwartzman, "Hate Speech, Illocution, and Social Context: A Critique of Judith Butler." *Journal of Social Philosophy* 33, no. 3 (2002): 421–41. https://doi.org/10.1111/0047-2786.00151 . Judith Butler, *Excitable Speech: a Politics of the Performative*. New York: Routledge, 1997. Leslie Green, "Pornographizing, Subordinating, Silencing." In *Censorship and Silencing*, edited by Robert C. Post, 285–311. Los Angeles: Getty Research Institute, 1998.

14. Daniel Jacobson, "Freedom of Speech Acts? A Response to Langton." *Philosophy & Public Affairs* 24, no. 1 (1995).

15. David Lewis, "Scorekeeping in a Language Game." *Journal of Philosophical Logic* 8, no. 1 (1979). https://doi.org/10.1007/bf00258436.

16. As Schwarzman notes, the distinction between illocution and perlocution is always a tricky and unstable one, which sometimes causes more confusion than clarity.

17. Schwartzman, "Hate Speech, Illocution, and Social Context: A Critique of Judith Butler." *Journal of Social Philosophy* 33, no. 3 (2002): 421–41. https://doi.org/10.1111/0047-2786.00151.

18. Joan Mason-Grant, *Pornography Embodied: From Speech to Sexual Practice*. Rowman & Littlefield, 2004.

19. A point Judith Butler emphasizes. Butler, *Excitable Speech: a Politics of the Performative*. New York: Routledge, 1997. Lisa H. Schwartzman, "Hate Speech, Illocution, and Social Context: A Critique of Judith Butler." *Journal of Social Philosophy* 33, no. 3 (2002): 421–41. https://doi.org/10.1111/0047-2786.00151.

20. Mason-Grant. Also, Butler, Judith. *Excitable Speech: A Politics of the Performative*. New York: Routledge, 1997.

21. Mason-Grant. A point that also draws upon Butler's critique.

22. Nancy Bauer. *How to Do Things with Pornography*. Cambridge: Harvard University Press, 2015.

23. Mason-Grant.

24. Mason-Grant and A. Levin, *Cost of Free Speech: Pornography, Hate Speech, and Their Challenge to Liberalism*. Palgrave Macmillan, 2014. Schwarzman would likely challenge such an interpretation, arguing that an analysis of the "total speech situation" would inevitably require an analysis of social power, thereby placing the one act within a broader structural context.

25. Mason-Grant and Levin.

26. Mason-Grant and Levin.

27. Lisa H. Schwartzman, "Hate Speech, Illocution, and Social Context: A Critique of Judith Butler." *Journal of Social Philosophy* 33, no. 3 (2002): 421–41. https://doi.org/10.1111/0047-2786.00151.

28. Lisa H. Schwartzman, "Hate Speech, Illocution, and Social Context: A Critique of Judith Butler." *Journal of Social Philosophy* 33, no. 3 (2002): 421–41. https://doi.org/10.1111/0047-2786.00151 , 13.

29. Lisa H. Schwartzman, "Hate Speech, Illocution, and Social Context: A Critique of Judith Butler." *Journal of Social Philosophy* 33, no. 3 (2002): 421–41. https://doi.org/10.1111/0047-2786.00151 .

30. Lisa H. Schwartzman, "Hate Speech, Illocution, and Social Context: A Critique of Judith Butler." *Journal of Social Philosophy* 33, no. 3 (2002): 421–41. https://doi.org/10.1111/0047-2786.00151 . Levin, *Cost of Free Speech: Pornography, Hate Speech, and Their Challenge to Liberalism* . Palgrave Macmillan, 2014.

31. Lisa H. Schwartzman, "Hate Speech, Illocution, and Social Context: A Critique of Judith Butler." *Journal of Social Philosophy* 33, no. 3 (2002): 421–41. https://doi.org/10.1111/0047-2786.00151.

32. Lisa H. Schwartzman, "Hate Speech, Illocution, and Social Context: A Critique of Judith Butler." *Journal of Social Philosophy* 33, no. 3 (2002): 421–41. https://doi.org/10.1111/0047-2786.00151.

33. Lisa H. Schwartzman, "Hate Speech, Illocution, and Social Context: A Critique of Judith Butler." *Journal of Social Philosophy* 33, no. 3 (2002): 421–41. https://doi.org/10.1111/0047-2786.00151.

34. Lisa H. Schwartzman, "Hate Speech, Illocution, and Social Context: A Critique of Judith Butler." *Journal of Social Philosophy* 33, no. 3 (2002): 421–41. https://doi.org/10.1111/0047-2786.00151.

35. Martha C. Nussbaum, "The Professor of Parody." *The New Republic*, February 22, 1999. https://newrepublic.com/article/150687/professor-parody.

36. Levin, *Cost of Free Speech: Pornography, Hate Speech, and Their Challenge to Liberalism*. Palgrave Macmillan, 2014. Schwartzman, "Hate Speech, Illocution, and Social Context: A Critique of Judith Butler." *Journal of Social Philosophy* 33, no. 3 (2002): 421–41. https://doi.org/10.1111/0047-2786.00151.

37. A. W. Eaton, "A Sensible Antiporn Feminism." *Ethics* 117, no. 4 (2007): 674–715. https://doi.org/10.1086/519226.

38. See also Andrew Kernohan, "Accumulative Harms and the Interpretation of the Harm Principle." *Social Theory and Practice*, vol. 19, ser. 1, 1993, pp. 51–72. Kernohan argues for an accumulative harms understanding of pornography's harms and their causal effects. He further asserts that this notion of accumulative harms is not only regulatable but consistent with J.S. Mill' s harm principle. Mill 's harm principle famously states that an individual's liberty is regulatable by the government when that liberty harms another.

39. Rae Langton, "Comments on A. W. Eaton's 'A Sensible Antiporn Feminism.'" http://web.mit.edu/sgrp. MIT, 2008. http://web.mit.edu/sgrp/2008/no2/Langton0508.pdf, 1-2.

40. Langton, "Comments on A. W. Eaton's 'A Sensible Antiporn Feminism,'" http://web.mit.edu/sgrp. MIT, 2008. http://web.mit.edu/sgrp/2008/no2/Langton0508.pdf , Eaton, "A Sensible Antiporn Feminism." *Ethics* 117, no. 4 (2007): 674–715. https://doi.org/10.1086/519226, 677.

41. Eaton, "A Sensible Antiporn Feminism." *Ethics* 117, no. 4 (2007): 674–715. https://doi.org/10.1086/519226 . Eaton, 2007, 676, borrowing from May.

42. See also Joan Mason-Grant, *Pornography Embodied: From Speech to Sexual Practice*. Rowman & Littlefield, 2004, 15.

43. Eaton, "A Sensible Antiporn Feminism." *Ethics* 117, no. 4 (2007): 674–715. https://doi.org/10.1086/519226 , 696-97.

44. Eaton, "A Sensible Antiporn Feminism." *Ethics* 117, no. 4 (2007): 674–715, 702. https://doi.org/10.1086/519226.

45. Eaton, "A Sensible Antiporn Feminism." *Ethics* 117, no. 4 (2007): 674–715. https://doi.org/10.1086/519226 , 702.

46. Eaton, "A Sensible Antiporn Feminism." *Ethics* 117, no. 4 (2007): 674–715. https://doi.org/10.1086/519226 . Don Adams, "Can Pornography Cause Rape?" *Journal of Social Philosophy* 31, no. 1 (2000): 1–43. https://doi.org/10.1111/0047-2786.00029.

47. Langton, "Comments on A. W. Eaton's 'A Sensible Antiporn Feminism.'" http://web.mit.edu/sgrp. MIT, 2008. http://web.mit.edu/sgrp/2008/no2/Langton0508.pdf , 2.

48. Langton, "Comments on A. W. Eaton's 'A Sensible Antiporn Feminism.'" http://web.mit.edu/sgrp. MIT, 2008. http://web.mit.edu/sgrp/2008/no2/Langton0508.pdf , 2.

49. A point that Ariel Levy's book notes.

50. Langton, "Comments on A. W. Eaton's 'A Sensible Antiporn Feminism.'" http://web.mit.edu/sgrp. MIT, 2008. http://web.mit.edu/sgrp/2008/no2/Langton0508.pdf , 3.

51. Shira Tarrant, *The Pornography Industry: What Everyone Needs to Know*. Oxford University Press, 2016. Pamela Paul, *Pornified*. Owl, 2006.

52. David Hume, *A Treatise of Human Nature*. Edited by David Fate Norton and Mary J Norton, Oxford University Press, 2000. Linda M. Alcoff, "How Is Epistemology Political?" In *Radical Philosophy*. Philadelphia, PA: Temple University, 1993. Linda M. Alcoff, *Real Knowing: New Versions of the Coherence Theory*. Ithaca, NY: Cornell University Press, 2008.

53. A point that both Rae Langton and Lori Watson make.

54. Tarrant, (2016). *The Pornography Industry: What Everyone Needs to Know*. Oxford University Press, 89 of 196. Despite Tennant's efforts to present an unbiased review of data, it seems only the only scholars described as "activist" are those arguing the side that pornography harms women.

55. S. Tarrant (2016). 89 of 196.

56. Arnold I. Davidson, *Foucault and His Interlocutors*. University of Chicago Press, 1997.

57. Sandra Harding, *Science and Social Inequality: Feminist and Postcolonial Issues*. University of Illinois Press, 2006.

58. Hilary Putnam, *Reason, Truth and History*. Cambridge University Press, 1998. Linda Alcoff, *Real Knowing: New Versions of the Coherence Theory*. Cornell University Press, 2008.

59. Ronald Dworkin, "Pornography and the New Puritans: Letters From Andrea Dworkin and Others," *The New York Times*, May 3, 1992. https://www.nytimes.com/1992/05/03/books/l-pornography-and-the-new-puritans-letters-from-andrea-dworkin-and-others-720092.html.

60. Mari J. Matsuda, Charles R. Lawrence, Richard Delgado, and Kimberle Williams Crenshaw, eds. *Words That Wound Critical Race Theory, Assaultive Speech and the First Amendment*. Westview Press, 2011.

61. Ronald Dworkin, "Pornography and the New Puritans: Letters From Andrea Dworkin and Others," *The New York Times*, May 3, 1992. https://www.nytimes.com/1992/05/03/books/l-pornography-and-the-new-puritans-letters-from-andrea-dworkin-and-others-720092.html.

SIX
Discursive Effects

A Different Framework to Understand the Harm from Speech

This chapter attempts to introduce a different conceptual framework to evaluate the anti-pornography feminist claim that pornography constitutes discrimination, thereby undermining women's citizenship rights. The claim is a difficult one to advance, and many other theorists have attempted to do so. Instead of assessing the "porn constitutes discrimination" claim from the perspective of an Austinian speech act or a sophisticated model of probabilistic causality, the chapter offers a different approach: namely, a theory of discursive effects.

Why utilize discursive effects to elaborate how pornography, according to antipornography feminists, silences and subordinates? MacKinnon herself has expressed hostility toward poststructuralism and its theoretical ability to elucidate the harm from pornography. She writes:

> Postmodernism is an academic theory, originating in academia with an academic elite, not in the world of women and men, where feminist theory is rooted.[1]

An added complication, one might argue, is that poststructural theory, even if it provides the tools to understand how pornography constitutes discrimination, is incompatible with our liberal constitutional tradition and our libertarian understanding of free speech doctrine. Debates within the liberal tradition have ignored Foucault's theories of discourse and power. The exclusion may stem from Foucault's hostility toward liberalism as well as the fact that analytic and continental philosophy historically "have a long history of antagonism and thus a propensity to talk past each other."[2]

However, both the egalitarian liberal tradition and Foucault's ideas about discourse and power share a common concern around the significance of unequal discourses in shaping the citizen subject. In egalitarian liberal language, culturally oppressive discourses distort the constitution of personhood and undermine one of the necessary preconditions to justice: namely, the primary good of self-respect. Those culturally oppressive discourses also make reciprocity in political liberalism an impossibility.[3] In Rawls's *Political Liberalism*, reciprocity is an agreement on minimal shared values necessary for government to function.[4] Political liberalism eschews comprehensive moral understandings as a foundation for government, preferring instead moral pluralism. Yet, if individuals are so degraded due to their membership in a group, then their ability to negotiate areas of fundamental minimal agreement is undermined. Put differently, negotiation based upon a deprecated ego is not possible.[5]

DEFINING DISCURSIVE EFFECTS

What is discourse and what are discursive effects? Discourse is all that is written, spoken, and communicated about a subject. Poststructuralists argue that discourses construct personhood. Put differently, discourses produce and constitute the public meaning about a subject, and everything that is depends on the structure of the discursive fields of which it is a part.[6] As such, discourses maintain their own premises, structuring and analyzing the world through those organizing first principles. Discourse, however, does more than establish meaning: it does *things*, as Austin would say. Michel Foucault tells us that:

> Discourse—the mere fact of speaking, of employing words, of using the words of others (even if it means returning them), word that others understand and accept (and, possibly, return from their side)—this fact is in itself is a force. Discourse is, with respect to the relation of forces, not merely a surface of inscription, but something that brings about effects.[7]

Discourse is a way of producing events and of producing decisions.[8] In this respect, Foucault shares a fundamental insight with the speech act tradition: namely, that speech "does things."

A theory of discursive effects, then, contends that speech does not simply cause hurt feelings or offense, as suggested by those defending pornography. Words and images are not categorically distinct from acts.[9] Pornography, as a discourse, connects with power, regulates conduct, constructs identities, and defines the way culture represents and thinks about women and sexuality.[10] In effect, when we say that discourse produces effects, we mean that it produces ideological, material, and epistemological effects. In other words, oppressive discourses misrepresent reality, generate deprivations in the quality of material well-being, and create social meaning.[11] Discursive effects circulate through society influencing the constitution of the self and how others view the individual.

In Levin's words, discourse is more than descriptive. It is the primary means by which power operates, and it forms subjects. Put more straightforwardly, power forms subjects while operating primarily through the production of discourse.[12] Nancy Hirshmann, paraphrasing Wittgenstein tells us that "'thinking subjects'—are themselves constructed by and through language."[13] Discourses are organized bodies of knowledge, creating human subjects as we have come to know them. Foucault famously writes about the discourse of psychiatry that formed the subjects of the deviant, the hysteric and the narcissist. Levin writes:

> One paradigmatic example [of discourses creating subjects] would be the discourse of psychiatry, which began in the nineteenth century. Through that organized body of knowledge, we derive such subjects as the hysteric, the narcissist, and others thus labeled by their mental disorders. These kinds of people were produced by the discourse of psychiatry and could not be said to exist without that discourse...[14]

Prior to the creation of the psychiatric discourse on the deviant, then, we had no categories in which to understand and act upon such individuals. For Foucault, "power is operationalized through discourse, and discourse is a necessary and crucial condition of power."[15] To paraphrase Levin, discourses produce truth, create, and rule us. When we interrogate discourse, we necessarily interrogate truth, power, and the very constitution of the self. The antipornography feminist claim is at its most compelling when asserting that pornography constitutes discrimination at the very construction of the subject.

The primary mechanism by which discursive effects operate is the process of social construction.[16] Nancy Hirschmann tells us that discourse is central to understanding who we are: it is the mechanism of social construction.[17] She quotes Gayatri Spivak:

> We know no world that is not organized as language, we operate with no other consciousness but one structured as language—languages that we cannot possess, for we are operated by those languages as well.[18]

Discourse, as central to the process of social construction, radiates outward. These different levels of social construction—the ideological, the material, and the epistemological—influence the way we live our lives. What we see (the ideological) has real-world tangible effects (the material) and shapes the ideas and concepts in which we think (the epistemological). If pornography produces a powerful, pervasive, and influential ideology about sexuality, one that constitutes and reinforces other patriarchal beliefs about women's capabilities and desires, it can influence our behavior, adversely affect our living conditions, and shape what we know and think is possible. These are the ideas that Judge Easterbrook accepts in his *American Booksellers v. Hudnut* (1985) decision even as he defends pornography as protected speech.

It is worth lingering on Nancy J. Hirschmann's argument in *The Subject of Liberty* where she discusses social construction in terms of layers. At level one, Hirschmann finds the "ideological misrepresentation of reality." Here she cites Marx's notion that capitalism distorts the most meaningful dimensions of labor, production, and relationships as an example of the "ideological misrepresentation of reality." She writes:

> Marx . . . talked about how capitalism inverted the truth of material reality so that, for instance, exchange was seen as more important than use; competition, rather than cooperation, was seen as the essential condition for production; and relationships between people took the form of relationships between things. In this inversion, ideology is more than simply party dogma; it is a picture of reality that comes to dominate lived experience by distorting it. [19]

The crucial point is that a discourse about capitalism and its workings generates an understanding that guides behavior and creates reality. Ideology isn't just about ideas but also a road map to action. At the second level of social construction, Hirshmann refers to "materialization." To demonstrate the meaning of materialization, Hirshmann appeals to Marx again. She writes:

> [H]ow we think about, talk about, interpret, and understand social phenomena produces material effects on the phenomena themselves . . . Marx . . . notes that capitalist ideology not only distorts the reality of the relations of production but actually produces those relations and constitutes empirical reality; workers become alienated from their labor, from each other, from themselves, and are reduced to the exchange value of their labor. [20]

To use Hirschmann's words, patriarchal discourse not only distorts the way women and men understand women's abilities, but actually produces the very conditions of their inequality. When women adhere to patriarchal discourses about their "proper" role in the private rather than the public realm, they fulfill the ideological tenets of gender inequality in very material ways. All repressive socialization processes work by moving through the ideological to the materialization stages. If women are socialized to choose nursing over becoming a doctor because the former is more feminine than the latter, we should not be surprised to find that most women are nurses, and indeed want to become nurses, rather than doctors.

The final layer of social construction is the epistemological stage. Hirschmann tells us that at the third level, "construction of reality takes root in our very language, where it establishes the parameters for understanding, defining, and communicating about reality, about who women are, what we are doing, what we desire." [21] Hirshmann notes that Fou-

cault in *The History of Sexuality* argues that the way we construct problems affects how we think about the world and define reality. While
Hirschmann refers to this third layer as the "discursive construction of
social meaning," the chapter refers to this process as an epistemological
one.

The difficulty in citing Foucault's understanding of discourse and its
relation to power is that he did not conceptualize power as centralized or
vertical in the way that some would posit law. As a result, one might
argue that a Foucauldian analysis as applied to law is inappropriate.
Foucault even contends that we do not need another study on the prohibition of laws and the state. He says that power circulates through the
social body producing not only dominant but counter discourses. Nonetheless, as Levin suggests, Foucault's view of the law is too circumscribed. While Foucault focused on discourses that disciplined the body
outside of law like schools, prisons, and psychiatry, he also recognized
that law was more coextensive with these other sites of power rather than
distinct. Schools, prisons, and the asylum carried out the discourses of
law. As such, studying law is a necessary component of the original
discourses disciplining the body.

Hirschmann too believes it is important to utilize Foucault's understanding of power in studying practices involving sexuality, gender and
law. Unlike more traditional views of power, Foucault helps us to understand its productive, permissive, and inescapable dimensions. Power is
not simply about forcing someone to do something or preventing them
from doing something. Nor is power about getting someone to desire
what you want them to do. Instead, power forms the very subject upon
which desires and choices are determined and we are all subject to it: no
one can avoid the circulation of power through the social body. Power is
everywhere; it is inescapable; and it constitutes our self-hood.

The concept of discursive effects is better suited to discussing the way
in which power is expressed through speech: the way it produces and
maintains inequality. For discourses to produce ideological, material, and
epistemic effects, no single authorial voice need be present, no one cultural production (movie, film, show) need be responsible in order for the
power relations within the discourse to re-instantiate itself and shape
what we desire.

As noted above, poststructuralists have a particular understanding
about the relationship of discourses to social power, truth, and objectivity. For poststructuralism, all discourses are imbricated with power. Power influences, forms, and creates discourses, which produce "the truth"
and subjects. As Michel Foucault forcefully and persuasively argues,
power is exercised through discourses, and resources are distributed according to the tenets of those discourses.[22] In order to assess "the truth,"
we must analyze the relations of power involved in creating the discourse. Complex academic debates discuss the implications of recogniz-

ing power's relationship to the truth. For example, is there no such thing as truth, only power? Foucault himself rejects this relativistic perspective, as do many feminists who seek to use the theoretical insights of post-structuralism to advance the liberatory goals of feminism. Nor is power totalizing: ideological fissures always exist within discourses, allowing for liberatory movements to exploit their inconsistencies.

THE PHENOMENOLOGY OF OPPRESSION, PSYCHIC ALIENATION, AND RECOUPING SUBALTERN KNOWLEDGE

Beyond the concept of discursive effects, we can look to postcolonial theory's description of psychic alienation to more deeply explore the notion that discourses shape subjectivity in oppressive ways. Psychic alienation is a concept that draws from a scholarly tradition involving the phenomenology of oppression. The philosophy of phenomenology provides an even fuller understanding of how discourse is experienced as constituting discrimination. In Foucauldian language, the phenomenology of oppression is "local knowledge" of the lived experience of racism, sexism, and homophobia, and it supplements an understanding of discursive effects.[23] Abigail Levin in *The Cost of Free Speech* writes:

> This type of lived experience—of being silenced and being subordinated as a consequence of racism, sexism, and homophobia—is exactly what the feminists and critical race theorists who have advanced the silencing and subordination arguments aim to reveal.[24]

In Levin's view, the silencing and subordinating argument follows Foucault's understanding of counter-discourse, which he sees as part of the genealogical project. A genealogical process entails identifying the resisting discourses that challenge the more dominant discourses. Our culture often sees those dominant, primary discourses as true. The workings of the dominant power structure hide counterdiscourses. These local, subaltern knowledges, if recouped by genealogy, challenge hegemonic discourses' claims to truth and universality.[25] Local knowledges remind us of the experience of women and minorities in the case of culturally oppressive speech that occludes their perspectives and lived experiences. In law, such "local knowledges" could help us better understand the depth of the harm from pornography from the very women who are injured rather than on a misdirected concept of causality.

To be clear, phenomenology studies the structures of first-person experience and consciousness. MacKinnon's ordinance in *Hudnut* is crafted around the first-person experience of women with pornography: she starts with how women describe and experience pornography—not as free speech but as sexual harassment, subordination, and degradation.[26] Drucilla Cornell makes a similar point about women who find themselves confronted with violent pornography.[27] Rather than approach pornography with our predetermined conceptions—that pornography is free speech—MacKinnon and Cornell give voice to the way many women, although certainly not all, experience inegalitarian pornography. In using the experience of women, MacKinnon grounds her definition in the empirical. Legal categories do not precede or de-center experience. Instead, the experience drives the legal definition, not vice versa. The phenomenological approach to defining pornography and explaining oppression stands in contrast to the causal approach. Phenomenology takes first-person experiences and the internal consciousness seriously and seeks to ascertain the collective structure of that experience. The first-person experiences, cumulatively understood and grounded in the empirical, build an understanding of pornography's meaning, adverse effects, and use. As such, the approach is compatible with the idea that porn "does things" as Wittgenstein, Austin, MacKinnon, Langton, and others suggest.

When anti-porn feminists focus on the notion that porn constitutes discrimination, they are, in my view, not only recouping a local knowledge or utilizing phenomenology, but are describing a process of psychic alienation that contributes or makes possible the effects described above (ideological, material, and epistemic effects). The process of psychic alienation takes place in two distinct ways. First, inegalitarian pornography as a discourse shapes the subject or personhood causing what Sandra Lee Bartky calls "psychic alienation" or psychological oppression. Second, pornography shapes how others (men) view women. In turn, both dimensions of these psychologically oppressive mechanisms produce a distorted ideology, material deprivation, and epistemic effects.[28] Crucial to understanding this psychic alienation is that the discourse of pornography, the inegalitarian version, is both the one that feminists are reacting to and the one that is dominant in the heterosexual variant in our culture.

Bartky, then, through her discussion of psychic alienation, significantly seeks to alter, expand, and deepen our concept of oppression. It supplements and augments our understanding of how discursive effects function to maintain oppression. Bartky contends that psychological oppression is dehumanizing and depersonalizing: it attacks the person in their personhood.[29] The chapter applies that concept to the harms anti-porn feminists articulate.[30] This expanded notion of oppression integrates the damage to the psyche and the effects of these distorted understandings on the individual's social, cultural, economic, and political lives.

In developing the theory of psychic alienation, Bartky borrows the concept from Frantz Fanon in *Black Skin, White Masks*. She attempts to explore "the ways in which the psychological effects of sexist oppression resemble those of racism and colonialism."[31] Oppression, Fanon tells us, not only has political and economic effects but psychic effects too. Bartky says:

> It is possible to be oppressed in ways that need involve neither physical deprivation, legal inequality, nor economic exploitation (Bartky summarizing Fanon).[32]

Those facing psychological oppression internalize the limitations of inferiority, becoming their own oppressions in a sense by exercising a harsh dominion over their self-esteem. Later, Bartky clarifies that political and economic oppression are often integral to one another. Oppression, properly understood, involves all three: namely, the political, economic, and psychological. They are, in effect, interrelated.[33] In our own liberal legal tradition, we unfortunately have de-emphasized or overlooked the psychological effects of discrimination and what those effects may mean for citizenship rights or full participation in public life. Part of the transformative re-understanding of *Brown v. Board of Education* (1954) as articulated by Charles Lawrence is his emphasis on the psychic harm from the message of discrimination.[34] The degrading message of segregation denies African Americans the primary good of self-respect and the principle requirement of reciprocity in liberalism: it robs them of the dignity to which every individual in a liberal democracy is entitled and depends upon.

Bartky elaborates the unique modes of oppression from psychological alienation. Fanon's descriptions of alienation operationalize in three different ways: stereotyping, cultural domination, and sexual objectification. Although Bartky uses the language of "stereotyping," we can easily see that discourses form stereotypes and they influence the formation of the self. Those holding stereotyped beliefs about women, she says, can hardly be expected to understand a woman's needs or respect her rights. Stereotypes embody an ideology and can ultimately influence what we know about ourselves as well. The effect of stereotyping, in essence, to use Charles Lawrence's words about African Americans in his groundbreaking *Brown v. Board of Education* (1954) analysis, is to "defame" women. In yet another way, stereotyping harms by causing psychic alienation. If I am the object of a stereotype that everyone else or the culture generally believes, why should I not believe it myself?[35] In internalizing the pejorative stereotype, whether partially or wholly, I have difficulty achieving an authentic choice of self. A depreciated ego, or in John Rawls's words, one that lacks the *primary good* of self-respect, can't achieve full self-determination. Simply put, you come to believe what they say, in whole or part, despite yourself. Even if you reject those negative stereotypes, a complex internal negotiation unfolds, one that the individual must process and combat with the knowledge that others expect less from you given your membership in the degraded group. Nor can such a depreciated ego negotiate the fair terms of social agreement, a fundamental requirement in a liberal democracy that seeks to find shared values without reference to comprehensive moral doctrines.[36]

In the case of cultural domination, Bartky acknowledges that women experience that phenomena a bit differently than those victimized by colonization. Women can look to no previous time before the colonizers came. "All the items in our general life of the people—our art and literacy, our language, our institutions are sexist"—they manifest male supremacy.[37] In contrast, even if colonizers degrade the culture, it is our own. Women, Bartky argues, lack *cultural autonomy.* I want to make that same claim with respect to pornography in our culture. In the area of pornography, the hegemonic inegalitarian variety, women lack cultural autonomy. Porn, the inegalitarian variant, remains dominant. As a result, women see a degraded, distorted sexual image of themselves reflected in a patriarchal culture and cultural practice.

In fact, this is the very image that a young Naomi Klein sees in the documentary written by her mother, *Not a Love Story.*[38] The young girl in the documentary walks by a storefront on the way to taking the bus. The storefront is littered with inegalitarian pornographic images of women. For young girls growing up in our culture, the incident is not isolated or relegated to a time in the 1970s. While the pornography may not appear in the local corner store, it does find its way onto the internet and influences mainstream cultural productions. The pornographic images at issue in *Not a Love Story* confound the young girl's sense of self-respect and undermine a developing sense of her own sexuality. Instead, those images reflect a cultural reality that presents a hegemonic and inegalitarian view of sexuality. While other more egalitarian forms of pornography exist, they are not the dominant images in our culture.

Bartky reminds us that it is through cultural life that a group is able to affirm its values and grasp its identity in acts of self-reflection. When we catch ourselves in that dominant culture, it is distorted or demeaning and it reflects the heterosexual male gaze. For the young girl in *Not A Love Story,* the dominant cultural view of women's sexuality—woman as object—distorts who she is. In Drucilla Cornell's words, the dominant cultural view violates the degradation principle, which derives from Rawls's notion of self-respect as a primary good. A patriarchal cultural ideology, then, guides behavior and shapes the criteria we have for knowledge: It becomes a method of subjugation. The girl's experience of pornography as a practice that depicts the heterosexual male experience of sexuality is culturally ignored and underexplored. A geneological, phenomenology-based approach can recoup her experience and dislodge the dominant cultural understandings of pornography as either liberatory or prurient.

Sexual objectification is the final dimension of psychic alienation presented by Bartky's elaboration of Fanon. Bartky explains that sexual objectification maintains dominance when sexualization becomes habitually extended and imposed into every area of a woman's experience.[39] Sexual objectification entails being the object of a kind of perception, unwelcome and inappropriate, that takes the part for the whole. It occurs independently of what a woman wants. She says that sexualization is a way of fixing disadvantaged persons in their disadvantage to their detriment within a narrow and repressive eros.[40] In such circumstances, one's own sexual self-definition is at odds with the oppressor, who's imposed projection dominates, confines, constricts, and represses.

To be sure, Bartky argues, we can be both the object and the objectifier in noticing our bodies in the mirror as sex objects. And, she continues, women learn to evaluate themselves as sex objects for the male connoisseur first, best, and, sometimes, most brutally. We, as women, have been taught to make ourselves as pleasing to the eye as possible and to take pleasure in it.[41] Yet sexual objectification, she says, psychically alienates an individual from her personhood. Sexual objectification places the object in the position of being both human and not quite human. The object is associated with the body and therefore human. But, the object is separated from personality, thereby estranging a person from the essential attributes of personhood.[42]

Bartky introduces the important notion that we can, in a sense, choose or even revel in our own oppression as women.[43] Linda Hirschmann discusses this same phenomenon when explaining the social construction of the subject and the centrality of discourse to that construction of personhood. Hirschmann complicates traditional liberal-theory notions about individual liberty and choice. Choice is the definitional core of liberty in traditional liberal treatises on the subject (Berlin 1969 as the quintessential example).[44] Hirschmann argues that the dominant theoretical conception of liberty is inadequate to account for the experience of women. Choice, she argues, is complicated by a complex relationship between internal factors of "will and desire" and factors outside of the self (the kind of and number of choices available, obstacles, and available power to pursue those choices). Hirschmann writes:

> Who I am and what I want are also to a significant degree a function of discursive categories of meaning and ideological pictures of social relations that produce the material conditions within which choice is exercised.[45]

Context, discourse, and language constitute the "choosing subject" and the choice matrix itself. Like Bartky, individual choice as expressed by "will and desire" is shaped by the very power relations embedded in discourses which stereotype, sexually objectify, and distort cultural representations.

Hirschmann's insights about social construction (and discourse) and Bartky's application of psychic alienation throw into relief precisely how pornography undermines women's citizenship rights. Pornography's discourse constructs desire, structures social relations between men and women, reifies gender by producing different truths about men and women, and constructs material reality in terms of everything from pay discrimination to sexual violence. This is not to say that pornography is determinative of women's material reality, but it is, anti-porn feminists contend, significant, relevant, and regulatable. Inegalitarian pornography as a discourse acts to shape a matrix of possibilities; while not eliminating individual choice, it can prime the subject to willingly desire its own oppression and even take pleasure in it, as well as structure a field of possibilities.

If the process described above is accurate, then it does not matter if individual women believe that pornography has not adversely affected the construction of their desire. As Foucault notes, sexual discourse is not simply repressive but also productive. Bartky writes that her own book "pay[s] particular attention to those modes of consciousness that can be shown to arise from oppressive intersubjective relationships and which tend at the same time to reproduce and to reaffirm these very relationships: feminine 'narcissism' and 'masochism'; female shame; sexual self-objectification; loss of self in the sense of merger with another."[46] Some women, of course, may not experience pornography in the way described by anti-pornography feminists. Similarly, not all African Americans introjected the negative racist stereotypes upon which segregation depended. Nonetheless, no one would argue that those pernicious racist discursive effects had no adverse cumulative statistical impact on the culture, politics, or citizenship rights of the group as a whole. Irrespective of whether those damaging stereotypes were internalized, African Americans had to interact with others who imposed those meanings onto them. In the same way, inegalitarian pornography's effects, if anti-porn feminists are right, has macrolevel reverberations beyond individual experiences. Women must interact with those who apply stereotypical sexual notions to women.

These subjective phenomenological experiences of discrimination that provide a fuller picture of the way oppression works are not solipsistic either. Intersubjectivity is confirmed within a web of public meaning. As Clyde Willis notes, subjectivity never leaves the realm of empirical fact and it is matched against other experiences and understandings of the world.[47] Foundations of intersubjective validity must be found in experience, he says, not beyond it. Yet facts don't come complete with their own interpretive framework. Until one places facts within some hermeneutical structure of understanding, they are meaningless. Principles are made intelligible by and as part of a person's conscious lived experience. Lived experience gives meaning, not the other way around. It is important then to discuss the way women experience pornography before simply categorizing pornography as protected speech: women may experience it as discrimination, a violation of the degradation principle, or, as Bartky explains it, taking pleasure in our own objectification and subordination.[48] Finding out women's and men's experiences with pornography means not only examining some vocal workers within the industry who see pornography as a liberatory choice but also listening to the experiences of women at rape crisis centers who discuss the ways in which pornography has been used in sexual violence against them.[49] Moreover, given the complexity of the formation of desire in a patriarchal system, no one is free from the oppressive forces that shape who we are and what we *willingly* desire.

The question remains whether free speech doctrine can conceptualize and operationalize the type of harm feminists (and hate speech code proponents) describe.[50] These harms stem from speech and produce discursive effects. The notion that pornography, or hate speech, has discursive effects conflicts with the current state of free speech jurisprudence in the United States, and frankly, the libertarian notion to which we are all acculturated. The libertarian sentiment is encapsulated in the childhood retort: "Sticks and stones will break my bones, but names will never hurt me." Hirschmann, while not specifically discussing pornography, tells us otherwise.[51] So do Bartky, McKinnon, Langton, McGowan, Eaton, Austin, Wittgenstein, Foucault, and others. Under current First Amendment jurisprudence, however, even if we tend to agree that pornography produces discursive effects and psychic alienation, we have no causal proof. Yet as Clyde Willis eloquently states:

> Everyone carries some enduring pain administered by words. The damage from words may be different, but it is just as real. . . . Yet people are loath to admit the hurt caused by words, and even less inclined to do anything about it, not because the hurt does not exist but because people adhere to an epistemological paradigm that recognizes only scientific evidence as real data, hence the protest that non-physical manifestations of pain are too subjective to be considered real, hence the need for phenomenology.[52]

The concept of discursive effects tells us that causality is a spurious, misleading, and ill-appropriated concept to help us understand how speech "does things" or the link between oppression and speech. Bartky and Willis supplement that understanding of harm through their use of phenomenology to explain psychic injury stemming from ineqalitarian discourse. To register that injury, free speech law must experience an epistemological shift about the relationship between speech and action.

CONCLUSION

Under a theory of discursive effects, the obstacles faced by speech act theory are removed. A theory of discursive effects need not rely upon a sovereign voice or locate the subordination in an isolated act. Instead, discourse is imbricated with power, enabling it to establish a dominance about cultural meaning and sexual practice. With an understanding of discursive effects, the intent of individual pornographers and the degree of authority they have to convey a message are not analytically necessary for harm to occur. It is this theory that we should apply to understanding the harms from discursive practices like pornography and hate speech.

NOTES

1. Catharine A. MacKinnon, "Points Against Postmodernism." *Chicago-Kent Law Review* 75 (2000): 687, p. 711.

2. A. Levin, *Cost of Free Speech: Pornography, Hate Speech, and Their Challenge to Liberalism*. Palgrave Macmillan, 2014, 119.

3. Lori Watson, "Pornography and Public Reason." *Social Theory and Practice* 33, no. 3 (2007): 467–88. https://doi.org/10.5840/soctheorpract200733318.

4. John Rawls, *Political Liberalism*. New York: Columbia University Press, 1993.

5. Watson, "Pornography and Public Reason." *Social Theory and Practice* 33, no. 3 (2007), 467–88. https://doi.org/10.5840/soctheorpract200733318

6. This citation and insight comes from an earlier iteration of this topic in a joint paper with Professor Georganna Ulary. Ernesto Laclau and Chantal Mouffe, *Hegemony and Socialist Strategy: towards a Radical Democratic Politics*. Verso, 2014.

7. Arnold I. Davidson, *Foucault and His Interlocutors*. University of Chicago Press, 1997. (Foucault in Davidson 1997.)

8. Davidson, *Foucault and His Interlocutors*. University of Chicago Press, 1997. (Foucault in Davidson 1997.)

9. Stuart Hall, ed. *Representation—Cultural Representations and Signifying Practices*. SAGE Publ., 1997.

10. Hall, ed. *Representation—Cultural Representations and Signifying Practices*. SAGE Publ., 1997.

11. Nancy J. Hirschmann, *The Subject of Liberty: Toward a Feminist Theory of Freedom*. Princeton University Press, 2003.

12. Levin, *Cost of Free Speech: Pornography, Hate Speech, and Their Challenge to Liberalism*. Palgrave Macmillan, 2014, 124.

13. Hirschmann, *The Subject of Liberty: Toward a Feminist Theory of Freedom*. Princeton University Press, 2003, 81.

14. Levin, *Cost of Free Speech: Pornography, Hate Speech, and Their Challenge to Liberalism*. Palgrave Macmillan, 2014, 124.

15. Levin, *Cost of Free Speech: Pornography, Hate Speech, and Their Challenge to Liberalism*. Palgrave Macmillan, 2014, 124. Levin citing Foucault.

16. A. W. Eaton, "A Sensible Antiporn Feminism," *Ethics* 117, no. 4 (2007): pp. 674-715, https://doi.org/10.1086/519226. As Anne Eaton notes, the very idea of social construction is a contested one. So does Nancy J. Hirschmann, *The Subject of Liberty: toward a Feminist Theory of Freedom*. Princeton University Press, 2003, 77.

17. Hirschmann, *The Subject of Liberty: Toward a Feminist Theory of Freedom*. Princeton University Press, 2003.

18. Hirschmann, *The Subject of Liberty: Toward a Feminist Theory of Freedom*. Princeton University Press, 2003, 81.

19. Hirschmann, *The Subject of Liberty: Toward a Feminist Theory of Freedom*. Princeton University Press, 2003, 77-78.

20. Hirschmann, *The Subject of Liberty: Toward a Feminist Theory of Freedom*. Princeton University Press, 2003, 79.

21. Hirschmann, *The Subject of Liberty: Toward a Feminist Theory of Freedom*. Princeton University Press, 2003, 80.

22. Rabinow, Paul, ed. *The Foucault Reader*. New York: Pantheon Books, 1984. Foucault, Michel. *The Archaeology of Knowledge and the Discourse on Language*. Translated by A.M. Sheridan Smith. New York: Pantheon Books, 1972.

23. Levin, *Cost of Free Speech: Pornography, Hate Speech, and Their Challenge to Liberalism*. Palgrave Macmillan, 2014, 126.

24. Levin, *Cost of Free Speech: Pornography, Hate Speech, and Their Challenge to Liberalism*. Palgrave Macmillan, 2014, 126.

25. Levin, *Cost of Free Speech: Pornography, Hate Speech, and Their Challenge to Liberalism*. Palgrave Macmillan, 2014, 126.

26. C.E. Willis, "The Phenomenology of Pornography: A Comment on Catharine MacKinnon's Only Words." *Law and Philosophy*, 16(2) (1997), 177-199.

27. Drucilla Cornell, *Feminism and Pornography*. Oxford University Press, 2007.

28. Joan Mason-Grant, *Pornography Embodied: From Speech to Sexual Practice*. Rowman & Littlefield, 2004.

29. Sandra Lee Bartky, *Femininity and Domination: Studies in the Phenomenology of Oppression*. Taylor & Francis, 2015, 29.

30. Bartky, *Femininity and Domination: Studies in the Phenomenology of Oppression*. Taylor & Francis, 2015, 23.

31. Bartky, *Femininity and Domination: Studies in the Phenomenology of Oppression*. Taylor & Francis, 2015, 22.

32. Bartky, *Femininity and Domination: Studies in the Phenomenology of Oppression*. Taylor & Francis, 2015, 22.

33. Bartky, *Femininity and Domination: Studies in the Phenomenology of Oppression*. Taylor & Francis, 2015, 23.

34. *Brown v. Board of Education* (1954).

35. Bartky, *Femininity and Domination: Studies in the Phenomenology of Oppression*. Taylor & Francis, 2015, 24.

36. Lori Watson, "Pornography." *Philosophy Compass*, vol. 5, no. 7, 2010, pp. 535–550.

37. Bartky, *Femininity and Domination: Studies in the Phenomenology of Oppression*. Taylor & Francis, 2015, 25.

38. *Not a Love Story: a Film about Pornography*. VHS, Canada, 1982.

39. Bartky, *Femininity and Domination: Studies in the Phenomenology of Oppression*. Taylor & Francis, 2015, 26.

40. Bartky, *Femininity and Domination: Studies in the Phenomenology of Oppression*. Taylor & Francis, 2015, 27.

41. Bartky, *Femininity and Domination: Studies in the Phenomenology of Oppression*. Taylor & Francis, 2015, 28.

42. Bartky, *Femininity and Domination: Studies in the Phenomenology of Oppression*. Taylor & Francis, 2015, 30.

43. See Bartky, pp. 46-47, where she discusses the story of P.

44. I am indebted to Professor Georganna Ulary for emphasizing the significance of problematized "choice." This insight comes from an early iteration of a joint paper with Professor Ulary.

45. Hirschmann, *The Subject of Liberty: toward a Feminist Theory of Freedom*. Princeton University Press, 2003, 202.

46. Bartky 2.

47. C. E. Willis, "The Phenomenology of Pornography: A Comment on Catharine MacKinnon's Only Words." *Law and Philosophy*, 16(2) (1997), 177-199.

48. Bartky, *Femininity and Domination: Studies in the Phenomenology of Oppression*.

49. Shira Tarrant, *The Pornography Industry: What Everyone Needs to Know*. Oxford University Press, 2016. C. A. MacKinnon and Dworkin, A., *In Harm's Way: The Pornography Civil Rights Hearings*. Cambridge, MA: Harvard University Press, 1998.

50. Jeremy Waldron, *The Harm in Hate Speech*. Harvard University Press, 2014.

51. Hirschmann, *The Subject of Liberty: Toward a Feminist Theory of Freedom*. Princeton University Press, 2003.

52. Willis, "The Phenomenology of Pornography: A Comment on Catharine MacKinnon's Only Words." *Law and Philosophy, 16*(2) (1997), 177-199. 197.

III

Liberal Law and a New Theory of Harm

SEVEN

Discursive Effects and Liberal Law

The previous chapter introduced the concept of discursive effects as a better way to understand how pornography undermines women's citizenship rights. It, along with previous chapters, critiqued different approaches like speech act theory and a probabilistic causal model, and it defined discursive effects. This chapter will consider whether discursive effects is compatible with liberal philosophy, and more specifically liberal law. Can concepts from egalitarian liberal theorists such as John Rawls, Joseph Raz, and Ronald Dworkin embrace poststructuralism's analysis of discourse's role in forming subjectivity?[1] In more liberal language, can we say that pornography (or white supremacy) are discourses that affect the formation of the subject citizen, adversely influencing an individual's dignity of social standing in a liberal democracy? Can pornography (and hate speech) undermine the primary good of self-respect in the words of John Rawls; or "equal concern and respect" in the words of Ronald Dworkin; or the dignity required for equal social standing in the words of Jeremy Waldron? Foucault's insights about discourse, power, and the shaping of subjectivity are shared with egalitarian liberalism whether explicitly recognized or not. More specifically, the principles of liberal *law* can embrace the poststructural model of discursive effects. In doing so, law will better reflect the actual workings and doings of language in constituting subjectivity and maintaining inequality.

Additionally, the philosophical insights of egalitarian liberals will be connected to constitutional precedent through Charles Lawrence's reinterpretation of *Brown v. Board of Education* (1954) as a case about speech.[2] *Brown* relies upon an unrecognized and unelaborated understanding of speech's relationship to inequality. The concept of discursive effects as applied to Lawrence's interpretation of *Brown* can help us better articulate how the message of segregation "does things" that violate the

Fourteenth Amendment. If *Brown* is understood as speech of the sort that produces discriminatory discursive effects, then the case provides a precedent for a civil damage–type ordinance in the *Hudnut* case and hate speech cases. We can indeed balance free speech and equality concerns based upon our past constitutional decisions, and we already understand how speech can constitute discrimination.

THE RELATIONSHIP BETWEEN DISCURSIVE EFFECTS AND EGALITARIAN LIBERALISM

Discursive effects as elaborated by Foucault, Bartky, and Hirschmann provide a richer sense of how oppression, through language, operates at the level of forming the subject. The argument thus far is that the inegalitarian form of pornography, as a dominant discourse, shapes the subjectivity of both men and women, undermining the latter's citizenship rights. Importantly, discursive effects help us to understand how discourse not only shapes the understandings, actions, and beliefs of others, but also ourselves.

Classical liberalism typically spends little time analyzing the emergence of subjectivity or personhood.[3] The power described by Hobbes or Locke is one involving the state restricting the ability of the citizen to act. The solution is to remove the obstacle inhibiting action: stop the state from unfairly squashing choice. Classical liberalism assumes that all individuals are free-choosing, autonomous actors. Insufficient time is spent analyzing from whence desires come and how power might shape those desires.[4] Beyond vainglory, competitiveness, or a propensity toward attaining private property, power's influence on the formation of the self is left unanalyzed. At best, only "thin" descriptions of the self are offered in order to ground community in truths that all can share in a pluralistic society.[5] The notion that personhood is constructed is left undiscussed. Classical liberalism, then, provides scant insight into the main argument presented in the chapter: it is at the very level of constructing the citizen subject through oppressive discourses that women's citizenship rights are most threatened because of discourses shaping both the subjectivity of the oppressed and the oppressor.

While classical liberalism, as conceived by Hobbes or Locke, cannot adequately analyze the psychic injury from oppression, egalitarian liberalism can. Egalitarian liberals tend to reject the classic distinction between negative and positive liberty. Whereas negative liberty is the right to be left alone, positive liberty entails the obligation of the state to protect the equality rights of individuals. Moreover, egalitarian liberals are far more concerned with the constitution of the person and its implications for liberty.[6] The construction of the subject (or personhood) and the way others view that subject is not just the preoccupation of feminists and poststructuralists. Instead, it deeply concerns egalitarian liberals as well.

Egalitarian liberalism helps us to examine the essential components of citizenship in a liberal democracy. Ronald Dworkin writes that liberalism has as its core commitment the "equal concern and respect" of all citizens—a principle for which John Rawls uses the phrase "primary goods."[7] Egalitarian liberalism asserts that primary goods—self-respect, liberty, equality, dignity, bodily autonomy—should extend to each citizen regardless of immutable characteristics such as gender, sexual orientation, and race. Under egalitarian liberal theory, people who lack primary goods as a result of oppression have an altered/diminished conception of the self and of its possibilities as well as more limited life opportunities.[8] Furthermore, without the full panoply of primary goods, dominant groups are able to devalue and stigmatize culturally oppressed individuals more readily and effectively, particularly through speech.[9] Thus, those without primary goods suffer due to their own self-understandings (they internalize what others say) and the understandings of others (dominant groups apply prejudiced conceptions), which, in turn, adversely affects their exercise of basic rights and the distribution of resources. Traditional liberals, of course, focus less on equality and more on liberty.[10]

It should be noted that relying on Ronald Dworkin to make the case that egalitarian liberalism is compatible with a reconceptualization of free speech law, one that takes into account the harm to the female subject from pornographic discourse, is problematic. Dworkin believes that the group deserving law's equal concern and respect is the men consuming pornography rather than women as a class. Yet, Dworkin's arguments about the primacy of equality and what's required to uphold it are inconsistent. Moreover, his claims about which group requires equal concern and respect belie history, context, and power. Dworkin explains the primacy of equality in the following manner:

> Government must treat those whom it governs with concern, that is, as human beings who are capable of suffering and frustration, and with respect, that is, as human beings who are capable of forming and acting on intelligent conceptions of how their lives should be lived. Government must not only treat people with concern and respect, but with equal concern and respect.[11]

Dworkin tells us that liberalism's traditional understanding of a tension between liberty and equality is misplaced. In fact, liberty is derived from equality. Fundamental liberties are only important to the extent that they protect something else, namely equality. Yet what does equality require for its principles to be upheld? Equal concern and respect demands government neutrality concerning conceptions of the good life. Everyone should have an equal opportunity to promote their conception of the good life in the public sphere. As Langton says, Dworkin's notion of equality appears to have a principle of neutrality at its heart.[12] What citizens need most is freedom of speech—liberty—in order to paradoxically achieve equality.

Dworkin's argument assumes what it must defend. Feminists and critical race theorists have consistently asserted that systemic and institutionalized racism and sexism prevent discrete and insular minorities from sufficiently advocating for their perspectives in the public realm. Racism and sexism distort, corrupt, and close off traditional channels of participation: prejudice implicates the very channels of participation themselves in failing to extend an equal opportunity for concern and respect. Under those circumstances, government cannot remain neutral in order to protect one's liberty to advocate the ideal conception of the good life. Government, to achieve equality, must intervene, leveling the playing field.

Levin seeks to recoup the liberatory aspects of Dworkin's egalitarian liberalism with a caveat: the cultural-oppression principle. Levin explains:

> [W]hat it means to live in a society where cultural oppression takes place is to have victims unable to be recipients of respect, in the sense that they cannot, due to the social forces at work in their situations, take advantage of the freedom and self-determination that the liberal state's stance of respect is supposed to provide.[13]

A cultural-oppression caveat would better account for the way that power and oppression operate in a society subject to historical and systematized discrimination. With such a caveat in place, government actions would have to be more substantive than a mere commitment to neutrality. A commitment to equality with the cultural-oppression caveat demands that government intervene to level the playing field, including potentially restricting forms of hate speech and inegalitarian pornography.

While Dworkin's articulation of egalitarian liberalism is inconsistent and lacking in a deep understanding of the corrosive effects of cultural oppression, his rejection of the notion that liberty and equality are in tension and his foregrounding of equality over liberty are worth keeping. Egalitarian liberals such as Joseph Raz share a similar view that individual rights are not at odds with community interests. Levin suggests that in Raz's formulation, the common good often meets the condition of harmony with individual interest.[14] The ascendent narrative traditional liberal philosophy—that we must protect individuals from government abuse of their fundamental rights—is both partial and longstanding. Yet Raz, like Dworkin, holds that we protect individual liberties precisely because in doing so we better advance the community's interests. When we face hard cases such as whether to regulate pornography or hate speech, we should cede individual rights to community interests.

In addition to what may initially seem an odd use of Dworkin, one might also argue that the chapter uses Rawls in a way with which he would disagree. Jeremy Waldron notes a similar problem in *The Harm in Hate Speech*.[15] In that book, Waldron relies on the Rawlsian notion of a well-ordered society to defend regulations on hate speech. A well-ordered society, for Rawls, is one that relies upon basic principles of justice that both government and the people uphold.[16] In such a well-ordered society, minorities have the assurance that our culture is one that is committed to justice and dignity. This assurance is a public good and becomes undermined by the visibility of hate speech, particularly in a culture with a long history of brutal racial discrimination. Hate speech in such a historical context is meant to proliferate and coordinate hate-inspired groups with animus toward minorities in an effort to degrade, humiliate and undermine the public good of assurance so vital in a well ordered and just society. Yet Rawls would seem to agree with American libertarian free speech orthodoxy, not Waldron's interpretation.[17] Nonetheless, like Waldron, the aim here is to discuss the implications of Rawls's theoretical ideas, which are open to interpretation beyond his specific intentions. Waldron describes his use of Rawlsian ideas despite Rawls's own position on free speech as taking his (Rawls's) notion and running with it in a direction that Rawls himself may have rejected. We will follow Waldron's lead in using both Rawls's and Dworkin's ideas in ways with which both might disagree.

We will return to a more extended discussion of both Waldron and Dworkin's argument about the supposed tension between liberty and equality in a bit. For now, it suffices to acknowledge that Dworkin's egalitarian liberalism poses some problems that should be addressed and remedied before grounding an argument in his theory. Similarly, we should recognize that we are making connections between Rawls's principles required for a just society and free speech in a way he most likely would not support.

In another way too, we must modify egalitarian liberalism's concepts with regard to speech. Egalitarian liberals tend to use the word "speech" rather than "discourse." Yet, when examining how speech can corrode an individual's primary goods, we must go beyond our understanding of speech. The more precise term to use in this discussion is "discourse," which serves as a primary mechanism for exercising oppression or denying individuals primary goods where formal legal barriers to equality no longer exist. Pornography, like hate speech, constitutes not just speech, then, but a *discourse* as a means to maintain inequality based upon immutable characteristics like race, gender, or sexual orientation. Put more directly, ascriptive discourses help limit the individual's access to primary goods. Importantly, the shift in language from *speech* to *discourse* signals a philosophically and politically significant move in understanding speech's real-world effects: it links liberalism to poststructuralism and considers speech's relationship to power, material effects, and discrimination. Phenomenology too helps us to foreground the experience of the target of inegalitarian discourse in understanding harm and developing legal remedies. Egalitarian liberalism allows poststructuralism's concern about power and language's role in constituting the subject into the discussion about equality and fairness.[18] It also requires that we take psychic alienation seriously in evaluating harm.

As Hirschmann reminds us, not only does that social construction of the subject through language inform others, it also, most powerfully and sometimes perniciously, defines our very notion of what we want. The theory of social construction maintains that our ideas, desires, aspirations, and self-understandings are deeply and profoundly constituted by the world in which we live.[19] Discourses and the power imbricated within them shape our subjectivity or personhood. We have no hermeneutically sealed, fully formed desires: there is no "pre-discursive material reality."[20] Desires are always already enmeshed, expressed, and shaped by our social surroundings. In short, discourse has subject producing capability through the process of social construction. Moreover, when liberals like Rawls discuss primary goods—the foundational senses of self that we all must have to begin political life on equal footing—he opens a larger discussion about social construction and the role that language plays in that construction of the person.

When we link the concept of social construction to poststructuralism's emphasis on discourse and its centrality in constituting our subjectivity or personhood, we find that speech and discourse play a tremendously important role in shaping the subject-citizen and maintaining oppression. Historically, liberalism understands the subject as unified and autonomous, whereas the continental tradition from which poststructuralism emerges deconstructs the subject, understanding it as constituted through multiple and conflicting ideologies, discourses, and disciplines.[21] Unlike traditional liberalism, egalitarian liberalism requires us to scrutinize the formation of personhood more closely because subjectivity (especially understood as "free agency") is a vital aspect of our primary goods. While traditional liberal theory attempts to avoid a thick description of subjectivity or personhood, egalitarian liberals like Rawls demand that liberalism pay attention to the formation of the subject-citizen (personhood) as central to upholding core values such as fairness and equal opportunity.[22] Without a sense of self-respect, for example, citizens come to the public sphere with a crucial disadvantage that results in unequal citizenship, unequal life opportunities, and unequal distribution of resources.

When it comes to questions about subjectivity, egalitarian liberals bridge a gap between traditional liberalism's scant description of personhood and poststructuralism, fuller articulation of subjectivity. If we take the tenets of egalitarian liberalism seriously—that unequal discourses like pornography connect to social status, equality of opportunity, and the distribution of material resources—we can no longer understand speech as simply offending or hurting the feelings of free-choosing, equal, and autonomous individuals. Egalitarian liberals demand a more thorough analysis of the subject and how it is formed, and speech's centrality to its formation. The theory of harm articulated by anti-pornography feminists and elaborated here, a theory of discursive effects combined with an understanding of psychic alienation, requires a more complex, nuanced, and accurate understanding of speech than modern libertarian US free speech jurisprudence currently permits. Yet the chapter argues that this alternative theory of harm based upon the concept of discursive effects is one that is compatible with the concerns of egalitarian liberals and ultimately US free speech law.

The connection between speech and the formation of the self has already been made by other egalitarian liberals. In *A Theory of Justice*, Rawls argues:

> ...the social system shapes the wants and aspirations that its citizens come to have. It determines in part the sort of persons they want to be as well as the sort of persons they are. . . . These matters are, of course, perfectly obvious and have always been recognized.[23]

In this passage, Rawls tacitly recognizes the idea of social construction. Rawls, and other egalitarian liberals, hold that the idea of a freely choosing subject unaffected by systems of power is not reflective of reality.[24] Put boldly, we are not free to be whomever we want. In shaping who we are and in shaping our desires, discourse forms internal barriers limiting our imaginations and our possibilities for choice.

In *The Imaginary Domain*, Drucilla Cornell connects pornography to the corrosion of citizenship rights and the formation of the self in the language of liberalism.[25] She argues that the role of violent or degrading pornography is analytically relevant in the construction of women's self-understandings.[26] Cornell writes:

> No woman should be forced to view her own body as it is fantasized as a dismembered, castrated other, found in bits and pieces. She should also not be forced to see her "sex" as it is stereotypically presented in hard-core porn through explicit depictions of sex acts. In hard-core porn, the woman is only there as her "sex." She should not, in other words, be forced to see her "self," her "sexed self," since a woman is always sexed, as reducible to an object, and thus as inherently unworthy of personhood.[27]

According to Cornell, imposing porn on another violates the "degradation prohibition," the idea that some of us are "unworthy of personhood" or are a "lesser being."[28] Forced viewing of pornography violates the degradation prohibition, which in turn affects a person's self-respect. Cornell extends the Rawlsian notion of self-respect, a primary good, to unwanted exposure to pornography. Most recently, Jeremy Waldron makes a similar Rawlsian argument about how hate speech undercuts the primary goods of minorities.[29]

Women exposed to pornography against their will are affected by pornography in a way that alters their own self-understandings and the self-understandings of the men with whom they must interact. If Hirschmann's understanding of social construction is correct, the importance of "willingness" may be less relevant given that pornographic discourse shapes will or desire.

The Rawlsian character of the "self-respect" claim commands us to not turn a morally irrelevant difference (like gender) into systemic disadvantage.[30] In this view, the "corrosive" effects of pornography on women's self-understandings and pornography's ability to alter the perceptions of men influence the distribution of social goods such as education, health, political representation, political influence, and wealth.[31] Further, pornography makes women more susceptible to sexual violence in the public and private spheres. Cornell translates Hirschmann's insights about the discursive social construction of the subject into the language of egalitarian liberalism. Forced viewing of pornography (and, in the book's view, even willing viewership) affects our ideology, women's material well-being, and the epistemology of sexuality: all points that Judge Easterbrook makes in his *Hudnut* decision.

Ultimately, though, Cornell fails to follow the logic of her argument. While Cornell makes a very important point about the subjection women face from forced exposure, she does not believe that pornography equates with discrimination or ripples outward in ways that undermine women's citizenship rights: law can contain the effects of pornography through zoning. This argument, then, redirects her argument on a path that she would not advocate.

Nonetheless, the chapter contends that Cornell's argument movingly describes why and how pornography constitutes discrimination and undermines self-respect, which is vital to forming the kinds of citizens which liberalism requires. Cornell favors zoning as a content-neutral means of regulation that both allows for women to avoid forced viewing of pornography and provides access for those who wish to consume pornography. Cornell's insights about pornography's harm to women's self-understanding are truncated by her failure to grasp pornography's pervasiveness—its hegemony—and the impossibility of containing it. Moreover, Cornell's attempt at a content-neutral means to address pornography's harms misconstrues neutrality itself. As Abigail Levin notes, neutrality in a culturally oppressive society fails to remedy the harm.[32]

> In a culturally oppressive society, if the liberal state is indeed commit-
> ted to facilitating each citizen's ability to realize her good, then the state
> must take steps to remedy the conceptions of the good that deny the
> equal moral worth of persons, rather than maintain neutrality about
> such conceptions.[33]

A neutral approach to regulating speech in an unequal environment only
serves to reinforce inequality rather than to remedy it. In her attack on
liberalism's commitment to neutrality, Levin goes much further than
Cornell, who retreats from addressing pornography's threat to women's
citizenship rights by relying on a libertarian, ostensibly neutral, understanding of the First Amendment.

In contrast, Levin understands that the harms from pornography occur on several different levels that parallel those discussed by Hirschmann.

> First, the dominant culture comes to believe what I will argue is the
> message of pornography and hate speech—that women and minorities
> have inferior moral worth. Second, women and minorities themselves
> come to believe this message. Finally, if women and minorities believe
> this message, they will be less likely to attempt to rebut it in the mar-
> ketplace, or their attempted rebuttals will be disregarded by the domi-
> nant culture.[34]

Levin uses different language than Hirschmann and Bartky but is
pointed in a similar direction.

A discussion of Cornell and her connection to Rawls's concept of the
primary goods necessary for citizenship brings us back onto the terrain of
liberal constitutional law. Cornell provides a missing piece in the puzzle
about how pornography harms and whether liberal constitutional law
may do anything about it. She connects Rawls to US constitutional law,
and, specifically, the First and Fourteenth Amendments. We've already
connected poststructuralism's concept of discursive effects to Rawls.
With Cornell, we can see precisely how a theory of discursive effects
could operate when assessing the harm from pornography, which is currently protected under the First Amendment.

BROWN V. BOARD OF EDUCATION (1954), DIGNITY, AND SPEECH

The previous chapter traveled a long philosophical distance to make the
case that discursive effects can better help us understand antipornography feminist claims that pornography discriminates and undermines
women's citizenship rights. It argues that poststructuralist concerns
about the social construction of the subject, and the way others understand that subject, creates negative real world material, ideological, and
epistemic consequences: discourses like pornography can constitute discrimination by affecting what we know, what we believe is ideal, and

how, in turn, we act. In Jeremy Waldron's language, pornography, like hate speech, undermines women's dignity and assurance about their citizenship status, which maintains that both groups may move through life without the threat of degradation, violence, and harassment.[35] MacKinnon describes the assault to women's dignity from pornography in the following manner:

> the hundreds and hundreds of magazines, pictures, films, videocassettes, and so-called books now available across America in outlets from adult stores to corner groceries, [include representations which] women's legs are splayed in postures of sexual submission, display, and access for all to see . . . [36]

Waldron's dignity claim, I believe, can be embraced by Rawls' argument about self-respect as a primary good.[37] Drucilla Cornell makes a similar point, arguing that Rawls's principle of self-respect can be extended to what she calls the degradation principle.

For those critics who contend that the very concept of dignity is far too broad, Waldron takes pains to distinguish a harm to dignity from a mere personal offense. Offense, Waldron contends, is not a legitimate rationale for regulation.[38] However, the undermining of an individual's dignity on the basis that they share ascriptive characteristics of a discrete and insular minority deserves regulation. Ascriptive characteristics are those that are immutable or unchanging, such as one's race, sex, or even one's sexual orientation. While race is not a biological category, we have historically assigned sociological characteristics to phenotypes like skin color using those assignations as a rationale to discriminate. Similarly, feminists argue that we should regulate pornography not because it offends but because it constitutes discrimination, undermining citizenship rights. Dignity is a significant basis for social standing where a person is entitled not to self-esteem or honor but to be regarded as a member of society in good standing.[39] Dignity as a public good ensures fair and decent treatment in society, not a reprieve from hurt feelings.[40] Waldron says:

> We protect people's basic dignity because it matters: it matters to society in general, inasmuch as society wants to secure its own democratic order and its character as a society of equals.[41]

We can legitimately analyze beliefs but not attack members of a group based on their immutable and morally irrelevant characteristics. Moreover, an emphasis is placed upon attacks to the dignity of those groups with a long, clear history of systematic discrimination at the hands of both government and private individuals. To emphasize this distinction, Waldron makes an analogy to religion. We can disagree with religious doctrine, critiquing it and thereby offending some believers. What we should not do, if we are to take this distinction between offending dignity as social status versus personal offense seriously, is to say that all members of a religious group are evil, unintelligent, subhuman, and second-class citizens. In short, Waldron, like Charles Lawrence, Mary Matsuda, and others in *Words that Wound,* argues that hate speech—and here again, I will extend the argument to pornography—harms the dignity of its targets.[42] Lawrence goes a step further in suggesting that if we interpret *Brown v. Board of Education* (1954) properly, we will find that it is specifically the message of segregation that harms dignity, the core of the Fourteenth Amendment. Dignity, then, is at the center of citizenship rights, and speech is a mechanism that may undermine that dignity.

In Charles Lawrence's interpretation of *Brown*, he asserts that the key to understanding this iconic case is that the practice of segregation is speech.[43] The injuriousness of segregation is in the message it conveys, which is white supremacy. To illustrate the point, Lawrence examines the public accommodations provisions in the Civil Rights Act of 1964. In Title II, the Civil Rights Act prohibits restaurant owners from segregating whites and blacks at places of public business. Even if owners disregard segregated facilities signs and provide the same service to all groups, they still violate the statute. The harm is in the message conveyed by the sign, not whether owners enforce the sign's commands. The very message of segregation undermines the central meaning of the equal protection clause, which is designed to protect dignity: the message, to use the language of the previous chapter, has discursive effects, including real psychic injuries, thereby violating equal protection of the laws. As John Rawls tells us, dignity and self-respect are primary goods in a liberal democracy. Without them, individuals come to the public realm disadvantaged both in terms of how they understand their life opportunities and in terms of the opportunities available to them.

In reinterpreting *Brown*, Lawrence focuses on Chief Justice Warren's claim that segregated public schooling harms African-American children's self-esteem. By grounding *Brown* in the experience of African-American school children, like MacKinnon, Warren begins the legal analysis with the lived experience of the oppressed. Unlike *Plessy v. Ferguson*, the argument presented is not that African-American school children misunderstand the message of segregation, but rather the starting premise of the opinion validates their experience of degradation from that demeaning message. In this sense, *Brown* addresses one of the most egregious arguments in *Plessy*. Justice Brown argues in *Plessy* that no public consensus exists around segregation's meaning. Justice Brown writes:

> We consider the underlying fallacy of the plaintiff's argument to consist in the assumption that the enforced separation of the two races stamps the colored race with a badge of inferiority. If this be so, it is not by reason of anything found in the act, but solely because the colored race chooses to put that construction upon it. The argument necessarily assumes that if, as has been more than once the case and is not unlikely to be so again, the colored race should become the dominant power in

the state legislature, and should enact a law in precisely similar terms, it would thereby relegate the white race to an inferior position. We imagine that the white race, at least, would not acquiesce in this assumption.[44]

Yet Justice Brown could only come to such a conclusion by willfully ignoring the historical context in which the meaning of social practices takes shape. Tangible equalities cannot undo the meaning of the act. In *Brown*, Chief Justice Warren challenges *Plessy's* argument, which denied the commonly understood meaning of segregation.[45] Chief Justice Warren counters the argument in *Plessy* by noting what we all know: namely, that the public meaning behind the practice is white supremacy.

Justice Brown is engaged in what Ludwig Wittgenstein would identify as a language game. In order to understand the true meaning of segregation, we would have to see how separate but equal works in everyday life.[46] In practice, we know that segregation limited African Americans access to full political and civil life in a number of deeply invidious ways. Justice Brown's argument challenging the meaning of segregation is the quintessential example of what James Baldwin would identify as "white innocence," denying the invidious meaning and purpose of segregation to maintain the virtue of whites.

As Lawrence points out, the harm in *Brown* was psychic and reputational.[47] He contends that, in the decision, plaintiffs overturned the principle of separate but equal by establishing that segregated schools caused psychological harm to African-American children. Children in such schools felt segregation was a "badge of inferiority" that translated into an inability to achieve. To quote Chief Justice Warren:

> Does segregation of children in public schools solely on the basis of race, even though the physical facilities and other "tangible" factors may be equal, deprive the children of the minority group of equal educational opportunities? We believe that it does. . . . To separate them from others of similar age and qualifications solely because of their race generates a feeling of inferiority as to their status in the community that may affect their hearts and minds in a way unlikely ever to be undone. . . . Separate educational facilities are inherently unequal.[48]

The harm done to African American children, then, was to negatively affect their own self-understandings, which in turn circumscribed their horizon of life opportunities. Segregation also harmed the reputation of African Americans by defaming Black school children. *Brown*, Lawrence argues, is a case about group defamation, and defamation is about speech. The message of segregation stigmatized Black children, depriving them of dignity and self-respect. To be labeled unfit to attend school with white children injured the reputation of Black children, thereby foreclosing employment opportunities and the right to be regarded as respected members of the body politic.[49] Thus, the demand for equality in this case is only facially about equal education, and a dual harm is inflicted. The first harm is that the message of segregation injured the school children's own self-understandings. The second is that it affected the perception of others about their abilities. The discourse of white supremacy whose meaning is imbricated in the practice of segregation harms equal rights.

Lawrence's reinterpretation of *Brown* as speech has clear implications for antipornography cases (and hate speech cases). In his interpretation, speech triggers a violation of the equal protection clause, and the harm that results is psychological and reputational in nature. That harm relies on expressive content to injure and leads to discrimination and material disadvantage. Segregation, like pornography, is a practice that depends upon expressive content to induce effects, more specifically ideological, material, and epistemic effects. Lawrence's interpretation makes the reader confront the entanglement of the liberty claims inherent in the right to association with the equal respect necessary for full citizenship. If Lawrence's interpretation is correct, liberty cedes to equality.

In interpreting *Brown* as speech, Lawrence seeks to argue in favor of the constitutionality of hate speech regulations. In doing so, Lawrence must address several critiques that could also apply to anti-pornography claims. The first critique concerns the conduct/speech distinction typically applied in First Amendment jurisprudence. The conduct/speech distinction separates regulatable conduct from the protected message. For example, you may protest the draft, but you may not burn your draft card.[50] The message that one disagrees with the draft is protected speech, but the conduct is prohibited. One may express that dissent in a myriad of ways, including burning the flag in protest, but one may not engage in the conduct of burning a draft card.[51] Following the same logic, a critic may argue the message of segregation is protected while the conduct is prohibited. In Lawrence's words, the critic here is suggesting a conflation between speech and conduct where the First Amendment has consistently held that they are separate.

Of course, Lawrence notes that under the Civil Rights Act of 1964 all signs segregating patrons had to be discarded even if the places of business were not actively separating customers. Lawrence says, "Outlawing these signs graphically illustrates my point that antidiscrimination laws are primarily regulations of the content of racist speech."[52] He adds that "racism is simultaneously speech (a socially constructed meaning or idea) and conduct."[53] As a social construction, race must continually be re-enacted "through millions of ongoing contemporaneous speech/acts." As such, we are "raced" as race must be consistently constructed and reconstructed in an ongoing process. As noted in the previous chapter, the primary means through which we are socially constructed is through discourse. Moreover, discourse produces effects that flow through our ideology, the material world, and in our understanding of social reality. In the case of socially constructing race, an ongoing process requiring daily reinstantiations, speech's actions are analytically entangled and inseparable from the message.

Judith Butler has explored the ways in which gender, masculinity, and femininity are unstable categories requiring ongoing performative reiterations to shape our lives. When any individual dresses in a way that undermines those unstable categories, society often reacts to punish the transgressor. Racial categories, like gender categories, are unstable and subject to rupture, reordering the status quo and the hierarchy within it.

Lawrence is also faced with the state action doctrine of the Fourteenth Amendment. The state action doctrine essentially holds that government may only address state-sponsored discrimination. It may not regulate purely private forms of discrimination. The Civil Rights Cases (1883) established the state action doctrine, which the Supreme Court handed down at a moment when it played an integral role in retrenching from the commitment of equality mandated in the Fourteenth Amendment.[54] While the state action doctrine has been in place as precedent for a long period of time, critics argue that the decision ignores the abolitionist Republican's original intent in framing the amendment.[55] Legal scholar Robin West contends that the abolitionist original understanding of the Fourteenth Amendment requires the following interpretation:

> The message that I suggest we should take . . . is that the plainest possible meaning of the Fourteenth Amendment mandate that no state shall deny to any citizen "equal *protection* of the law" is that no state may deny to any citizen the protection of its criminal and civil law against private violence and private violation. Put differently, no state may, through denials of protection, permit any citizen to live in a state of "dual sovereignty." The equal protection clause on this reading is at root a guarantee not of equal justice nor of substantive equality, but of sole sovereignty: the state, and only the state, shall be sovereign over each and every citizen. Only the state shall have access to the use of unchecked and uncheckable violence to effectuate its will (and then, of course, only with due process). No citizen shall be subject to uncheckable violence by anyone other than the state; no citizen shall be under the will and command of anyone other than the state.[56]

West interprets the beginning phrase of the Fourteenth Amendment, "no state shall," as meaning that government is required to provide every individual the full force of the law (criminal and civil) to eliminate all forms of discrimination, whether public or private. Instead, we are left with a cramped and decontextualized reading of "State," an interpretation put forth for overtly racist reasons. On this interpretation, the Civil Rights Cases elaboration of the state action doctrine violates the originalist understanding of the Fourteenth Amendment and limits government action to state-sponsored discrimination in a distorting and unintended manner.

If West and other scholars are correct about a more appropriate reading of the Fourteenth Amendment, then we can dispense with an unwieldy and warped construction of the state action doctrine. The application of the state action doctrine has caused great legal distortions in the attempt to eliminate segregation and discrimination generally. In *Heart of Atlanta Motel Inc. v. United States* (1964), in an effort to avoid the state action doctrine, the federal government argued that segregation in motor lodging adversely affected the national economy, thereby enabling Congress under the commerce clause to prohibit discrimination.[57] The holding is a silly one given that we all know that the real harm from segregation is not damage to commerce but instead to the dignity of individual African-American citizens, a dignity which the core of the Fourteenth Amendment is designed to protect.

Finally, Lawrence argues that understanding *Brown* as speech as a way to defend the constitutionality of hate speech regulations has support within free speech law as well. First, Lawrence contends that hate speech regulations of the sort found on college campuses simply ban face-to-face insults, which law already regulates under the fighting words doctrine. Under that doctrine, face-to-face insults that lead to violence may be regulated. Of course, Lawrence documents that the way in which fighting words is really based upon the experience of white heterosexual men who tend to respond to emotionally assaultive speech with violence. Women and minorities, given their historical experiences, typically leave a situation where they have been verbally assaulted rather than engage in violence. In their historical experience, such assaultive speech precedes violence.[58] As such, hate speech conceptualized as fighting words simply bans a subcategory of already proscribable speech. As we know from *R.A.V. v. St. Paul* (1992), the Court finds regulating hate speech as a problematic subcategory of fighting words is viewpoint-based, violating the First Amendment.[59]

A previous chapter extensively critiques the strong reaffirmation of the content and viewpoint neutrality principle that results from the ruling in *R.A.V.* The content-neutrality principle articulated in *R.A.V.*, with its roots in *Brandenburg v. Ohio* (1969), is hardly neutral.[60] In short, an ahistorical and acontextual approach to assessing the harm from racist speech is biased, ignoring a long, clear brutal history of the relationship between hate speech and racial subordination. We can only assess meaning, and harm, within a context of history. Without the use of history and political context, we make a deliberate choice, a biased choice, to obscure meaning in the way that Justice Brown willfully ignored the meaning of segregation in *Plessy v. Ferguson* (1896).

Another case, separate from the fighting words doctrine, bolsters the notion that hate speech is regulatable under the First Amendment. Under the concept of group libel established in *Beauharnais v. Illinois* (1952), citizens can be harmed by speech that targets all members of a racial group by defaming them and undermining their dignity.[61] In *Beauharnais*, which is no longer considered good law after *New York Times v. Sullivan* (1964), a man circulated a leaflet in Chicago asking government officials to stop the encroachment of blacks against whites.[62] In the pamphlet, Beauharnais wrote that he feared the mongrelization of the white race and that whites should be motivated to defend against the aggressions of the Black race including rape, thievery, and murder. The Illinois ordinance that prohibited the group libel was essentially what we would now call a hate speech law.[63] Illinois sought to prohibit the description of "depravity, criminality, unchastity or lack of virtue of a class of citizens of any race, color, creed or religion."[64] The Supreme Court upheld the statute, a remarkable outcome given the status of the Court's current libertarian jurisprudence on free speech.

Critics argue that the decision in the *Sullivan* case undermines the holding in *Beauharnais*. In *Sullivan*, the Supreme Court handed down a more speech-protective decision. In the decision, the Court held that libel against public officials required proof of a reckless disregard for the truth. Thus, under the *Sullivan* decision, public officials would not only have to prove that a statement was false, but also that the purveyor of the statement recklessly and maliciously chose to report the falsehood. Waldron suggests that applying the *Sullivan* decision to undermine *Beauharnais* is wrong. Waldron writes:

> So there is a carelessness about the consensus of modern First Amendment jurists that *Sullivan* implicitly overturns *Beauharnais*, a carelessness that I suspect is really the product of nothing more scholarly than wishful thinking.[65]

The *Times* decision applies to public figures, not groups of private citizens. Therefore, in the view of scholars such as Waldron, the application of *Sullivan* to invalidate *Beauharnais* is sloppy and wrong-headed.

The claim that pornography harms women's citizenship rights bears some similarities to the *Beauharnais* instance of racial group libel. In order to make the case that pornography undermines Fourteenth Amendment rights, one would have to acknowledge that the message from inegalitarian pornography sends a message about women as a class. The force of the harm emanates from a message about women, their value, and their worth to the political compact. In MacKinnon's words, women as a class are worthy of sexual violence, degradation, and submission. Again, we can argue about whether pornography as a genre provides diverse representations of sexuality. The market suggests otherwise. While those other versions exist, they are not the dominant cultural products.

BROWN, PORNOGRAPHY, AND DISCURSIVE EFFECTS

But how does Lawrence's re-interpretation of *Brown* share anything in common with the concepts such as discursive effects and psychic aliena- tion introduced in the previous chapter? To use the language and con- cepts of this earlier chapter, Lawrence is outlining the ways in which segregation, its message, produces psychic alienation and socially con- structs race. Through that psychic alienation and its reverberations through social constructs like race, we see discursive effects rippling out- ward-creating ideological distortions, epistemic inaccuracies, and materi- al disadvantage. If Lawrence's understanding of *Brown* as speech is cor- rect, we already understand that speech "does things" in maintaining inequality of the sort that violates one's citizenship rights. Moreover, law has regulated such discourse based upon its corrosion of citizenship rights. The degrading and humiliating message from segregation meant that African Americans entered civil society with less respect, a vital primary good in a liberal democracy. And, at least for some African Americans, the message of segregation adversely affected their own self- understandings, resulting in a kind of psychic alienation with adverse real world material effects. Moreover, in *Brown*, speech (liberty) did not trump equality as we are told that it should in *American Booksellers v. Hudnut* (1985). Instead, following the insights of Joseph Raz, liberty and equality are not at odds but rather coextensive. Dworkin goes so far as to argue that all liberty is derived from equality.[66] Fundamental liberties are only important, he says, to the extent that they protect something else, namely equality.[67] Speech, then, should be viewed through the organiz- ing lens of equality.

In certain respects, Judge Easterbrook's understanding of pornogra- phy in maintaining women's inequality is remarkably similar to Law- rence's key insight in reinterpreting *Brown*: expressive content harms the standing of the citizen in public life, violating his or her equal protection rights. In the quote below, Judge Easterbrook agrees that pornography generates what we've termed earlier as discursive effects that are ideo- logical, material, and epistemic in nature.

> Men who see women depicted as subordinate are more likely to treat them so. Pornography is an aspect of dominance. It does not persuade people so much as change them. It works by socializing, by establish- ing the expected and the permissible. In this view, pornography is not an idea; pornography is the injury.[68]

This quote makes MacKinnnon's argument that pornography constitutes discrimination. Pornography is not just speech: it is discrimination (the injury). Pornography is ideological in establishing what is to be wanted, and it is epistemic in determining the outer boundaries of permissible behavior. Here, he concedes much to MacKinnon and effectively makes

the same argument as Rae Langton in that pornography has perlocutionary effects.

He continues,

> There is much to this perspective. Beliefs are also facts. People often act
> in accordance with the images and patterns they find around them. . . .
> Pornography affects how people see the world, their fellows, and social
> relations. . . . Racial bigotry, anti-Semitism, violence on television, re-
> porter's biases—these and many more influence the culture and shape
> socialization. . . . Yet all is protected as speech, however insidious. [69]

Judge Easterbrook's quote, taken together, reinforces a theory of discursive effects. Pornography, he admits, influences how people see the
world, triggering ideological effects. In turn, how we see the world
shapes our actions. Men who watch inegalitarian pornography are more
likely to treat women in a subordinate manner, leading to injury and
abuse at home and in the streets as well as lowering pay at work. Pornography shapes the expected and what we know. The discourse of pornography, just like the discourse of white supremacy conveyed through the
message of segregation, socially constructs us. Judge Easterbrook concedes, however tacitly through the logic of his opinion, that pornography
"does things." In the case of *Brown*, we face a different starting point. We
begin with the practice (segregation) to find the core of the injury (segregation's message) is speech. Whereas in the case of pornography, at least
in *Hudnut*, we begin with the speech—pornography is protected under
the First Amendment—and deny the injuries—that pornography corrodes citizenship rights.

Unlike Warren in *Brown*, Judge Easterbrook spends no time analyzing
the effects of pornography on women's subjectivity or the formation of
the self, which is key to understanding some of the most devastating
effects of the anti-pornography feminists' Fourteenth Amendment
claims. Lawrence's reinterpretation of *Brown* draws out the psychic alienation and phenomenological implications of segregation implicit in Chief
Justice Warren's opinion. In Judge Easterbrook's decision, the idea that
pornography may psychically alienate women in ways that violate their
citizenship rights is wholly unexplored. Yet Judge Easterbrook does
understand that pornography generates these other serious harms in
terms of sexual violence, abuse on the streets, and lesser pay at work. In
the terms that Lawrence uses, Judge Easterbrook seems to grasp the defamation argument but leaves unexplored the ways in which pornography
may undermine the primary good of self-respect or Cornell's variant, the
degradation principle.

A key missing element to Easterbrook's opinion, then, involves the
phenomenology of oppression. Judge Easterbrook travels part of the distance to understand the real harms from pornography but stops short.
Like Justice Brown in *Plessy*, Ronald Dworkin in "The New Puritans,"

and Justice Scalia in *R.A.V. v. St. Paul*, he failed to take a hermeneutic leap to see the world from the position of the marginalized and to begin the analysis with that experience.[70] The cases that most fulfill our obligations under equal protection, such as *Brown* or *Beauharnais*, take that hermeneutic leap, beginning with the experience of the disadvantaged. They write from the perspective of the victim of discrimination rather than the perpetrator, taking sub-altern or "local" knowledges more seriously. Unfortunately, Judge Easterbrook started down the path toward seeing the world from the position of those subject to discrimination, but failed to follow the logic of his premises.

By accounting for power, the concept of discursive effects helps us to better understand the perspectives and experiences of the oppressed. It takes seriously the cultural dominance of discourses and their effects on our subjectivity as well as on the subjectivity of the oppressor. It can recoup marginalized counter-narratives, centering them in an analysis of harm. Discursive effects avoid the mystification of causality when considering how speech influences the world around us, maintaining inequality.

CONCLUSION

This chapter has attempted to provide a rich theoretical basis for better understanding why Judge Easterbrook's insights about the real world harm to women stemming from pornography are accurate and corrosive of the role that women play in public life. Moreover, if *Brown* is about speech, Judge Easterbrook had a precedent for upholding the civil damage ordinance. Speech, expressive content, and discourse can indeed maintain inequality in violation of citizenship rights as MacKinnon, Langton, McGowan, and others have so powerfully argued elsewhere. The ways in which Judge Easterbrook describes the harms from pornography are best understood through the concept of discursive effects. Discourse does far more than cause hurt feelings and, if we are to seriously combat inequality, we must move away from a simplistic libertarian conception of speech and better balance liberty with equality.

In fact, through Lawrence's reinterpretation of *Brown* and the application of concepts like discursive effects and psychic alienation, we have a more poignant and painful understanding of precisely how speech, messages, and meaning can undermine a sense of our dignity, value, and worth both to ourselves and to others. Without that dignity, vital negotiations in the public realm falter. A re-reading of *Brown* and *Hudnut* through the lens of discursive effects helps us to more fully comprehend why the libertarian notion of speech is faulty: harmful speech at issue is not limited to hurt feelings. Speech maintains inequality through discursive effects.

This reading of *Brown* and its comparison to pornography regulation invokes many powerful criticisms. One such criticism is that Lawrence's reinterpretation of *Brown* as speech is not accepted in courts and is wrong.[71] However, my purpose in discussing Lawrence's interpretation of *Brown* is to show that courts could and should understand *Brown* in this way, and, if *Brown* is speech, courts need to reconsider notions of harm in pornography cases. Courts could conclude that the harm in *Brown* occurs through speech and that the harm in pornography is similar enough to the practice of segregation in *Brown* to find regulations justified. But, they do not, and this fact is worth examining. This comparison between *Brown* and *Hudnut* highlights that our understanding of free speech is a contested political battleground.

NOTES

1. John Rawls, *A Theory of Justice*. Universal Law Publishing Co Ltd, 2013. Ronald Dworkin, *Life's Dominion: An Argument about Abortion, Euthanasia, and Individual Freedom*. Vintage Books, 1994. Ronald Dworkin, *Taking Rights Seriously*. Harvard University Press, 1978. Joseph Raz, "On The Nature of Right." *Mind* 93 (1984): 194–214.

2. *Brown v. Board of Education*, 347 U.S. 483 (1954).

3. Donald J. Moon, *Constructing Community: Moral Pluralism and Tragic Conflicts*. Princeton University Press, 1993.

4. Nancy J. Hirschmann, *The Subject of Liberty: Toward a Feminist Theory of Freedom*. Princeton University Press, 2003.

5. Moon, 12.

6. Hirschmann, *The Subject of Liberty: Toward a Feminist Theory of Freedom*. Princeton University Press, 2003. A. Levin, *Cost of Free Speech: Pornography, Hate Speech, and Their Challenge to Liberalism*. Palgrave Macmillan, 2014.

7. Ronald Dworkin, *Taking Rights Seriously*. Harvard University Press, 1978. Levin, *Cost of Free Speech: Pornography, Hate Speech, and Their Challenge to Liberalism*. Palgrave Macmillan, 2014.

8. See Cynthia Stark's understanding of what the Rawlsian concept of self-respect entails. She tells us that "justice as fairness" requires that we address the self-respect of citizens who face discrimination on account of class, race, gender, or other morally irrelevant immutable characteristics. Cynthia Stark, "Rawlsian Self-Respect." *Oxford Studies in Normative Ethics*, edited by Mark Timmons, vol. II. Oxford University Press, 2013, pp. 238–261. Oxford Series in Normative Ethics II. DOI:10.1093/acprof:oso/9780199662951.003.0010. Levin, *Cost of Free Speech: Pornography, Hate Speech, and Their Challenge to Liberalism*. Palgrave Macmillan, 2014. Dworkin, *Taking Rights Seriously*. Harvard University Press, 1978. Rawls, *A Theory of Justice*. Universal Law Publishing Co Ltd, 2013.

9. Levin, *Cost of Free Speech: Pornography, Hate Speech, and Their Challenge to Liberalism*. Palgrave Macmillan, 2014. Dworkin, *Taking Rights Seriously*. Harvard University Press, 1978. Rawls, *A Theory of Justice*. Universal Law Publishing Co Ltd, 2013.

10. Levin, *Cost of Free Speech: Pornography, Hate Speech, and Their Challenge to Liberalism*. Palgrave Macmillan, 2014.

11. Dworkin 2005, 272, and Levin quoting Dworkin 29.

12. Rae Langton, 121.

13. Levin 36.

14. Levin, 25.

15. Jeremy Waldron, *The Harm in Hate Speech*. Harvard University Press, 2014.

16. Jeremy Waldron, *The Harm in Hate Speech*. Harvard University Press, 2014, 66.

17. Waldron 69-70.

18. Hirschmann, *The Subject of Liberty: Toward a Feminist Theory of Freedom*. Princeton University Press, 2003.

19. Hirschmann, *The Subject of Liberty: toward a Feminist Theory of Freedom*. Princeton University Press, 2003.

20. Hirschmann,*The Subject of Liberty: toward a Feminist Theory of Freedom*. Princeton University Press, 2003.

21. Paul Rabinow, ed. *The Foucault Reader*. Pantheon Books, 1984. Hirschmann, *The Subject of Liberty: Toward a Feminist Theory of Freedom*. Princeton University Press, 2003. Levin, *Cost of Free Speech: Pornography, Hate Speech, and Their Challenge to Liberalism*. Palgrave Macmillan, 2014. J. Donald Moon, *Constructing Community: Moral Pluralism and Tragic Conflicts*. Princeton University Press, 1993.

22. Levin, *Cost of Free Speech: Pornography, Hate Speech, and Their Challenge to Liberalism*. Palgrave Macmillan, 2014.

23. Levin, *Cost of Free Speech: Pornography, Hate Speech, and Their Challenge to Liberalism*. Palgrave Macmillan, 2014. Dworkin, Ronald. *Taking Rights Seriously*. Harvard University Press, 1978. Rawls, John. *A Theory of Justice*. Universal Law Publishing Co Ltd, 2013. Rawls, John. *A Theory of Justice*. Universal Law Publishing Co Ltd, 2013, 259.

24. I am indebted to Professor Georganna Ulary for highlighting this connection where it was developed in an earlier paper on a similar topic.

25. Drucilla Cornell, *Feminism and Pornography*. Oxford University Press, 2007. Also *The Imaginary Domain*.

26. Cornell, *Feminism and Pornography*. Oxford University Press, 2007, 8-10. Also, *The Imaginary Domain*.

27. Cornell, *The Imaginary Domain: Abortion, Pornography & Sexual Harassment*. New York: Routledge, 1995, 103.

28. Cornell, *Feminism and Pornography*. Oxford University Press, 2007, 10. Also *The Imaginary Domain*.

29. Waldron, *The Harm in Hate Speech*. Harvard University Press, 2014.

30. Levin, *Cost of Free Speech: Pornography, Hate Speech, and Their Challenge to Liberalism*. Palgrave Macmillan, 2014, 1-2. Cass R. Sunstein, "Words, Conduct, Caste," *University of Chicago Law Review* 60 (1993): p. 800, 802.

31. Cass R. Sunstein, "Words, Conduct, Caste," *University of Chicago Law Review* 60 (1993): p. 802.

32. Levin, *Cost of Free Speech: Pornography, Hate Speech, and Their Challenge to Liberalism*. Palgrave Macmillan, 2014, 2.

33. Levin, *Cost of Free Speech: Pornography, Hate Speech, and Their Challenge to Liberalism*. Palgrave Macmillan, 2014, 2.

34. Levin, *Cost of Free Speech: Pornography, Hate Speech, and Their Challenge to Liberalism*. Palgrave Macmillan, 2014, 2.

35. Waldron, J., *The Harm in Hate Speech*. Harvard University Press, 2014.

36. MacKinnon quoted in Waldron, 90. Waldron, Jeremy. *The Harm in Hate Speech*. Harvard University Press, 2014.

37. Based upon Cyntia Stark's understanding of Rawlsian self-respect. Cynthia Stark, "Rawlsian Self-Respect," in *Oxford Studies in Normative Ethics*, ed. Mark Timmons, vol. II. Oxford University Press, 2013, pp. 238-261.

38. Waldron, *The Harm in Hate Speech*. Harvard University Press, 2014, 105-111.

39. Waldron, 105.

40. Waldron, 107.

41. Waldron, 111.

42. In Charles Lawrence's interpretation of *Brown*, he asserts that the key to understanding the iconic case is that the practice of segregation is speech. The injuriousness of segregation is in the message it conveys, which is white supremacy. Recently, Bruce Ackerman, in *We The People: The Civil Rights Revolution*, argues that the appropriate way to interpret *Brown* is to understand that it elaborated the "anti humiliation principle" as the core of equal protection jurisprudence. While Lawrence and Ackerman

emphasize different ways to understand the iconic *Brown* case—one as a case about speech the other as a way to find the core meaning of the equal protection clause— both interpretations converge on the idea that dignity is at the center of citizenship rights. This dignity argument is consistent with Rawls's demand for self-respect as a necessary primary good in a liberal democracy. Bruce Ackerman, *We The People: The Civil Rights Revolution.* Cambridge, MA: Belknap Harvard, 2018.

43. Lawrence, 59.

44. *Plessy v. Ferguson,* 163 U.S. 537 (1896), 551.

45. *Plessy v. Ferguson,* 163 U.S. 537 (1896). *Brown v. Board of Education* (1954).

46. N. Warburton, (2006); Ludwig Wittgenstein in *Philosophy: The Classics.* Routledge. The notion of language games is described.

47. Lawrence, 74.

48. *Brown,* 493-94.

49. Lawrence, 75.

50. United States v.O'Brien, 391 US 367 (1968)

51. *Texas v. Johnson,* 491 US 397 (1989)

52. Lawrence, "If He Hollers Let Him Go," in *Words That Wound,* 61.

53. Here, Lawrence invokes the argument of Professor Kendall Thomas, 61.

54. *The Civil Rights Cases,* 109 U.S. 3(1883).

55. See Jacobus Tenbroek, *Equal Under the Law* (1965). John P. Frank and Robert F. Munro, "The Original Understanding of 'Equal Protection of the Laws,'" 1972 *WASH. U. L.Q.* 421. Robin West, "Toward an Abolitionist Interpretation of the Fourteenth Amendment," 94 *W. VA. L. Rev.* 111 (1991).

56. West, 129.

57. *Heart of Atlanta Motel Inc. v. United States,* 379 U.S. 241 (1964).

58. See both Matsuda and Lawrence in *Words That Wound.*

59. *R.A.V. v. St. Paul,* 505 U.S. 377 (1992).

60. *Brandenburg v. Ohio,* 395 U.S. 444 (1969).

61. *Beauharnais v. Illinois* 343 U.S. 250 (1952)

62. *New York Times v. Sullivan* 376 US 254 (1964).

63. Waldron, 47.

64. Beauharnais and Waldron, 47.

65. Waldron, 63.

66. Dworkin eventually diminishes the power of his claim that liberty is derived from equality when he argues that equality simply means equal access to promoting your worldview to other citizens. He never seriously accounts for differentials in social status and the need to remedy deep structural inequality. See Levin.

67. Levin.

68. *Hudnut,* 328.

69. Judge Easterbrook in *American Booksellers Association, Inc. v. Hudnut,* 771 F2d. 323 (1985), 329.

70. Ronald Dworkin, "Pornography and the New Puritans: Letters From Andrea Dworkin and Others." *The New York Times,* May 3, 1992. https://www.nytimes.com/1992/05/03/books/l-pornography-and-the-new-puritans-letters-from-andrea-dworkin-and-others-720092.html.

71. Not only is Lawrence's interpretation of *Brown* contested, but the reasoning in the Warren Court's opinion itself is also questioned. Judith Baer in *Our Lives Before the Law* on page 114 writes: "But the constitutional doctrine of *Brown* got the Court in trouble. The conclusion rests on a questionable interpretation of the facts." In a later effort to "ground racial decisions on neutral principles," the Warren Court found a law forbidding interracial marriage unconstitutional because the law was an example of "racial discrimination." The subtle shift from racism to racial discrimination established that "law forbids not oppression but classification." Discussion found on page 114. On page 121, she characterizes the Warren Court's *Brown* decision as one that "was committed to certain results," and freed itself from traditional ways of jurisprudential thinking, creating new law. I would not characterize the *Brown* decision in this

way. *Brown* is a hard case given the long-standing precedent upholding segregation, but as Stephen Macedo writes: "moral principles underlie and help justify the law, and by extending to cover the gaps between legal rules these principles help settle hard cases, cases not settled by reference to explicit legal rules." See Stephen Macedo, *Liberal Virtues*. New York: Oxford University Press, 1990, 84. Judith A. Baer, *Equality Under the Constitution: Reclaiming the Fourteenth Amendment*. Cornell University Press, 2018.

EIGHT

Reconsidering the Tension between Liberty and Equality

The final chapter addresses the appropriate relationship between liberty and equality, which is the philosophical question at the center of the pornography regulation debate. The previous chapter noted that egalitarian liberals like Raz, Dworkin, and Waldron emphasized a coextensive rather than zero-sum relationship between liberty and equality.[1] How should we appropriately understand and balance the liberty of speech against the right of equal protection of the law? May we recalibrate the balance without sliding into the tyranny of political correctness or regulating too much speech in the name of equality? In attempting to re-evaluate this historically perceived tension, the arguments of Isaiah Berlin, Benjamin Constant, and Ronald Dworkin will be addressed.[2] The chapter also investigates two precedential Canadian Supreme Court decisions on hate speech and pornography, comparing the ways in which that court balanced liberty and equality with our own US Supreme Court. In the end, these debates about the tension between liberty and equality fail to capture the complexity of the experiences of women and minorities, a point that Nancy Hirschman makes so eloquently. Liberty, as Hirschmann argues, cannot simply be understood as the absence of an obstacle.[3] Instead, the argument in the chapter opts for avoiding the dichotomous narrative on liberty as being at odds with equality, borrowing instead a notion of freedom as non-domination and autonomy from scholars such as Nancy Hirschmann and Philip Pettit.[4] It is these alternate understandings of freedom and its relationship to equality that are at play in the Canadian Supreme Court's decisions in *R. v. Keegstra* (1990), a hate speech case, and *R. v. Butler* (1992), a pornography case.[5] It is the understanding of freedom and equality we should embrace in US constitutional jurisprudence.

THE CLASSIC LIBERAL FORMULATION OF
LIBERTY VERSUS EQUALITY

Isaiah Berlin in his "Two Concepts of Liberty" lecture famously outlines the tension between negative and positive liberty. Negative liberty, according to Berlin, is the absence of interference with one's activities.[6] No entity, public or private, should introduce an obstacle preventing choice. Berlin carefully distinguishes between thwarting choice and incapacity. Liberty is unfairly sacrificed when fellow human beings prevent me from achieving my goal (choice). If no such interference exists, and yet, I do not have the skills or resources to achieve that goal, Berlin sees no violation of liberty (capacity). People are not free if they can't do something, they are only unfree if interfered with.[7] A lack of money to craft and air a political campaign ad, for example, is not a violation of negative liberty: it simply indicates a lack of resources or capabilities. A law prohibiting pornography, on the other hand, reflects an attack on negative liberty: the state obstructs my choice to obtain inegalitarian pornography. While no absolute sphere of liberty exists, a commitment to authentic liberty requires a generous sphere of private freedom for self-development and choice, even absent capacity. Liberty, Berlin continues, should not be traded simply for greater economic fairness or a quiet moral conscience, meaning that even if my liberty undercuts another's equality, we must choose liberty.[8] Others may lose when we exercise our negative liberties. Nonetheless, with an absence of interference, we pursue our conception of the good life in our own way.

In contrast, Berlin argues positive liberty derives from the notion of self-mastery. Berlin describes it this way:

> I wish my life and my decisions to depend on myself, not on external forces of whatever kind. I wish to be the instrument of my own, not of other men's acts of will. I wish to be a subject, not an object; to be moved by reasons, by conscious purposes, which are my own, not by causes which affect me, as it were, from outside.[9]

Positive liberty requires not just a lack of interference but a gaining of mastery over one's less rational, more libidinous self. The more irrational, sensual self desires may, on a higher plane of self-fulfillment, be at odds with the development of our best selves.[10] Berlin warns that the quest for positive liberty can too easily slide into tyranny by way of the state mandating a better path in order to achieve that best self. The state may rationalize the imposition of choice as helping one to achieve true liberty of the kind that an individual may be unable to see or lack the discipline to attain. Berlin writes:

> Once I take this view, I am in a position to ignore the actual wishes of men or societies, to bully, oppress, torture them in the name, on behalf, of their "real" selves, in the secure knowledge that whatever is the true

goal of man (happiness, performance of duty, wisdom, a just society, self-fulfillment) must be identical with his freedom—the free choice of his "true," albeit often submerged and inarticulate, self.[11]

For Berlin, the cost of positive liberty on freedom is far greater than the conflicts that emerge when modestly calibrating negative liberty for the greater good, as in the case of mandating that we all stop at a traffic light.

In fact, Berlin associates negative liberty with political liberalism and positive liberty with totalitarianism.[12] Berlin believes in a world of deep pluralism and where no comprehensive agreement on ultimate ends exist, thus finding that the freedom to choose is the penultimate value.[13] For Berlin, the real culprit behind the tyranny of positive liberty is the rationalism of eighteenth-century thinkers like Voltaire and Rousseau.[14] Nancy Hirschman writes that "Hegel in particular lent the 'fear factor' to the idea of positive liberty. . . . By declaring that the state, as an independent entity rather than a democratic collective, was the ultimate repository of the collective will and thereby of the individual's true will."[15] In the history of ideas, then, positive liberty's totalitarianism is rooted in the mistaken notion of rationalism.

Benjamin Constant, in "The Liberty of the Ancients and the Liberty of the Moderns," connects positive liberty to the Greeks, who prioritized not choice, but the ability to participate in the governing decisions of the community.[16] To be free, to attain positive liberty, is to govern. What follows from that political involvement is a sense of belonging and concord that comes from the ties that bond communities together. We see this sensibility or understanding of freedom elaborated in Aristotle's *The Politics* where liberty is grounded in participation in self-governance. Nonetheless, in the modern world, the opportunity to directly participate in the actual decision-making of the community is not possible with vast territories and large populations.[17] Yet the ability to participate in the governing decisions of one's community does not necessarily mean that a private realm of choice will be protected. It is moderns, according to Constant, that emphasize the individual's pursuit of their own version of the good life that defines the most refined form of liberty in carving that private sphere. In this sense, Constant rejects Rousseau's attempt to reconcile the individual with the body politic.[18] The liberty of the ancients problematically amounts, according to Constant, to the complete subjection of the individual to the collective, communal will.[19] The individual should not bury desires and choices that lead to self-fulfillment within the demands of the collective will, irrespective of whether one has participated in the shaping of that will or not. Democracy understood as majority rule may not be coterminous with liberty in Constant's modern sense, a point that Berlin makes as well. For Constant, like Scottish Enlightenment figures, modern liberty emerges from commercial relations and not purely citizenship. [20]

The tension between liberty and equality described above overlays the pornography debate in modern free speech jurisprudence. Within that debate over the balance between free speech and equality, law draws the boundaries around a libertarian understanding of the First Amendment. Yet the tension described by Berlin and embraced by First Amendment jurisprudence, in my view, sacrifices nuance and depth of understanding for simplicity. Berlin's description of negative and positive liberty is rooted in a deep skepticism about our metaphysical ability to find the collective agreement about core values in a deeply pluralistic society and an old fear about the overwhelming power of the state to squash the individuals' right to pursue their own version of self-fulfillment and truth. The slippery slope of fear is foregrounded in the discussion of positive liberty, while this sense that negative liberty should entail only reasonable and limited sacrifices dominates the debate. On the slippery slope side of the Berlinian argument, the quest for self-mastery ineluctably leads to state tyranny. Berlin engages in no sustained analysis of the cost of liberties on the rights of minorities and women even though those groups are least powerful in our society and most susceptible to pay the price associated with protecting a crude version of negative liberty. Instead, Berlin notes that reasonable limitations on negative liberty produce an overall increase in the kinds of freedom we find most valuable. In that scenario, we prioritize higher over lower values: the sacrifice of liberty to run a traffic light in order for increased safety.

These values, however, are not the tough issues to balance. The hard cases involve balancing one's liberty to burn a cross with one's right to equal dignity under the law. Does burning a cross undermine the equal citizenship of African Americans, or is such an action an exercise of a tough-minded negative liberty? Difficult cases involve the liberty to prohibit minorities and women from attending private elite schools versus the right of every citizen to pursue an education based on ability rather than being barred based upon their morally irrelevant immutable characteristics. It concerns the liberty to eat in a "privately-owned" restaurant that segregates whites from blacks versus equal access to public accommodations irrespective of any individual's skin color. These are the penumbral cases where trade-offs become much more serious than the simplistic sacrifice of the liberty to run a traffic light.

Berlin spends too little time weighing the cost to minorities when government opts to prioritize liberty over equality. Instead, Berlin consistently focuses on the cost to the dominant group in society who loses the liberty to discriminate. Yet, for minorities and women, when equality is better balanced with liberty, they gain greater liberty to pursue their own ideas about self-fulfillment. Comparably speaking, one group loses the ability to disadvantage others for arbitrary, irrational reasons while another gains a liberty taken for granted by historically dominant groups. In short, historically oppressed minority groups gain equal liberty.

Berlin forgets that liberal democracies are not value neutral with respect to the balance between liberty and equality either. The Fourteenth Amendment is a value commitment that requires the government to undermine racial hierarchy and invidious discrimination. The US Constitution ratified a commitment to equality after the Civil War when millions died for this substantive principle. Moreover, the meaning and weight we assign to the principle of equality emerged from the crucible of conflict and debate rather than some purely metaphysical commitment to self-mastery. While we still struggle to define what the commitment to equality requires, it is simplistic and polemical to characterize that guarantee as one rooted in the state's tyranny alone. Tyranny is not limited to the government exercising its power over individuals but also private individuals brutalizing and terrorizing fellow private citizens. While we may not have settled on an understanding of equal protection, the meaning of that equality commitment is nonetheless subject to ongoing debate in a political community that struggles to "get it right." We revise our understandings in light of new understandings and facts on the ground. The metaphysical should be rooted in the dialogical and the material conditions on the ground.

Moreover, Berlin's commitment to negative liberty is no less metaphysical than the positive liberty he defines. If self-mastery is metaphysical chicanery that justified tyranny, so is the belief that conflict is so deep and irresolvable that the only means toward resolution is for some to sacrifice equality for the fuller exercise of negative liberty. This conception seems to me wrong and it defies the very purpose of civil society, which attempts to harmonize interests and perspectives by means outside of the powerful hands of government. Healthy civil societies do a better job at harmonizing those interests and deeper values than unhealthy ones where polarization and alienation take over. Furthermore, in a liberal polity, government requires a minimal sacrifice from those with competing comprehensive moral doctrines. While one may believe a different worldview is morally wrong, what one may not do, at a minimum, is demand allegiance to their moral doctrine. On this matter, liberalism demands tolerance from all.[21] Therefore, we manage deep disagreement about the good life all the time and there are limits and demands placed upon the liberty of believers. While liberal democracy allows for the expression of plural values, it too requires a minimal commitment to equal dignity. Moreover, it is unclear why we must conclude that some individuals exercise of liberty should trump another's opportunity for equal liberty.

Another conceptual limitation in Berlin's argument is in the way that Berlin conceives the individual. Berlin assumes and leaves unanalyzed the assumption that the individual is free choosing and autonomous. "Freedom is being able to do what you want, where what you want is unproblematically understood as what the agent can identify as his desires."[22] Negative liberty is presented in a crude and uncomplicated fashion. Yet communitarians, feminists, and critical race theorists, to name a few, complicate the assumption that liberty can only be measured on the basis of such a simplistic conception of freedom from constraints. Individuals are not free from social construction, for example, which affects the parameters of choice and the social construction of desire.[23] The options available to us as "free choosing" subjects to consider include why we have one plate of options available to us but not others. "Who we are—the 'choosing subject'—exists within and is formed by particular contexts; the ideal of the naturalized and unified subject utilized by most freedom theory is thus deeply problematic and simplistically over-drawn."[24] The options, then, have little to do with nature, inevitability, or any other metaphysical explanation and more to do with our collective decisions to fund particular policy positions or prioritize some values over others. The options as well as the power available to women—women's very agency—has everything to do with the patriarchal, social context in which we live.[25] Similarly, desire is constructed at the level of our subjectivity. What are the social conditions that lead to the structuring of desire? If those conditions change, will desires change? One need only look to Title IX to see how government institutions can change underlying social conditions, changing desires. If women are given the opportunity to play soccer because of government investment in sports programs, they will often find that they like it and will pursue a future in the game. Freedom becomes far more complicated than a simple conversation about Berlinian choice.

Those social conditions are, of course, imbricated with power as well. To demonstrate these points, Nancy Hirschmann asks, why does a battered woman wish to stay with her batterer, and, are we obligated to respect her decision as a matter of her exercising her liberty? Should the state impose their conception of equality upon her despite her wishes, particularly if we believe that "living under oppressive conditions is antithetical to freedom"?[26] Hirschmann's response is to acknowledge that desires are motivated by many social forces and factors. If we can account for those factors, analyzing them, we would be better able to consider those concerns and move toward contexts that allow for authentic rather than compromised freedoms—those that are facially about negative liberty but fail to fulfill any real or profound criteria for effective or functional freedom.

Charles Taylor tells us, like Hirschmann, that obstacles to action are both internal and external. If we are in some sense self-deceived or cannot properly discriminate between the ends we seek—we can't identify our wants—then we are entrenching our unfreedom.[27] "You are not free if you are motivated, through fear, inauthentically internalized standards, or false consciousness, to thwart your self-realization."[28] Doing what one wants is no longer a sufficient condition of being free.

Moreover, we can discriminate between the kinds of obstacles that government should remove and those it should leave alone, finding that some restrictions would be far more significant than others. The crude version of negative liberty, the Hobbesian scheme, allows for no qualitative judgments about the discriminations to be made.[29] Yet freedom, says Taylor, is important to us because we are purposive beings who make these sorts of discriminations. Taylor asks us if freedom isn't at stake when we find ourselves carried away by some insignificant goal to override a highly significant one? The obstacle to freedom then is not simply external but internal. A position that the subject cannot be wrong or mistaken about their purposes, Taylor explains, seems mistaken and untenable. The question of our freedom or unfreedom is bound up with our frustration or the fulfillment of purposes.[30] As we all know, significant purposes can be frustrated by our own desires, which we experience as fetters. Negative liberty then cannot simply be measured on the presence or absence of external factors alone. The elimination of internal factors matters too, and the elimination of those kinds of factors requires a degree of self-realization.

A THIRD WAY

Philip Pettit suggests that the Berlinian taxonomy of liberty at odds with equality masks a third conceptual alternative.[31] If liberty is not non-interference simpliciter and equality is not understood as self-mastery, an alternative understanding of liberty as non-domination emerges. Under a theory of liberty as non-domination, no one lives at the mercy of another, where one's arbitrary will directs your life. Pettit explains that if you find yourself in the "shadow of another's presence" or in a position of vulnerability where you are demeaned or forced to fawn or flatter to ingratiate, you are unfree. Unfreedom, so to speak, does not consist in being restrained but instead being subject to capricious will. The experience of women and minorities speaks to the conditions of unfreedom where one is dependent upon a job, for example, where one is demeaned, harassed, or even evaluated with stereotypical preconceptions of one's abilities based upon their gender or race.

Petit criticizes the liberal conception of negative liberty, arguing that it remains indifferent to power and domination. As a result, liberals under the sway of such a conception of negative liberty are unable to recognize relationships in the workplace, home, and electorate as paradigms of domination and unfreedom. Moreover, liberals conflate interference with an automatic reduction in liberty. Under the Republican understanding of liberty as non-domination, it is possible to have domination without interference and interference without domination.[32] To use a paradigmatic example of a master-slave relationship, I may find that my master is laissez-faire, Petit elaborates, leaving me to make choices on my own. Yet, despite the master who leaves me alone, I am still dominated as a slave in the sense that I am subject to the capricious whim of another. If someone interferes with me to help further my own interests, this interference is not domination. Petit's description best describes the idea of power of attorney. Liberal liberty as non-interference in the Berlinian sense is structurally unsafe because it disregards power relationships and norms in which citizens and political authorities operate.[33] In such a system, those with the least power are the most vulnerable, experiencing very little substantive negative liberty or any real functional liberty.

In the Republican tradition, liberty is frequently described within the conceptual framework of slave/master relationships. The slave/master dynamic is an extreme one that helps throw into relief the conceptual parameters of domination. Petit writes: "[I]n the Republican tradition, . . . liberty is always cast in terms of opposition between liber and servus, citizen and slave."[34] Machiavelli is one of the first to see liberty-as-non-domination as central to freedom. To him, tyranny and colonization are violations of liberty-as-non-domination. In the Anglo-American tradition of republican thought, James Harrington gives voice to the idea that non-domination requires economic resources or wealth.[35] For Harrington, depending on another for money is to be under the arbitrary rule of another. In contrast, the Berlinian notion of liberty is private or individualistic outside of and against law.[36] Republican liberty, on the other hand, requires a structure of constitutional law where members of a political community may express their liberty within boundaries.[37] Liberty, then, is never simply "freedom from."

In the case of pornography, the argument regarding liberty as non-domination amounts to an acknowledgment that inegalitarian pornography contributes to conditions of domination. As a discourse, pornography generates discursive effects (ideological, material, and epistemic in nature) that subject women to both public and private forms of domination. We see the connection between porn and conditions of domination most clearly in hostile environment sexual harassment cases where porn creates those very conditions of domination prohibited by law under Title VII. Similarly, hate speech as part of a discourse of white supremacy subjects African Americans to comparable forms of both public and private forms of domination. Such republican understanding of liberty as non-domination not only undermines the simplistic dichotomy of negative versus positive liberty, but also frustrates the state action doctrine of the Fourteenth Amendment.

The state action doctrine holds that the equal protection clause of the Fourteenth Amendment pertains only to state-sponsored discrimination rather than private forms of discrimination. Scholars such as Robin West reject that limited conception of state action, suggesting instead that a proper understanding requires the state to use the full force of its power to protect citizens against public and private forms of domination.[38] Any public or private relationships that subject citizens to an arbitrary or capricious will, a condition of "dual sovereignty," undermines their sovereignty as a citizen and requires regulation.[39] Private forms of domination under totalizing systems like Jim Crow create a situation where some citizens live under two sovereigns—the state and, in the case of white supremacy, white citizens. Under an abolitionist interpretation of the Fourteenth Amendment, white supremacy functions as a kind of tyrannical regime akin to the "state" that must be dismantled. Conditions of patriarchy would similarly function in a comparable manner, requiring affirmative efforts by institutions to undo the tyranny.

The notion of non-domination does not exclude insights from feminist scholars such as Nancy Hirschmann either. The concept of domination is not limited purely to external physical barriers as Hirschman elaborates. Domination may play out in the shaping of one's subjectivity and desires, both internal barriers. The patriarchal context, the social structures, produce subjectivities rather than simply limit them. These conditions both enable and restrain women. The concept of social construction helps us to understand that even the dichotomy between negative and positive liberty is a socially and artificially constructed one. The construction of that dichotomy is motivated by power structures that favor men over women and it is rooted in the political/historical conditions of the Cold War. Yet, such an acknowledgment of the social construction of the negative versus positive liberty debate enables us to identify the ways that power operates in a particular social context and to devise political strategies to dismantle them.[40] Liberty as non-domination is compatible with these insights about both internal and external barriers as constructed and with the method of deconstruction. In comparison, the crude dichotomy between negative and positive liberty cannot account for the construction of internal barriers as interrelated to external barriers. Such a positive/negative dichotomy leaves us with a paltry understanding of the true nature of liberty and its relationship to equality and citizenship, a relationship crucial to understanding the feminist critique of pornography.

THE CANADIAN WAY: A BETTER BALANCE BETWEEN EQUALITY AND LIBERTY

In *R. v. Keegstra* (1990) and *R. v. Butler* (1992), we see the Canadian Supreme Court confront a hate speech and pornography regulation case.[41] In both instances, the Canadian Supreme Court balances liberty with equality differently than US courts. In those cases, the Canadian high court finds the hate speech and pornography regulations at issue compatible with the Canadian Charter of Rights. These two cases share remarkable similarities with *R.A.V. v. St. Paul* (1992) and *American Booksellers v.*

Hudnut (1985) respectively, despite their differing outcomes in the US context.

In *Keegstra*, the Canadian Supreme Court upheld a portion of the criminal code prohibiting incitement of hatred in public on the basis of color, race, religion, or ethnic origin. Mr. Keegstra, a high school teacher, violated the code by communicating anti-semitic statements to his students. In attributing evil intentions to Jews, Justice Dickson writes the following: "He [Mr. Keegstra] . . . described Jews to his pupils as 'treacherous,' 'subversive,' 'sadistic,' 'money-loving,' 'power hungry,' and 'child killers.'"[42] He contrasted Jews to Christians who he described as "open and honest," contending that the former had created the Holocaust to "gain sympathy." The criminal code allowed for "truth" as a defense if in good faith an individual believed the statement's veracity. The Canadian Charter of Rights and Freedoms holds that "the freedoms set out in it [are] subject only to such reasonable limits prescribed by law as can be demonstrably justified in a free and democratic society . . . "; that everyone has the fundamental "freedom of thought, belief, opinion, expression"; that every individual is equal before and under the law and has the right to equal protection and equal benefit of the law without discrimination"; and that the "Charter shall be interpreted in a manner consistent with the preservation and enhancement of the multicultural heritage of Canadians."[43]

From the moment of a first analysis, we see crucial differences between the Canadian Charter of Rights and Freedoms with our own US Constitution. The values that provide a context in which to interpret clauses are not explicitly articulated in the United States Constitution.[44] The Supreme Court in *Jacobson v. Massachusetts* (1907) found that the preamble, one possible contextual guidepost, was irrelevant to constitutional interpretation.[45] The preamble states:

> We the People of the United States, in Order to form a more perfect Union, establish Justice, insure domestic Tranquility, provide for the common defence, promote the general Welfare, and secure the Blessings of Liberty to ourselves and our Posterity, do ordain and establish this Constitution for the United States of America.[46]

The preamble arguably furnishes a context for interpreting the scope, purposes, and objectives of the Constitution. Every clause in the Constitution requires interpretation, even the most absolutist like the First Amendment, which states "Congress shall make no law . . . abridging the freedom of speech."[47] Yet, we regulate speech all the time, including commercial speech, fighting words, libel, obscenity, and sedition.

To explain why those regulations do not violate the First Amendment, we resort to background theories to help us understand the limits of the First Amendment. Those background theories may be informed, for example, by a republican philosophical understanding of the purposes of free speech, which would entail strongly protecting political speech while balancing less significant, low-value speech such as commercial speech. The purpose of speech, then, is to protect political dialogue, and that purpose sets the boundaries for legitimate and illegitimate regulation of speech. We can see echoes of this two-tiered approach to First Amendment jurisprudence in Justice Stevens's *R.A.V. v. St. Paul* (1992) concurrence.

According to the distinction between high- and low-value speech, dissident speech falls into a category of high-value speech in that it analyzes the powerful institutions of government. The animating purpose of speech for those committed to republican understandings of liberty is to promote meaningful political exchanges: any kind of hate speech that silences, degrades, assaults, or demeans individuals based upon their morally irrelevant immutable characteristics could be regulated without violating free speech rights. In contrast, if liberal values in the form of Berlin's definition of negative liberty animate the background context of the First Amendment, then no regulation of hate speech is tolerable because the individual's liberty to discriminate is curtailed. As we know, the First Amendment prohibits government from evaluating speech unless a causal harm can be identified.

In contrast to such Berlinian interpretive assumptions, the Canadian government articulates what law professor Kathleen Mahoney calls an "equality approach" to freedom of expression.[48] Unlike US law, interpretive background assumptions are articulated in their foundational document. Professor Mahoney describes the equality approach to freedom of expression in the following manner:

> The connections the Canadian Supreme Court makes between institutional arrangements, collective and individual harms, human relations, and equality are very important elements in its equality approach to freedom of expression. The centrality of equality to the enjoyment of individual as well as group rights emphasizes that the main constitutional consideration surrounding extremist speech is the harm it causes to equality interests. The Court is clear that if we are to live in a society without discrimination, the harm of hate speech must be redressed.[49]

The Canadian approach explicitly considers the need for a more inclusive, democratic, and egalitarian society when considering the constitutionality of hate speech or pornography. Professor Mahoney writes that with such a conscious balancing of liberty and equality, Canada avoids "the more limited view of freedoms . . . that in the past have emphasized the autonomy of individuals" while ignoring the power differences and unequal social context in which they operate.[50] It is exactly analytical components like power and context that US First Amendment jurisprudence ignores in the *R.A.V.* and *Hudnut* cases. It is also the analytical components that scholars like Petit and Hirschmann believe are crucial to better understanding and defining liberty.

While the US Supreme Court sometimes balances concerns about free speech and public safety, it has been reluctant to balance liberty versus equality in cases such as *R.A.V. v. St. Paul* (1995) or *Virginia v. Black* (2003).[51] As we know, in the case of *American Booksellers v. Hudnut* (1985), a lower federal court struck down the ordinance regulating pornography arguing that liberty interests outweighed equality interests. In the case of the Canadian Supreme Court, not only is the balance between liberty and equality weighted differently, but the background conditions that help us to understand the scope of free speech as well as a clear commitment to equal protection are made explicit. Specifically, the Canadian Charter of Rights and Freedoms states clearly that free speech has "reasonable limits" in a democratic society committed to the "preservation and enhancement of the multicultural heritage of Canadians." Free speech rights must be weighed against these specifically cited larger values: whereas, in the United States, we debate about the necessary starting assumptions or values operating in the background to help give meaning to the text of the Constitution. As discussed above, in the US context, we consider whether the background interpretive theories are committed to a libertarian understanding of freedom, a democratic commitment to pluralism, a conception of liberty as non-domination or some other philosophy? No such debate about background values is necessary in the Canadian Charter because those background commitments are stated clearly.[52]

In the Canadian Charter, the values that provide a frame in which to interpret the meaning, expanse, and limitations of fundamental rights like free speech are explicit in the document itself. The right to free speech, while fundamental, doesn't exist in isolation, and must be balanced against a commitment not only to equality, but also is also driven by a fidelity to multiculturalism.[53] In the US context, the commitment to multiculturalism and diversity as an interpretive lens is contentious while, again, it is plainly mandated in the Canadian context. The clear commitment to equality is buttressed by the commitment to multiculturalism and it leads to a significantly different decision-making calculus in the context of a hate speech case than in comparison to American courts.

The Canadian Charter is different from the United States in another way despite our mutual commitments to democracy and free speech as a path toward open democratic discourse and self-development. As law professor Kent Greenawalt notes, both nations are at separate points of development in the evolution of free speech doctrine.[54] In the United States, we spend little time incorporating the judicial rulings and reasonings of other nations, whereas Canada has drawn extensively from the traditions and principles of international law.[55] In particular, Canada revamped the entire charter in 1982, specifically including insights from international jurisprudence. Professor Yves Motigney writes that the

Charter revision of fundamental rights as embedded in the Canadian Constitution was revolutionary in transforming Canadian law and political debate.[56] On rare occasions, the US Supreme Court may mention the views of international legal sources but rarely utilizes them as an authoritative interpretive foundation.

Due to the nature of the structural mandates of the Canadian Charter, the court analyzes the *Keegstra* case in two distinct stages. Section 1 of the Canadian Charter notes that the fundamental rights like free speech have limitations that can be sufficiently justified in a "free and democratic society." Although the charter identifies free speech as fundamental, section 1 also makes clear that the fundamental right will be balanced against other principles in Canadian society. In explicitly noting that fundamental rights are not absolute, Professor Mahoney writes that section 1 is distinctive among other fundamental rights, protecting documents like the Bill of Rights in the United States Constitution. The Canadian Charter unequivocally commands interpreters to balance competing values and ideals, whereas the US Constitution makes no such unambiguous demands.[57]

Under the Canadian standard of review, stage one determines the scope of the fundamental right and whether government has indeed violated that right. Once established that government violated the right, the second step analyzes whether the limitation may be justified as balanced against the Canadian Charter's other equally weighty principles. The two stage analytical approach embodies the Canadian Charter's recognition that no right is absolute.[58]

In concordance with the two-stage approach, Justice Dickson finds that the defendant's actions qualify as speech in the first stage. The court's first categorical choice is crucial when comparing the kinds of analysis that take place regarding hate speech in the US context. In finding that Keegstra's message was indeed speech, a forthright and honest balancing of values may take place in that second stage.[59] In the US context, all sorts of theoretical distortions arguing that regulations target only the effects indirectly related to the content of speech, for example, are often deployed in an attempt to distance us from the constraining libertarian understanding of free speech articulated in First Amendment jurisprudence. Such a libertarian understanding of speech chains the Supreme Court to a theoretically unsustainable and unrealistic understanding of speech's relationship to oppression. Thus, the Canadian court rather straightforwardly finds that the target of the regulation, hate propaganda, constitutes speech rather than "secondary effects" or the conduct part of the expression. Justice Dickson then begins the second evaluative stage in considering whether the speech can be limited in a "free and democratic society."

In the second analytical stage, the Canadian court explicitly weighs section 2b of the Charter (free speech) with section 15, the equality portion. In the same way that section 1 in the charter is distinctive in comparison to other national foundational documents like the US Constitution and Bill of Rights, section 15 is also unique.[60] Professor Mahoney writes:

> The most important substantive provision relevant to the egalitarian approach to freedom of expression is section 15, the equality section. It, like section 1, is distinctive compared to other national and international instruments that exist to prohibit discrimination. It actually contains four equality guarantees, an open-ended list of prohibited grounds, and an affirmative action provision to allow for beneficial programs for disadvantaged groups or individuals.[61]

Section 15 makes clear the boundaries of free speech rights, highlighting legitimate limitations on speech that government may enact in the name of equality. Section 15 is further aided by section 27 and section 28, which concern multiculturalism and gender equality respectively.[62] To be clear, sections 27 and 28 mandate a balance between free speech rights and a commitment to multiculturalism and gender equality rather than just emphasizing only the rights of an individual to speak in ways that undermine those values to equality.

Chief Justice Dickson's stage one analysis is not without criticism. Professor Mahoney argues that Chief Justice Dickson wrongly ignored the link between hateful propaganda and systematic discrimination in holding that the government provision prohibiting hate speech violated section 2b (the free speech portion) of the Canadian Charter. The progressive criticism stands even though Chief Justice Dickson goes on to balance speech, equality, and multiculturalism in stage two of the analysis. To critics of Chief Justice Dickson's stage-one analysis, Keegstra's willful public promotion of group hatred makes the hate speech more analogous to segregation, a practice of inequality, rather than pure speech, and should be recognized as such in stage one.[63] Professor Mahoney further explains that hate speech as espoused by Keegstra is better conceptualized as an "act" or "injury." Professor Mahoney writes:

> To promote group hatred is to practice discrimination, and discrimination is an act that contradicts one of the core values underlying freedom of expression, individual self-fulfillment and human flourishing—the very value we are told defines the environment in which all the goals of freedom of expression should be pursued. Under this view, regulation of hate propaganda should not be invalidated by the doctrine of free speech any more than legal regulation of racial segregation is invalidated by the same doctrine.[64]

In the Canadian court's failure to understand the link between speech and discrimination, the opinion, at least in the initial analytical stage, makes a hard content/form distinction in the same manner as US courts. Critics argue that such a strict categorical approach, one analogous to the content-neutrality principle in US law, ignores the link between speech and violence present in our national historical experience and collective consciousness with hate propaganda.[65] Professor Mahoney's critique of the Canadian court's stage-one analysis is compatible with the argument about pornography and harm throughout this book. Nonetheless, despite the court's invocation of a "strict categorical approach" in the step-one analysis, an explicit contextual balancing takes place in stage two, which does not occur with rigor in the US system. Professor Mahoney is correct to note that the court's stage-one argument leaves intact the traditional liberty versus equality tension only to reweight the traditional balancing with its stage two analysis.

In stage two, the court applies the Oakes test, finding by a vote of 4–3 that the law regulating hate propaganda is justifiable under the commitment to a free and democratic society that values equality and multiculturalism. The Oakes test considers several questions: whether the state has a pressing and substantial concern, the regulation has proportionality between the state's objective and the measure, and finally, the restriction will have a minimal impact on the fundamental right.

Justice Dickson reminds us that hate propaganda produces real harm, humiliating and degrading members and undermining their self-worth. Unregulated hate propaganda creates an environment conducive to discrimination and violence. In finding real harm from hate propaganda, the Canadian court adopts a line of reasoning similar to *Beauharnais v. Illinois* (1952), a case where the US Supreme Court upheld a group libel statute.[66] At the same time, the Canadian court specifically rejected the "clear and present danger" test articulated in U.S. free speech jurisprudence. Professor Mahoney writes that by rejecting the clear and present danger test, the Canadian court makes clear that "dry and sterile analytical techniques that effectively predetermine the issue will not be imported into Canada."[67] In Canadian free speech jurisprudence, charter law precedent acknowledges that hate propaganda produces no discrete, clearly identifiable moment of danger and that such speech instead works across time through fear, ignorance, and indoctrination, socializing, and establishing the expected and permissible.[68] Throughout this second stage of analysis in *Keegstra* and *Butler*, the Canadian court has stayed away from the conceptual tangles produced by US courts in explaining how speech moves from the expression of ideas to harm. In this second stage of analysis, the Canadian court approaches a more republican understanding of liberty.

As noted above, in the Canadian Charter, free speech rights are read against not only the commitment to a free and democratic society but also against the special role of equality and multiculturalism in Canadian society. It is worth reiterating that the US Constitution and its precedent has no equivalent to these explicit value commitments as lenses through which a commitment to free speech is interpreted. Justice Dickson further conveys that the Charter has a dual role to both activate and permit reasonable limitations on rights. "A Free and Democratic Society" is seen as one that has a respect for the inherent dignity of persons, a commitment to social justice and equality, and respect for cultural and group identity, as well as a faith in the social and political institutions that enhance the participation of individuals and groups.

The Canadian respect for multiculturalism differs from the American commitment to diversity in substantial ways. Unlike the melting pot metaphor, which best describes the US commitment to diversity, the Canadian commitment to multiculturalism invokes the image of a mosaic where the goal is respect for varying cultural practices rather than assimilation.

Furthermore, one section of the charter, Justice Dickson contends, cannot be read in isolation from another. A concern for equality means that all individuals are deserving of concern, respect, and consideration. Equality invokes a remedial component that if such concern, respect, and consideration are absent, society has an obligation to rectify the situation. In the United States, we debate whether the First Amendment must be read through the lens of the Fourteenth Amendment. We question whether amendments that follow from the previous ones must provide a frame around which to understand the earlier amendments. Moreover, we question the meaning of equal protection, debating whether the Fourteenth Amendment demands colorblindness, the elimination of racial hierarchy, or equal dignity to all regardless of morally irrelevant immutable characteristics.

Justice Dickson weighs many of the arguments considered in the context of US hate speech cases yet applies different values and methods to analyzing the controversy, coming to an opposite conclusion: hate speech may be reasonably regulated without violating the fundamental right of free speech. The core goals of free speech, the reason why democracies protect free speech, are to promote individual self-fulfillment through expression, allowing ideas to compete as a method to pursue truth and participate in the political process. Dickson concedes that hate speech regulations will muzzle some, suppressing their self-fulfillment, and hobbling their ability to participate in the democratic process. At the same time, he notes that hate speech undercuts the self-fulfillment and autonomy of those who find their identity through membership to a minority group targeted by hate.

Justice Dickson explains that all members of society are entitled to self-development. However, hate speech is wholly inimical to the democratic aspirations that free expression requires. A minimal concession from citizens in a democratic system committed to multiculturalism, fairness, and equality requires a willingness to see all as deserving of equality, dignity, and respect while not tolerating speech acts that undermine those core principled commitments. Canada's Charter of Rights is not neutral on such a matter, just as Locke's *Letter on Toleration* explains that liberalism is not neutral toward religion. A minimal concession that liberalism demands of religion is that they must teach the value of toleration. A disqualifying view in a multicultural democracy is one that undermines the very core principle of democracy as an openness to all, a position that makes free speech possible in the first instance. In regards to truth, Dickson acknowledges that the truth is difficult to ascertain. Yet, he contends that we have a greater degree of certainty that hate speech is mendacious, erroneous, and less valuable in terms of finding the truth. We know, he says, that hate speech will not lead to a better society, given our commitment to first principles like equality and democracy, and I might add, given our history. Without the distortions of the content-neutrality principle, Canada avoids the moral obtuseness involved in ignoring a history of white supremacy and it rejects a simplistic notion of liberty advanced in US constitutional civil rights and liberties cases.

The content of Chief Justice Dickson's decision reflects many of the same arguments in Justice Stevens's *R.A.V.* dissent. In particular, Justice Stevens, like Chief Justice Dickson, recognizes the historical context of hate speech and the unique role that it plays in maintaining inequality and discrimination. Justice Stevens also describes a First Amendment jurisprudence that has recognized a two-tiered approach to high and low value speech, where the latter is regulated with less anxiety, especially if the speech undermines other highly valued ideals like equality.

In *R v. Butler* (1992), the Canadian Supreme Court considered the constitutionality of a statute criminalizing obscenity. The statute read:

> For purposes of this Act, any publication a dominant characteristic of which is the undue exploitation of sex, or sex and any one or more of the following subjects, namely, crime, horror, cruelty, and violence shall be deemed obscene.[69]

Pornography falls into three categories, according to the decision: sex with violence, sex that is degrading and dehumanizing without violence, and explicit sex. The statute regulates only materials where the dominant theme is sex and the exploitation undue. In *Butler*, a shop owner selling hardcore pornography is charged with over 250 counts of selling obscenity.[70] The basis of the statute is a concern about societal harm and harm to women rather than offensiveness. In this sense, Canada seems to have retooled obscenity law to embrace both a traditional approach to speech regulation based on offensiveness with concerns about women's equality. *Butler* holds that a community standards test should be based upon the community as a whole rather than a small segment. Justice Sophinka suggested that material promoting anti-social behavior counted toward a violation of community standards, connecting anti-social behavior to violence and degradation.[71] Furthermore, the appearance of consent isn't determinative in making the porn at issue non-obscene, but rather can make it even more degrading.[72] Degradation and dehumanization are the principal indicators of undueness. Exceptions are made for those depictions where the portrayal of explicit sex is essential to a wider artistic, literary, or educational purpose.

Just as in *Keegstra*, *Butler* finds pornography protected free expression, yet goes on to balance the right of free speech with equality provisions (section 15 in the Charter).[73] The court in *Butler* applies the *Oakes* test, concluding that the statute had a rational connection to the state's objectives, minimally impaired freedom of speech, and balanced the effects of regulating pornography with an undue emphasis on exploitation and the legitimate object of achieving equality. Justice Sopinka, writing for the majority, notes that not all pornography is regulated, only the kind that links sex to violence and/or sex to degradation and dehumanization. Therefore, all pornography is not impugned or regulated. Materials with scientific, artistic, educational, and literary significance aren't covered by the statute. The focus is on a limited category of material that includes undue exploitation. The court identifies a clear rational relationship existing between degrading and dehumanizing pornography and societal harms, especially harms to women. While the court finds no causal link, they identified a "reasoned apprehension of harm."[74] Finally, the regulation of the most violent and degrading forms of pornography lie far enough from the core of free speech values to pose no threat to the place of free speech in Canadian society. Pornography, Justice Sopinka notes, appeals to our most base aspects of individual fulfillment and is primarily economically motivated.

Butler sees a clear connection to *Keegstra*: the precedent in *Keegstra* lends force to *Butler*. Hate speech and pornography are homologous in attacking freedom, democracy, and equality in Canadian society. Both forms of speech undermine competing values of the sort that make a free and open society where free speech is protected possible.[75] *Butler* takes a different approach to regulating pornography than *Hudnut*. *Butler* revises and reboots its obscenity doctrine to embrace concerns about gender equality, whereas *Hudnut* embarks down the path of a civil damage ordinance.

We can utilize the reasoning in these two cases to demonstrate that the regulation of hate speech and pornography does not take us down a slippery slope to tyranny. Canada protects all kinds of speech, including the highest form of free speech: political speech. In no way does Canada face the parade of horrors suggested by civil libertarians who tell us we must protect the speech we hate in order to protect the speech we love. The Canadian parliament and its high court have drawn a reasonable line distinguishing between the kinds of speech that undermine political community based upon irrational hatred, degradation, and dehumanization. They have done so without engaging in the theoretical gymnastics required to convince American libertarian free speech jurisprudence of the harm of pornography and, closely related, the harm of hate speech.

Part of the reasonableness of the Canadian decision in both *Keegstra* and *Butler* is that definitions of hate speech or pornography may rely upon content, which is balanced against other democratic values in its stage two analysis. Thus, in the case of pornography, the definition is not overly broad and seeks to make distinctions between the exploitive and demeaning versus the simply explicit. In the American context, such a definition that makes reasonable distinctions on the basis of content is disqualified. Yet we know that context, content, power, and history matter in assessing harm and that law considers those elements in the Canadian context without running afoul of a commitment to free speech. Nor does Canadian law become stymied by causality, a gender-coded and race-coded evidentiary standard. The Canadian court is also not driven by rigid levels of scrutiny in reviewing regulatory statutes.

Moreover, the Canadian Charter protecting free speech does not exclude the importance of truth. In the case of hate speech, truth is a defense. In the US system, the truth of speech is irrelevant to the First Amendment analysis. Government, in the United States, is neutral, making no assessment of the rightness of claims. Yet, surely, in the aftermath of historical experiences like the Holocaust, we might consider whether a commitment to free speech entails allowing Neo-Nazis to march in a town where Holocaust survivors have relocated. The US Constitution contains a commitment to equality in the Fourteenth Amendment. If we are to take that commitment seriously, it means that we might need to consider the ways in which free speech is connected to equality rather than opposed to it. We might consider the way that speech "does things." On discriminatory matters involving morally irrelevant characteristics like race, gender, and sexual orientation, the Supreme Court should not ignore context, power, and history in assessing harm. Neutrality in the face of cultural oppression reinforces subordination, unfairness, and injustice.[76] The Canadian Supreme Court better understands that the commitment to free speech doesn't require us to forgo equality. So do Hirschman and Petit as they describe a more co-extensive rather than zero-sum relationship between liberty and equality. The benefits that flow from free speech should not just accrue to privileged groups while minority groups pay for that free speech with their dignity.

CONCLUSION

Real liberty entails non-domination: the freedom from relationships in both the public and private realms that are characterized by conditions of subordination and subjection to an arbitrary or capricious will. Liberty as non-domination bypasses Berlin's reductive, historically cramped understanding of negative versus positive liberty, a distinction still alive and well in American First Amendment jurisprudence. Power that is arbitrary, leaving one servile to another, implicates equality. At the core of liberty as non-domination is a commitment to the equal dignity of all individuals. It is not based on a crude notion of formalistic choice, where we fulfill the definition when presented with either a plate of unwanted, undesired options or choices with no real capacity to execute them.

Liberty as non-domination entails both equality and freedom. For to be truly free, we must be equal in terms of our autonomy, social status, and power. Non-domination helps us to consider how our choices and desires are socially constructed; creating both internal and external barriers that must be analyzed and dismantled to move toward liberatory politics or, in different language, to achieve the primary good of self-respect. Berlin's understanding of liberty tells us nothing about internal barriers, only external barriers; it tells us nothing about how we can desire our own oppression, consenting to our own deprivation of liberty. Berlin cannot help us consider how choices are socially constructed, limiting our options even as we are presented with some cramped choices rather than a full panoply of options. Nor does Berlin's conceptualization of liberty versus equality fulfill liberal Rawlsian requirements for achieving the primary good of self-respect.

Liberty properly understood as non-domination undermines the choice between the free speech of liberty or the equality that comes with pornography or hate speech regulation. Speech that creates conditions of domination, subordination, and degradation is an abuse, not liberty. The decisions in *Keegstra* and *Butler* bring us closer to understanding liberty not as license or as freedom from external barriers. Anyone who experiences conditions of domination, conditions that subject us to the arbitrary will of another, experiences a loss of freedom. A discursive practice that perpetuates such unfreedom is not protected. The hate speech in *Keegstra* and the inegalitarian pornography in *Butler* are not properly conceived of as a liberty but rather as abuses. While the Canadian court's approach to regulating hate speech and inegalitarian pornography is imperfect, as Professor Maloney suggests, it's better than the US legal approach in the civil damage ordinance case. The Canadian court does not quite displace the traditional tension between liberty and equality, but it does place greater weight on the significance of equality in a multicultural democracy; it does leave philosophical openings for a much more substantive understanding of liberty advocated by republican philosophy. The measure of liberty is not being free to create conditions of inequality. Nor is liberty one sided, but instead requires considering and evaluating speech in the context of a commitment to democracy, multiculturalism, and gender equality. With these values in mind and without the theoretical and categorical contortions in American First Amendment jurisprudence, the Canadian courts have managed to protect free speech alongside the freedom of citizens targeted by ineqalitarian pornography and hate speech. The result is that the less valued and socially problematic discursive practices of pornography and hate speech are reasonably limited, while equal liberty more fully thrives.

NOTES

1. Ronald Dworkin, *Taking Rights Seriously*. Harvard University Press, 1978. Joseph Raz, "On The Nature of Right." *Mind* 93 (1984): 194–214. Jeremy Waldron, *The Harm in Hate Speech*. Harvard University Press, 2014.

2. Benjamin Constant and Biancamaria Fontana, *The Political Writings of Benjamin Constant*. Cambridge University Press, 1988. Isaiah Berlin, *Two Concepts of Liberty: An Inaugural Lecture Delivered before the University of Oxford on 31 October 1958*. Clarendon Press, 1958.

3. Nancy J. Hirschmann, *The Subject of Liberty: Toward a Feminist Theory of Freedom*. Princeton University Press, 2003. Also, Isaiah Berlin, "Two Concepts of Liberty." in *Law and Morality: Readings in Legal Philosophy*, Dyzenhaus, et al., editors, 3rd ed., University of Toronto Press, 2003, pp. 342–359, 345.

4. Phillip Pettit, *Republicanism: A Theory of Freedom and Government*. Oxford Univ. Press, 2010. Nancy J. Hirschmann, *The Subject of Liberty: Toward a Feminist Theory of Freedom*. Princeton University Press, 2003.

5. *R. v. Keegstra* (SCR 1990). *R. v. Butler* (SCR 1992).

6. Isaiah Berlin, "Two Concepts of Liberty." In *Law and Morality: Readings in Legal Philosophy*, Dyzenhaus, et al., editors, 3rd ed. University of Toronto Press, 2003, pp. 342–359, 345.

7. Paul Spicker, "Liberty." In *Liberty, Equality, Fraternity*, 5-42. Bristol: Bristol University Press, 2006. www.jstor.org/stable/j.ctt9qgkg5.6. 5.

8. Isaiah Berlin, "Two Concepts of Liberty." In *Law and Morality: Readings in Legal Philosophy*, Dyzenhaus, et al., editors, 3rd ed. University of Toronto Press, 2003, pp. 342–359, 345.

9. Berlin in Dyzenhaus, 349.

10. Charles Taylor, "What is Wrong with Negative Liberty," pp. 359-69.

11. Berlin in Dyzenhaus, 351.

12. Paul Franco, "Oakeshott, Berlin, and Liberalism" 31, no. 4 (2003): pp. 484-507, http://www.jstor.org.online.library.marist.edu/stable/3595669, 488.

13. Paul Franco, "Oakeshott, Berlin, and Liberalism," 31, no. 4 (2003): pp. 484-507, http://www.jstor.org.online.library.marist.edu/stable/3595669, 494.

14. Zeev Sternhell and David Maisel, "The Anti-Enlightenment of the Cold War." In *The Anti-Enlightenment Tradition*, 372-421. New Haven; London: Yale University Press, 2010, 6. www.jstor.org/stable/j.ctt5vm23x.12, 372-73. Also, Joshua L. Cherniss et al., *From the Twentieth Century to the Romantic Age*. Princeton University Press, 2014, p. xliii-xcii, https://doi.org/10.2307/j.ctv6zddd2.

15. Nancy J. Hirschmann, "John Stuart Mill: Utility, Democracy, Equality." In *Gender, Class, and Freedom in Modern Political Theory*, 213-73. Princeton; Oxford: Princeton University Press, 2008. www.jstor.org/stable/j.ctt7s271.9, 213.

16. Constant and Fontana. *The Political Writings of Benjamin Constant*. Cambridge University Press, 1988. See also Philip Pettit, *Republicanism: a Theory of Freedom and Government*. Oxford University Press, 2010.

17. Phillippe Raynaud, "Constant." In *New French Thought: Political Philosophy*, edited by Lilla Mark and Ann T. Gardiner, 82-90. Princeton University Press, 1994. www.jstor.org/stable/j.ctt7zvq8k.9, 87. In summarizing Constant, Raynaud characterizes modern politics as lacking the concrete richness of participation in the ancient republics.

18. Raynaud, "Constant." In *New French Thought: Political Philosophy*, edited by Lilla Mark and Ann T. Gardiner, 82-90. Princeton University Press, 1994. www.jstor.org/stable/j.ctt7zvq8k.9.

19. Jeremy Jennings, "Liberty." In *The French Republic: History, Values, Debates*, edited by Berenson Edward, Duclert Vincent, and Prochasson Christophe, 95-102. Cornell University Press, 2011. www.jstor.org/stable/10.7591/j.ctt7zbwr.13, 95.

20. Jennings, "Liberty." In *The French Republic: History, Values, Debates*, edited by Berenson Edward, Duclert Vincent, and Prochasson Christophe, 95-102. Cornell University Press, 2011. www.jstor.org/stable/10.7591/j.ctt7zbwr.13.

21. Locke's Letter Concerning Toleration. See Horacio Spector, "Four Conceptions of Freedom." *Political Theory* 38, no. 6 (2010): 780-808. www.jstor.org/stable/25749186 who argues that one can find two strands of thought in liberalism concerning civil liberty. One strand derives from Hobbes, while the other derives from Locke. While Hobbes's understanding of liberty better fits with Berlin's conception of negative liberty, Lockean liberty is closer to the republican philosophical understanding of liberty.

22. Taylor, in Dyzenhous. Charles Taylor, *Philosophy and the Human Sciences*. Cambridge: University Press, 1985, 362.

23. Hirschmann, *The Subject of Liberty: Toward a Feminist Theory of Freedom*. Princeton University Press, 2003, 93.

24. Hirschmann, 13.

25. Hirschmann, 13.

26. Hirschmann, *The Subject of Liberty: Toward a Feminist Theory of Freedom*. Princeton University Press, 2003, 96.

27. Taylor, in Dyzenhous, 362. See also Charles Taylor, *Philosophy and the Human Sciences*. Cambridge: University Press, 1985.

28. Taylor, in Dyzenhous, 362. And Taylor, *Philosophy and the Human Sciences*. Cambridge: University Press, 1985.

29. Taylor, in Dyzenhous, 362. And Taylor, *Philosophy and the Human Sciences*. Cambridge: University Press, 1985, 363.

30. Taylor, in Dyzenhous, 364.

31. Pettit, *Republicanism: A Theory of Freedom and Government*. Oxford Univ. Press, 2010.

32. Pettit, *Republicanism: A Theory of Freedom and Government*. Oxford Univ. Press, 2010, 22.

33. Nadia Urbinati, "Competing for Liberty: The Republican Critique of Democracy." *The American Political Science Review* 106, no. 3 (2012): 607-21. www.jstor.org/stable/23275436, 611.

34. Pettit, *Republicanism: A Theory of Freedom and Government*. Oxford Univ. Press, 2010, 31.

35. James Harrington, *The Commonwealth of Oceana and A System of Politics*. Edited by J. G. A. Pocock. Cambridge: University Press, 1992, 611 (paraphrasing Quentin Skinner).

36. Urbinati, "Competing for Liberty: The Republican Critique of Democracy." *The American Political Science Review* 106, no. 3 (2012): 607-21. www.jstor.org/stable/23275436.

37. Urbanati, "Competing for Liberty: The Republican Critique of Democracy." *The American Political Science Review* 106, no. 3 (2012): 607-21. www.jstor.org/stable/23275436 .

38. Robin West, *Progressive Constitutionalism: Reconstructing the Fourteenth Amendment*. Durham & London: Duke University Press, 1994.

39. Robin West, "Toward an Abolitionist Interpretation of the Fourteenth Amendment," *West Virginia Law Review* 94 (1991): 111. And also Jacobus TenBroeck, *The Antislavery Origins of the Fourteenth Amendment*. University of California Press, 1951.

40. Susanne Baer, "Lecture: Dignity Liberty, Equality: A Fundamental Rights Triangle of Constitutionalism." *The University of Toronto Law Journal* 59, no. 4 (2009): 417-68. www.jstor.org/stable/40542327. Baer proposes that rights of equality, liberty, and dignity should be framed as a triangle, inherently linked and balanced with one another rather than conceptualized in limited and isolated ways.

41. *R. v. Keegstra* (1990), 3 SCR 697 and *R. v. Butler* (1992), 1 SCR 452.

42. Justice Dickson in *Keegstra*.

43. Canadian Constitution, http://laws-lois.justice.gc.ca/eng/Const/page-15.html.

44. Kathleen Mahoney, "The Canadian Constitutional Approach to Freedom of Expression in Hate Propaganda and Pornography." *Law and Contemporary Problems* 55, no. 1 (1992): 77–106. https://doi.org/https://scholarship.law.duke.edu/lcp/vol55/iss1/.

45. *Jacobson v. Massachusetts* 197 U.S. 11 (1905), 11.

46. www.constitutionus.com.

47. www.constitutionus.com.

48. Mahoney, "The Canadian Constitutional Approach to Freedom of Expression in Hate Propaganda and Pornography." *Law and Contemporary Problems* 55, no. 1 (1992): 77–106. https://doi.org/https://scholarship.law.duke.edu/lcp/vol55/iss1/, 76.

49. Mahoney, "The Canadian Constitutional Approach to Freedom of Expression in Hate Propaganda and Pornography." *Law and Contemporary Problems* 55, no. 1 (1992): 77–106. https://doi.org/https://scholarship.law.duke.edu/lcp/vol55/iss1/, 87.

50. Mahoney, "The Canadian Constitutional Approach to Freedom of Expression in Hate Propaganda and Pornography." *Law and Contemporary Problems* 55, no. 1 (1992): 77–106. https://doi.org/https://scholarship.law.duke.edu/lcp/vol55/iss1/, 76.

51. *Virginia v. Black*, 538 U.S. 343 (2003), 343. In *Black*, The Supreme Court struck down a Virginia statute banning cross burning as a threat of intimidation. The Court argued that Virginia conflated the distinction between intimidation and symbolic speech.

52. Mahoney. See also Kent Greenawalt, "Free Speech in the United States and Canada." *Law and Contemporary Problems* 55, no. 1 (1992): 5–34. https://doi.org/https://scholarship.law.duke.edu/lcp/vol55/iss1/, 6.

53. Mahoney, "The Canadian Constitutional Approach to Freedom of Expression in Hate Propaganda and Pornography." *Law and Contemporary Problems* 55, no. 1 (1992): 77–106. https://doi.org/https://scholarship.law.duke.edu/lcp/vol55/iss1/, 76.

54. Kent Greenawalt, "Free Speech in the United States and Canada." *Law and Contemporary Problems* 55, no. 1 (1992): 5–34. https://doi.org/https://scholarship.law.duke.edu/lcp/vol55/iss1/, 6.

55. Greenawalt, "Free Speech in the United States and Canada." *Law and Contemporary Problems* 55, no. 1 (1992): 5–34. https://doi.org/https://scholarship.law.duke.edu/lcp/vol55/iss1/, 6-7.

56. Yves de Montigney, "The Difficult Relationship between Freedom of Expression and Its Reasonable Limits ." *Law and Contemporary Problems* 55, no. 1 (1992): 35–52.

57. Section 1 of the Charter is the central, preeminent provision. It states that the Charter "guarantees the rights and freedoms set out in it subject only to such reasonable limits prescribed by law as can be demonstratively justified in a free and democratic society." This is an unusual section if one compares it with other national or international rights-protecting instruments. The American Bill of Rights, for example, has no similar section. At first glance, section 1 may appear to be "inconsistent or contradictory..." Mahoney, "The Canadian Constitutional Approach to Freedom of Expression in Hate Propaganda and Pornography." *Law and Contemporary Problems* 55, no. 1 (1992): 77–106. https://doi.org/https://scholarship.law.duke.edu/lcp/vol55/iss1/, 76.

58. Mahoney, "The Canadian Constitutional Approach to Freedom of Expression in Hate Propaganda and Pornography." *Law and Contemporary Problems* 55, no. 1 (1992): 77–106. https://doi.org/https://scholarship.law.duke.edu/lcp/vol55/iss1/, 76.

59. Something Waldron advocates in the US context. Jeremy Waldron, *The Harm in Hate Speech*. Harvard University Press, 2014.

60. Greenawalt, "Free Speech in the United States and Canada." *Law and Contemporary Problems* 55, no. 1 (1992): 5–34. https://doi.org/https://scholarship.law.duke.edu/lcp/vol55/iss1/, 6-7.

61. Mahoney, "The Canadian Constitutional Approach to Freedom of Expression in Hate Propaganda and Pornography." *Law and Contemporary Problems* 55, no. 1 (1992): 77–106. https://doi.org/https://scholarship.law.duke.edu/lcp/vol55/iss1/, 77.

62. Mahoney, "The Canadian Constitutional Approach to Freedom of Expression in Hate Propaganda and Pornography." *Law and Contemporary Problems* 55, no. 1 (1992): 77–106. https://doi.org/https://scholarship.law.duke.edu/lcp/vol55/iss1/, 81.

63. Mahoney, "The Canadian Constitutional Approach to Freedom of Expression in Hate Propaganda and Pornography." *Law and Contemporary Problems* 55, no. 1 (1992): 77–106. https://doi.org/https://scholarship.law.duke.edu/lcp/vol55/iss1/, 81.

64. Mahoney, "The Canadian Constitutional Approach to Freedom of Expression in Hate Propaganda and Pornography." *Law and Contemporary Problems* 55, no. 1 (1992): 77–106. https://doi.org/https://scholarship.law.duke.edu/lcp/vol55/iss1/, 76 citing Kathleen A. Lahey, "The Canadian Charter of Rights and Pornography: Toward a Theory of Actual Gender Equality." *New England Law Review* 649 (1985).

65. Greenawalt, "Free Speech in the United States and Canada." *Law and Contemporary Problems* 55, no. 1 (1992): 5–34. https://doi.org/https://scholarship.law.duke.edu/lcp/vol55/iss1/, 6-7. Greenawalt explains that balancing approaches openly weigh values whereas conceptual approaches deploy categorical analysis.

66. *Beauharnais v. Illinois*, 343 U.S. 250 (1952).

67. Mahoney, "The Canadian Constitutional Approach to Freedom of Expression in Hate Propaganda and Pornography." *Law and Contemporary Problems* 55, no. 1 (1992): 77–106. https://doi.org/https://scholarship.law.duke.edu/lcp/vol55/iss1/, 77 citing Harlan F. Stone, "The Common Law in the United States," 50 *Harv L Rev* 4, 10 (1936) and *Keegstra* 3 SCR at 740-44.

68. Mahoney, "The Canadian Constitutional Approach to Freedom of Expression in Hate Propaganda and Pornography." *Law and Contemporary Problems* 55, no. 1 (1992): 77–106. https://doi.org/https://scholarship.law.duke.edu/lcp/vol55/iss1/, 77-78.

69. *R. v. Butler* (1992) 1 SCR 452.

70. Michelle Louise Atkin, "Examining the Limits of Free Expression through Canadian Case Law: Reflections on the Canadian Library Association's Code of Ethics and Its Supporting Statement on Intellectual Freedom." *Journal of Education for Library and Information Science* 53, no. 4 (2012): 239-53. www.jstor.org/stable/43686918, 245.

71. Michael Plaxton, "What Butler Did." Osgoode Digital Commons. *The Supreme Court Law Review: Osgoode's Annual Constitutional Cases Conference* , 2012. https://digitalcommons.osgoode.yorku.ca/sclr/vol57/iss1/14/, 324.

72. A point that Rae Langton makes.

73. Justin Juson and Brenda Lillington. "*R. v. Butler*: Recognizing the Expressive Value and the Harm in Pornography." *Golden Gate University Law Review* 23, no. 2 (1993). https://doi.org/https://digitalcommons.law.ggu.edu/ggulrev/vol23/iss2/7.

74. Juson and Lillington. "*R. v. Butler*: Recognizing the Expressive Value and the Harm in Pornography." *Golden Gate University Law Review* 23, no. 2 (1993). https://doi.org/https://digitalcommons.law.ggu.edu/ggulrev/vol23/iss2/7. Plaxton, "What Butler Did." Osgoode Digital Commons. *The Supreme Court Law Review: Osgoode's Annual Constitutional Cases Conference* , 2012.

75. Max Waltman, "Rethinking Democracy: Legal Challenges to Pornography and Sex Inequality in Canada and the United States." *Political Research Quarterly* 63, no. 1 (2010): 218-37. www.jstor.org/stable/27759897. Waltman notes that despite the decision in *Butler*, the actual conditions on the ground, the ability to remove the inegalitarian variety of pornography, has been less than effective.

76. A. Levin, *Cost of Free Speech: Pornography, Hate Speech, and Their Challenge to Liberalism*. Palgrave Macmillan, 2014.

Conclusion

This book has sought to examine the way we actually regulate pornography, comparing the reasons law accepts and rejects for regulating the practice. It argues that the rejected approach in *American Booksellers v. Hudnut* (1985) is the right one in that it specifically considers the effects of pornography on women's equality.[1] While recognizing that pornography as a genre is not necessarily unified or monolithic, it considers that the most problematic forms of pornography are the sort that fuse patriarchy, violence, degradation, and sex.

In analyzing how and why the Court argues for zoning pornography, the book examines the language and categorical choices of law. The book scrutizes how law defines pornography and determines which doctrinal approach to apply within free speech law, examining its underlying value commitments. Among the categories in law closely examined and criticized is the content-neutrality principle, especially for its gatekeeping function in disqualifying history, context and power in evaluating the harm from inegalitarian pornography and hate speech. The book offers an alternative theory to understand the harm from pornography and hate speech through the concept of discursive effects instead of causality or speech act theory. Speech—discourse—produces ideological, material, and epistemic effects of the kind that maintain inequality.

Moreover, the argument in the book holds that an understanding of discursive effects is compatible with US constitutional law and precedent if we utilize Professor Charles Lawrence's radical reinterpretation of *Brown v. Board of Education* (1954) as a case about speech.[2] Finally, the book ends by arguing that liberal law must also reconsider the traditional understanding of liberty being in tension with equality in a way that embraces the insights from republican philosophy and feminist theory. Liberty is not in tension with equality but rather the two are coextensive, a point that Justice Kennedy recognizes, however partially or briefly, in *Obergefell v. Hodges* (2015).[3] It is also a point that egalitarian liberals acknowledge.

In short the book is an attempt to consider how and why the gender-based approach to regulating pornography failed in *Hudnut* and what doctrinal changes in US constitutional law would need to occur in order to come to a different, more just and reasonable, outcome. By making an initial comparison to the zoning cases and *Hudnut*, the juxtaposition throws into relief what law will say and not say about pornography. It highlights the doctrinal obstacles that prevent serious consideration of the gendered nature of inegalitarian pornography and its effects. It attempts to shed light on the taken-for-granted theoretical assumptions in law regarding free speech and pornography. All the while, the arguments in the book aim to be guided by epistemic criteria in explaining why current free speech jurisprudence fails to register the real tangible harm to women from pornography. Measurements and studies alone will not resolve the debate about pornography regulation, but rather the hidden values and assumptions that underlie such endeavors must be discussed and debated in the open.

Epistemology cannot provide us with transcendent objectivity and the truth necessary to permanently and forever resolve contentious disputes like the one about pornography regulation and harm, but it can require us to consistently consider the bias in our prejudgments, to openly defend or revise them, and to connect the epistemic process with liberatory politics. If epistemic processes consistently lead to social and political injustices, then we may have to consider the role they play in not finding the truth but reifying structures of inequality and power.[4] These are the sorts of concerns applied to the epistemic gatekeeping function of doctrines within free speech law regarding pornography. In maintaining that inegalitarian pornography generates discursive effects, the book contends that law cannot simply adopt a libertarian approach to free speech. Those effects are connected to a vast system of gender inequality in the United States. While inegalitarian pornography may not be determinative of gender inequality, it does contribute, reinforce, reflect, and help maintain such unfairness. As a result, we can place reasonable gender-based regulations on inegalitarian pornography while upholding our most treasured commitments to dissident speech, just as other liberal democracies with strong free speech traditions have done.

NOTES

1. *American Booksellers v. Hudnut*, 771 F.2d. 323 (7th Cir. 1985).

2. *Brown v. Board of Education*, 347 U.S. 483 (1954). Charles R. Lawrence, "If He Hollers Let Him Go: Regulating Racist Speech on Campus," in *Words That Wound: Critical Race Theory, Assaultive Speech, and the First Amendment*, ed. Mari J. Matsuda (Westview Press, 1993).

3. *Obergefell v. Hodges*, 576 U.S. _____ (2015).

4. Satya P. Mohanty, *Literary Theory and the Claims of History: Postmodernism, Objectivity, Multicultural Politics.* Oxford University Press, 1998. Linda M. Alcoff, "How Is Epistemology Political?" In *Radical Philosophy*. Philadelphia, PA: Temple University, 1993. Linda Alcoff, *Real Knowing: New Versions of the Coherence Theory.* Ithaca, NY: Cornell University Press, 2008.

Bibliography

Abrams v. United States, 250 U.S. 616 (1919).

Ackerman, Bruce. *We The People: The Civil Rights Revolution*. Cambridge, MA: Belknap Harvard, 2018.

Ackerman, Elise. "Sex Sells. Latte Sells. But in the Same Store?" *U.S. News & World Report*, May 10, 1999.

Adams, Don. "Can Pornography Cause Rape?" *Journal of Social Philosophy* 31, no. 1 (2000): 1–43. https://doi.org/10.1111/0047-2786.00029.

Adler, Amy. "Problem's of Censorship in a New Technological Age: All Porn All the Time." *New York University Review of Law & Social Change* 31 (2007): 695.

———. "What's Left?: Hate Speech, Pornography, and the Problem for Artistic Expression." *California Law Review* 84 (1996): 1499.

Affidavit of Richard "Bo" Dietl at 2-3, *Stringfellow's v. City of New York*, No. 113049/96 (N.Y. App. Div. Sept. 12, 1996)., Affidavit of Richard "Bo" Dietl at 2-3, § (n.d.).

Alcoff, Linda M. "How Is Epistemology Political?" In *Radical Philosophy*. Philadelphia, PA: Temple University, 1993.

———. "Justifying Feminist Social Science." *Hypatia* 2, no. 3 (1987): 107–20. https://doi.org/10.1111/j.1527-2001.1987.tb01344.x.

———. *Real Knowing: New Versions of the Coherence Theory*. Ithaca, NY: Cornell University Press, 2008.

Allen, Leah Claire. "The Pleasures of Dangerous Criticism: Interpreting Andrea Dworkin as a Literary Critic." *Signs: Journal of Women in Culture and Society* 42, no. 1 (2016): 49–70. https://doi.org/10.1086/686977.

Allen, M., D. D'alessio, and K. Brezgel. "A Meta-Analysis Summarizing the Effects of Pornography, II." *Human Communication Research* 22 (1995): 258–83.

Allen, Mike, Tara Emmers, Lisa Gebhardt, and Mary A. Giery. "Exposure to Pornography and Acceptance of Rape Myths." *Journal of Communication* 45, no. 1 (1995): 5–26. https://doi.org/10.1111/j.1460-2466.1995.tb00711.x.

Althusser, Louis, Balibar Etienne, and David Fernbach. *Reading Capital: The Complete Edition*. London: Verso, 2016.

Althusser, Louis. *For Marx*. Verso, 2010.

Amar, Akhil Reed. "The Supreme Court, 1991 Term Comment—The Case of the Missing Amendments: *R.A.V. v. St. Paul*." *Harvard Law Review* 106 (1992): 124–61.

———. "The Supreme Court, 1999 Term–Foreword: The Document and the Doctrine." Yale Law School Legal Scholarship Repository. Harvard Law Review, 2000. https://digitalcommons.law.yale.edu/fss_papers/851.

American Booksellers v. Hudnut, 771 F. 2d. 323 (7th Cir. 1985).

American Psycho. Lions Gate Films, 2000.

Amsterdam, Anthony G., and Jerome Seymour Bruner. *Minding the Law*. Cambridge: Harvard University Press, 2000.

Andrew, Christopher J. "The Secondary Effects Doctrine: The Historical Development, Current Application, and Potential Mischaracterization of an Elusive Judicial Precedent." *Rutgers Law Review* 54 (2002): 1175.

Angier, Natalie. *Woman: an Intimate Geography*. Boston: Mariner Books/Houghton Mifflin Harcourt, 2014.

Aristotle. *The Politics*. Translated by Carnes Lord. Chicago: University of Chicago Press, 2013.

Ashcroft v. Free Speech Coalition, 535 U.S. 234 (2002).

Atkin, Michelle Louise. "Examining the Limits of Free Expression through Canadian Case Law: Reflections on the Canadian Library Association's Code of Ethics and Its Supporting Statement on Intellectual Freedom" 53, no. 4 (2012): 239–53. http://www.jstor.org.online.library.marist.edu/stable/43686918.

Baer, Judith A. *Equality Under the Constitution: Reclaiming the Fourteenth Amendment.* Ithaca, NY: Cornell University Press, 2018.

———. *Our Lives Before the Law: Constructing a Feminist Jurisprudence.* Princeton: Princeton University Press, 2001.

Baer, Susanne. "Lecture: Dignity Liberty, Equality: A Fundamental Rights Triangle of Constitutionalism" 59, no. 4 (2009): 417–68. http://www.jstor.org.online.library.marist.edu/stable/40542327.

Bagli, Charles V., and Randy Kennedy. "Disney Wished Upon Times Sq. And Rescued a Stalled Dream." *The New York Times.* April 5, 1998. https://www.nytimes.com/1998/04/05/nyregion/disney-wished-upon-times-sq-and-rescued-a-stalled-dream.html.

Baker, Peter. "Maintaining Male Power: Why Heterosexual Men Use Pornography." Essay. In *Pornography: Women, Violence and Civil Liberties, A Radical New View*, edited by Catherine Itzin. Oxford: Oxford University Press, 1993.

Balibar, Etienne. "The Infinite Contradiction." *Yale French Studies* 88 (1995): 142–64. https://doi.org/https://www.jstor.org/stable/i347914.

Barnes v. Glen Theatre, 501. U.S. 560 (1991).

Barr, Rachel Anne. "Watching Pornography Rewires the Brain to a More Juvenile State." The Conversation, December 4, 2019. http://theconversation.com/watching-pornography-rewires-the-brain-to-a-more-juvenile-state-127306?fbclid=IwAR32K5MLDhxnxV36ITbitcqt98nntmtyUDHtc4EYkKd2AIFUSdhY2ZMniwM.

Bartky, Sandra Lee. *Femininity and Domination: Studies in the Phenomenology of Oppression.* New York: Taylor & Francis, 2015.

Bauer, Nancy. *How to Do Things with Pornography.* Cambridge: Harvard University Press, 2015.

Baynes, Kenneth, James Bohman, and Thomas McCarthy. "Questions of Method: An Interview with Michel Foucault." In *After Philosophy: End or Transformation?*, 100. Cambridge, MA: MIT Press, 1987.

Beauharnais v. Illinois, 343 U.S. 250 (1952).

Benhabib, Seyla, Nancy Fraser, Judith Butler, Drucilla Cornell, and Nancy Fraser. "Pragmatism, Feminism, and the Linguistic Turn." In *Feminist Contentions: A Philosophical Exchange*, 157–71. New York: Routledge, 1995.

Benhabib, Seyla. *Situating the Self Gender, Community, and Postmodernism in Contemporary Ethics.* Boston: Polity Press, 2007.

———. *The Claims of Culture: Equality and Diversity in the Global Era.* Princeton: Princeton University Press, 2006.

———. *The Rights of Others: Aliens, Residents and Citizens.* Cambridge: Cambridge University Press, 2011.

———. *Critique, Norm and Utopia: A Study of the Foundations of Critical Theory.* New York: Columbia University Press, 1986.

Benjamin, Matthew. "Problems of Censorship in a New Technological Age: Possessing Pollution." *New York University Review of Law & Social Change* 31 (2007): 733.

Berger, James E. "Essay: Zoning Adult Establishments in New York: A Defense of the Adult-Use Zoning Text Amendments of 1995." *Fordham Urban Law Journal* 105 (1996): 24–135.

Berlin, Isaiah, Avishai Margalit, and Henry Hardy. "Liberty," 134–38. In *The Power of Ideas*, 2nd ed. Princeton: Princeton University Press, 1995. http://www.jstor.org.online.library.marist.edu/stable/j.ctt46n3xt.14.

Berlin, Isaiah, Joshua L. Cherniss, William A. Galston, and Henry Hardy. "Summaries of the Flexner Lectures," 333–48. In *Their Rise and Influence on Modern Thought—*

Updated Edition. Princeton: Princeton University Press, 2014. https://doi.org/10.2307/j.ctv6zddd2.13.

Berlin, Isaiah. "Two Concepts of Liberty." In *Law and Morality: Readings in Legal Philosophy*, edited by David Dyzenhaus, Sophia Reibetanz Moreau, and Arthur Ripstein, 3rd ed., 342–59. Toronto: University of Toronto Press, 2003.

Berlin, Isaiah. *Two Concepts of Liberty: An Inaugural Lecture Delivered before the University of Oxford on 31 October 1958*. Oxford: Clarendon Press, 1958.

Bernardin, Mark. "The Law and Politics of Dancing: Barnes v. Glen Theatre and the Regulation of Striptease Dance." *Hawaii Law Review* 14 (1992): 925–48.

Beth, Loren P. "Mr. Justice Black and the First Amendment: Comments on the Dilemma of Constitutional Interpretation." *The Journal of Politics* 41, no. 4 (1979): 1105–24. https://doi.org/10.2307/2129735.

Binnion, Gayle. "Feminist Jurisprudence and the First Amendment: Hearing Another Voice." *Southern California Review of Law and Women's Studies* 7 (1998): 269–98.

Bird, Sharon R. "Welcome To The Men's Club." *Gender & Society* 10, no. 2 (1996): 120–32. https://doi.org/10.1177/089124396010002002.

Blasi, Vincent. "Six Conservatives in Search of the First Amendment: The Revealing Case of Nude Dancing." *William and Mary Law Review* 33 (1992): 611–63.

Bollinger, Lee C., and Geoffrey R.. Stone. *The Free Speech Century*. New York: Oxford University Press, 2019.

Boos v. Barry, 485 U.S. 312 (1988)

Bordo, Susan. *The Male Body a New Look at Men in Public and in Private*. New York: Farrar, Straus and Giroux, 2015.

———. *Unbearable Weight Feminism, Western Culture, and the Body*. Berkeley: University of California Press, 2013.

Boye, Brett. "Obscenity and Community Standards." *Yale Journal of International Law* 33 (2008): 299.

Boyle, Karen. "The Pornography Debates: Beyond Cause and Effect." *Women's Studies International Forum* 23, no. 2 (2000): 187–95.

Brandenburg v. Ohio, 395 U.S. 444 (1969).

Brennan, William, James E. Fleming, Sortirios A. Barber, and Stephen Macedo. "The Constitution of the United States: Contemporary Ratification." In *American Constitutional Interpretation*, edited by Walter F Murphy, 4th ed. The Foundation Press, 2016.

Brown v. Board of Education, 347 U.S. 483 (1954).

Brown, Rebecca L. "The Harm Principle and Free Speech." by Rebecca L. Brown :: SSRN, March 25, 2015. http://papers.ssrn.com/sol3/papers.cfm?abstract_id=2584080#.

Buchwald, Emilie, Pamela R. Fletcher, Martha Roth, and Gloria Steinem. "Erotica vs. Pornography, in Transforming A Rape Culture." Essay. In *Transforming a Rape Culture*. Milkweed Editions, 1995.

Burchell, Graham, Collin Gordon, and Peter Miller, eds. *The Foucault Effect: Studies in Governmentality*. Chicago: University of Chicago, 1991.

Butler, Judith. *Excitable Speech: a Politics of the Performative*. New York: Routledge, 1997.

———. *The Psychic Life of Power: Theories in Subjection*. Stanford: Stanford University Press, 2006.

———. "Conscience Doth Make Subjects of Us All." *Yale French Studies*, no. 88 (1995): 6. https://doi.org/10.2307/2930099.

Butler, Melissa A., and Carole Pateman. "Early Liberal Roots of Feminism: John Locke and the Attack on Patriarchy." In *Feminist Interpretations and Political Theory*, edited by Mary Shanley, 74–94. University Park: The Pennsylvania State University Press, 1991.

Calvert, Clay. "Free Speech and Content-Neutrality: Inconsistent Applications of An Increasingly Malleable Doctrine." *McGeorge Law Review* 29 (1997).

Cameron, Deborah, Elizabeth Fraser, and Catherine Itzin. "On the Question of Pornography and Sexual Violence: Moving Beyond Cause and Effect." In *Pornography,*

Women, Sexual Violence and Civil Liberties: A Radical View, 359–83. Oxford: Oxford University Press, 1992.

Caputo, John D. *Radical Hermeneutics: Repetition, Deconstruction, and the Hermeneutic Project*. Bloomington: Indiana University, 1999.

Chaplinsky v. New Hampshire, 315 U.S. 568 (1942).

Chermerinsky, Erwin. "Content Neutrality as a Central Problem of Freedom of Speech: Problems in the Supreme Court's Application." *Southern California Law Review*, 49, 74 (2000): 61.

Cherniss, Joshua L., Isaiah Berlin, William A. Galston, and Henry Hardy. "From the Twentieth Century to the Romantic Age," xliii-xcii. *Their Rise and Influence on Modern Thought—Updated Edition*. Princeton: Princeton University Press, 2014. https://doi.org/10.2307/j.ctv6zddd2.6.

Church, Jennifer. "Ownership and the Body." Essay. In *Feminists Rethink the Self*, edited by Diana Tietjens Meyers, 85–103. Boulder, CO: Westview Press, 1997.

City of Erie v. Pap's A.M., 529 U.S. 277 (2000).

City of Renton v. Playtime Theatres, Inc., 475 U.S. 41 (1986).

The Civil Rights Cases, 109 U.S. 3 (1883).

Clark v. Community for Creative Non-Violence, 468 U.S. 288 (1982).

Code, Lorraine. *Rhetorical Spaces: Essays on Gendered Locations*. New York: Routledge, 1995.

Cohen v. California, 403 U.S. 15 (1971).

Colburn, David R. "Governor Alfred E. Smith and the Red Scare, 1919-20." *Political Science Quarterly* 88, no. 3 (1973): 423. https://doi.org/10.2307/2148992.

Cole, Kristen L. "Pornography, Censorship, and Public Sex: Exploring Feminist and Queer Perspectives of (Public) Pornography through the Case of Pornotopia." *Porn Studies* 1, no. 3 (2014): 227–41. https://doi.org/10.1080/23268743.2014.927708.

Collins, Patricia Hill. *Fighting Words: Black Women and the Search for Justice*. Minneapolis: University of Minnesota Press, 2007.

Committee on Technology, Gender, and Teacher Education. *Tech-Savvy: Educating Girls in the New Computer Age*. Washington, D.C.: American Association of University Women Educational Foundation, 2000.

Conkle, Daniel O. "Harm, Morality, and Feminist Religion—Canada's New—But Not so New—Approach to Obscenity." *Indiana Law Faculty Papers*, 722, 1993. https://doi.org/https://www.repository.law.indiana.edu/cgi/viewcontent.cgi?article=1725&context=facpub.

Constant, Benjamin, and Biancamaria Fontana. *The Political Writings of Benjamin Constant*. Cambridge: Cambridge University Press, 1988.

Cooke, Maeve. *Language and Reason: A Study of Habermas's Pragmatics (Studies in Contemporary German Social Thought)*. Cambridge: MIT Press, 1994.

Cooper, Alvin, Coralie R. Scherer, Sylvain C. Boies, and Barry L. Gordon. "Sexuality on the Internet: From Sexual Exploration to Pathological Expression." *Professional Psychology: Research and Practice* 30, no. 2 (1999): 154–64. https://doi.org/10.1037//0735-7028.30.2.154.

Cornell, Drucilla. *At the Heart of Freedom: Feminism, Sex, and Equality*. Princeton: Princeton University Press, 1998.

_____. *Feminism and Pornography*. Oxford: Oxford University Press, 2007.

_____. "Sexual Difference, the Feminine, and Equivalency: A Critique of MacKinnon's Toward a Feminist Theory of the State." *Yale Law Journal* 100 (1991): 2247-75.

_____. *The Imaginary Domain: Abortion, Pornography & Sexual Harassment*. New York: Routledge, 1995.

Costa, Gregg. "John Marshall, the Sedition Act, and Free Speech in the Early Republic." *Texas Law Review* 77 (1999): 1011-47.

Crenshaw, Kimberle, Neil Gotanda, Gary Peller, and Kendall Thomas, eds. *Critical Race Theory: The Key Writings That Formed the Movement*. New York: The New Press, 1995.

Crump, David. "Camouflaged Incitement: Freedom of Speech, Communicative Torts, and the Borderland of the Brandenburg Test." *Georgia Law Review* 29 (fall 1994): 1-80.

Curiel, Jonathan. "Gloves Are Off on Broadway: Angry S.F. Neighbors Say Owner of Adult Club Skirts Permit Process." *San Francisco Chronicle*, 28 March 2000, A1.

Curtis, Michael Kent. "Lincoln, Vallandigham, and Anti-War Speech in the Civil War." *William & Mary Bill of Rights Journal* 7 (December 1998): 105-91.

D'Amico, Robert. *Historicism and Knowledge*. London: Taylor & Francis, 2018.

Dancy, Jonathan. *An Introduction to Contemporary Epistemology*. Oxford: Blackwell, 2008.

Danielsen, Dan. "Identity Strategies: Representing Pregnancy and Homosexuality." In *After Identity: A Reader in Law and Culture*, eds. Dan Danielsen and Karen Engle, 38-60. New York & London: Routledge, 1995.

Darcy, R., Susan Welch, and Janet Clark. *Women, Elections, and Representations*. 2d ed. Lincoln & London: University of Nebraska Press, 1994.

Daum, Courtenay W. "The Relationship between Pornography and Racial Stereotypes: A Content Analysis of Hustler Magazine." Paper delivered at the Western Political Science Association, San Jose, Calif., 2000.

Davidson, Arnold I. ed. *Foucault and His Interlocutors*. Chicago: University of Chicago Press, 1997.

Davidson, Arnold I. "Structures and Strategies of Discourse: Remarks towards a History of Foucault's Philosophy of Language." In *Foucault and His Interlocutors*, ed. Arnold I. Davidson, 1-17. Chicago & London: The University of Chicago Press, 1997b.

Davis, R. Bauserman and C. "Exposure to Sexually Explicit Materials: An Attitude Change Perspective." *Annual Review of Sex Research* 4 (1993): 121-209.

Debs v. United States, 249 U.S. 211 (1919).

Delgado, Richard and Stefancic, Jean. "Essay On Hateful Speech, Loving Communities: Why Our Notion of 'A Just Balance' Changes So Slowly." *California Law Review* 82, no. 4 (1994): 851.

———. *Must We Defend Nazis?: Hate Speech, Pornography, and the New First Amendment*. New York: New York University Press, 1997.

Delgado, Richard, and David Yun. "'The Speech We Hate': First Amendment Totalism, the ACLU, and the Principle of Dialogic Politics." *Arizona State Law Journal* 27 (winter 1995): 1281-1300.

Delgado, Richard, and Jean Stefancic. "Pornography and Harm to Women: 'No Empirical Evidence?'" *Ohio State Law Journal*, 1992, 1037.

deMontigney, Yves. "The Difficult Relationship Between Freedom of Expression and Its Reasonable Limits." *Law and Contemporary Problems* 55, no. 1 (1992): 35–52. https://doi.org/https://scholarship.law.duke.edu/lcp/vol55/iss1/.

Dennis v. United States, 341 U.S. 494 (1951).

Dennis, Donna I. "The Law of Obscenity and Its Consequences in Nineteenth Century America." *Columbia Journal of Gender & the Law* 16 (2007): 43.

Dettmer, Jamie. "Gore Chastises Porn Industry on One Hand but Counts Campaign Cash with Other." *Insight on the News*, 23 October 2000, 6.

Dienstag, Joshua. "Between History and Nature: Social Contract Theory in Locke and the Founders." *The Journal of Politics* 58, no. 4 (1996): 985-1009.

Dietl, Richard "Bo," Founder and Principal of Beau Dietl & Associates. Affidavit. New York: New York Supreme Court, Appellate Division, 1996. Photocopied, index number 103568/96, 103569/96.

Dines, Gail, and Robert Jensen. "Feminist Debates on Pornography." *International Encyclopedia of Communication* 8 (n.d.): 3807–11.

Dines, Gail, Jean McMahon Humez, Bill Yousman, and Lori Bindig. *Gender, Race, and Class in Media: a Critical Reader*. Washington, D.C.: Sage, 2018.

Dines, Gail, Robert Jensen, and Ann Russo. *Pornography: The Production and Consumption of Inequality*. London: Routledge, 1998.

Dines, Gail. *Pornland: How Porn Has Hijacked Our Sexuality*. Beacon Press, 2014.
———. "The White Man's Burden: Gonzo Pornography and the Construction of Black Masculinity." *Yale Journal of Law and Feminism*, 2006.
Dionne, Elizabeth Harmer. "Why Obscenity Should Survive Lawrence." *George Mason Law Review* 15 (2008): 611.
Division, Environmental Management. Zoning Controls for Adults-Only Theaters. Seattle: Department of Community Development, 1976. Photocopied.
Doppelt, Gerrald. "The Place of Self Respect in a Theory of Justice." *Inquiry* 52, no. 2 (2009): 127–54. https://doi.org/https://doi.org/10.1080/00201740902790219.
Downey, Michael P. "The Jeffersonian Myth in Supreme Court Sedition Jurisprudence." *Washington University Law Quarterly* 76 (1998): 683-720.
Downs, Donald A. *Nazis in Skokie: Freedom, Community, and the First Amendment*. Notre Dame: University of Notre Dame Press, 1985.
Drabek, Matt L. "Pornographic Subordination, Power, and Feminist Alternatives." *Feminist Philosophy Quarterly* 2, no. 1 (2016).
Dreyfus, Hubert L., and Paul Rabinow. *Michel Foucault: Beyond Structuralism and Hermeneutics*. 2nd ed. Chicago: The University of Chicago Press, 1983.
Dryzek, John S. "Critical Theory as a Research Program." In *The Cambridge Companion to Habermas*, ed. Stephen K. White, 354. Cambridge: Cambridge University Press, 1995.
Duggan, Lisa, Nan D Hunter, and Carol S Vance. "False Promises: Feminist Anti-Pornography Legislation." *New York Law School Law Review* 38, no. 133 (1993).
Duggan, Lisa. *Sex Wars: Sexual Dissent and Political Culture*. Hoboken: Routledge, 2006.
Dunn, Jancee. "The Rock-Porn Connection: Featuring Limp Bizkit, Blink-182, Kid Rock, Korn and—Of Course—Barenaked Ladies." *Rolling Stone*, August 19, 1999, 44 [online]; available from Lexis-Nexis Academic Universe, News; accessed 2 March 2001.
Dworkin, Andrea, and Catharine MacKinnon. *Pornography and Civil Rights: A New Day for Women's Equality*. Minneapolis: Organizing Against Women's Inequality, 1988.
Dworkin, Andrea. *Intercourse*. New York: New York Free Press, 1987.
Dworkin, Ronald. *Life's Dominion: An Argument about Abortion, Euthanasia, and Individual Freedom*. New York: Vintage Books, 1994.
———. "Pornography and the New Puritans: Letters From Andrea Dworkin and Others." *The New York Times*, May 3, 1992. https://www.nytimes.com/1992/05/03/books/l-pornography-and-the-new-puritans-letters-from-andrea-dworkin-and-others-720092.html.
———. *Taking Rights Seriously*. Harvard University Press, 1978.
———. "Women and Pornography." *The New York Review of Books*, October 21, 1993. https://www.nybooks.com/articles/1993/10/21/women-and-pornography/.
Dyzenhaus, David, Sophia Reibetanz Moreau, and Arthur Ripstein. *Law and Morality: Readings in Legal Philosophy*. Toronto: University of Toronto Press, 2014.
Dyzenhaus, David. "Obscenity and the Charter: Autonomy and Equality." CR 1 (1991): 367.
———. "The Rule of Law as the Rule of Liberal Principle." *Ronald Dworkin*, n.d., 56–81. https://doi.org/10.1017/cbo9781139167109.003.
Eaton, A. W. "A Sensible Antiporn Feminism." *Ethics* 117, no. 4 (2007): 674–715. https://doi.org/10.1086/519226.
Economist, The. "Branded Flesh: Steven Hirsch is Recreating Hollywood's Old Studio System in the Pornography Business." August 14, 1999, [online].
Economist, The. n.d. https://www.economist.com/international/2015/09/26/naked-capitalism.
Egan, Timothy. "Erotica Inc.—A Special Report; Technology Sent Wall Street Into Market for Pornography." *The New York Times*, October 23, 2000, A1 [online]; available from Lexis-Nexis Academic Universe, News.
Ely, James R., Jr. *The Guardian of Every Other Right: A Constitutional History of Property Rights*. New York: Oxford University Press, 1991.

Eyal, Nir. "'Perhaps the Most Important Primary Good': Self-Respect and Rawls' Principles of Justice." *Politics, Philosophy, and Economics*. Sage, June 2005. http://journals.sagepub.com/doi/abs/10.1177/1470594X05052538.

Fahringer, Herald Price. "Zoning Out Free Expression: An Analysis of New York City's Adult Zoning Resolution." *Buffalo Law Review* 46 (spring 1998): 403-31

FCC v. Pacifica Foundation, 438 U.S. 726 (1976).

Feree, Myra Marx, and Beth B. Hess. *Controversy and Coalition: The New Feminist Movement Across Three Decades of Change*. New York: Twanye Publishers, An Imprint of Simon & Schuster MacMillan, 1995.

Ferguson, Ann. "Sex War: The Debate between Radical and Libertarian Feminists." *Signs* 10, no. 1 (1984): 106-12.

Foster, James C. "Justice Civility: William J. Brennan Jr.'s Free Speech Jurisprudence." *Judging Free Speech*, 2015, 123–46. https://doi.org/10.1007/978-1-137-41262-1_6.

Foucault, Michel, and Paul Rabinow. *The Foucault Reader: An Introduction to Foucault's Thought*. New York: Penguin, 1991.

Foucault, Michel. *Power/Knowledge: Selected Interviews & Other Writings 1972-1977*. Edited by Colin Gordon. New York: Pantheon Books, 1980.

———. *The Archaeology of Knowledge and the Discourse on Language*. Translated by A.M. Sheridan Smith. New York: Pantheon Books, 1972.

———. *The History of Sexuality*. New York: Penguin, 1990.

Franco, Paul. "Oakeshott, Berlin, and Liberalism," *Political Theory* 31, no. 4 (2003): 484–507. http://www.jstor.org.online.library.marist.edu/stable/3595669.

Fraser, Nancy. "False Antitheses: A Response to Seyla Benhabib and Judith Butler, in Feminist Contentions: A Philosophical Exchange." In *Feminist Contentions: A Philosophical Exchange*, edited by Nancy Fraser, 59–74. London: Routledge, 1995.

———. *Unruly Practices: Power, Discourse, and Gender in Contemporary Social Theory*. London: Polity Press, 2004.

Fredericks, Albert. "Adult Use Zoning: New York City's Journey on the Well-Traveled Road from Suppression to Regulation of Sexually Oriented Expression." *Buffalo Law Review* 46 (Spring 1998): 433-66.

Freedman, Estelle B. "The New Woman: Changing Views of Women in the 1920s." *Journal of American History* 61, no. 2 (1974): 372-393.

Frohwerk v. United States, 249 U.S. 204 (1919).

Fuller, Steve. *Social Epistemology*. Bloomington: Indiana University Press, 2002.

Geduldig v. Aiello, 417 U.S. 484 (1974).

Gibson, Pamela Church. *More Dirty Looks: Gender, Pornography and Power*. London: British Film Institute, 2004.

Gilmore, Jane. "Latest Porn Statistics Are Surprising." *The Sydney Morning Herald*. April 24, 2018. https://www.smh.com.au/lifestyle/life-and-relationships/latest-porn-statistics-are-surprising-20180424-p4zbd8.html.

Gitlow v. New York, 268 U.S. 652 (1925).

Glaser, Elizabeth M. "When Obscenity Discriminates." *Northwestern University Law Review* 102 (2008): 1379.

Gordon, Colin, Graham Burchell, Peter Miller, and Michel Foucault. *The Foucault Effect: Studies in Governmentality*. London: Wheatsheaf, 1991.

Gottlieb, Roger S. *Radical Philosophy: Tradition, Counter-Tradition, Politics*. Philadelphia: Temple University Press, 1993.

Grant, Joan Mason. *Pornography Embodied: From Speech to Sexual Practice*. Lanham, MD: Rowman & Littlefield, 2004.

Green, Leslie. "Pornographies." *Journal of Political Philosophy* 8 (2000): 44.

———. "Pornographizing, Subordinating, Silencing." Essay. In *Censorship and Silencing*, edited by Robert C Post, 285–311. Los Angeles, CA: Getty Research Institute, 1998.

Greenawalt, Kent. *Fighting Words: Individuals, Communities, and Liberties of Speech*. Princeton: Princeton University Press, 1995.

———. "Free Speech in the United States and Canada." *Law and Contemporary Problems* 55, no. 1 (1992): 5–34. https://doi.org/https://scholarship.law.duke.edu/lcp/vol55/iss1/.

Greer v. Spock, 424 U.S. 828 (1976).

Grosz, Elizabeth A. *Space, Time and Perversion*. New York & London: Routledge, 1995.

Gubar, Susan. "Representing Pornography: Feminism, Criticism, and Depictions of Female Violation." *Critical Inquiry* 13, no. 4 (1987): 712–41. https://doi.org/10.1086/448418.

Guest, Stephen. *Ronald Dworkin. Jurists: Profiles in Legal Theory*, ed. William Twining and Neil MacCormick. Stanford: Stanford University Press, 1991.

Hall, Kermit, James W. Ely Jr., Joel B. Grossman, and William M. Wiecek, eds. *Oxford Companion to the Supreme Court of the United States*. New York & Oxford: Oxford University Press, 1992.

Hall, Stuart, David Morley, and Kuan-Hsing Chen. *Stuart Hall: Critical Dialogues in Cultural Studies*. London: Routledge, 2007.

Hall, Stuart, ed. *Representation—Cultural Representations and Signifying Practices*. Washington, D.C.: Sage Publications, 1997.

Hall, Stuart. "Introduction." In *Representation: Cultural Representations and Signifying Practices*, ed. Stuart Hall, 1-11. London: Sage Publications, 1997a.

———. "The Emergence of Cultural Studies and the Crisis of the Humanities." *The Humanities as Social Technology* 53 (October 1990): 11. https://doi.org/10.2307/778912.

———. "The Problem of Ideology: Marxism Without Guarantees." In *Stuart Hall: Critical Dialogues in Cultural Studies*, eds. David Morley and Kuan-Hsing Chen, 25-46. New York: Routledge, 1996.

Hansell, Saul. "After Complaints, Yahoo to Close Access to Pornographic Sites." *The New York Times*, 14 April 2001. Available from http://www.nytimes.com/2001/04/14/technology/14YAHO.html?pagewanted=print; accessed 29 April 2001.

Harding, Sandra. *Science and Social Inequality: Feminist and Postcolonial Issues*. Champaign: University of Illinois Press, 2006.

Hardy, Simon. *The Reader, The Author, The Woman and Her Lover: Soft-Core Pornography and Heterosexual Men*. New York: Cassell, 1998.

Harrington, James. *The Commonwealth of Oceana and A System of Politics*. Edited by J. G. A. Pocock. Cambridge: University Press, 1992.

Harvard Law Review Association. "The Content Distinction in Free Speech Analysis After Renton." *Harvard Law Review* 102 (June 1989): 1904-24.

Heart of Atlanta Motel Inc. v. United States, 379 U.S. 241 (1964).

Hester, Helen. *Beyond Explicit*. Albany: State University Of New York Press, 2015.

Higgins, Tracy E., Gender, Why Feminists Can't (or Shouldn't) Be Liberals, 72 *Fordham L. Rev.* 1629 (2004). Available at: http://ir.lawnet.fordham.edu/flr/vol72/iss5/12.

Hindess, Barry. *Discourses of Power: From Hobbes to Foucault*. Cambridge & Oxford: Blackwell Publishers, Inc., 1996.

Hirschmann, Nancy J. *Gender Class and Freedom in Modern Political Theory*. Princeton: Princeton University Press, 2008.

———. *The Subject of Liberty: toward a Feminist Theory of Freedom*. Princeton: Princeton University Press, 2003.

———. "Utility, Democracy, Equality," 213–73. Princeton: Princeton University Press, 2008. http://www.jstor.org.online.library.marist.edu/stable/j.ctt7s271.9.

Hirshman, Linda. "Is the Original Position Inherently Male-Superior?" *Columbia Law Review* 94 (1994): 1860-75.

Hollis, Martin. "The Last Post?" In *International Theory: Positivism and Beyond*, ed. Steve Smith, Ken Booth, and Marysia Zalewski, 306. Cambridge: Cambridge University Press, 1996.

Hornsby, Jennifer, and Rae Langton. "Free Speech and Illocution." *Legal Theory* 4, no. 1 (1998): 21–37. https://doi.org/10.1017/s1352325200000902.

Hoy, David Couzens. "Power, Repression, Progress: Foucault, Lukes, and the Frankfurt School." In *Foucault: A Critical Reader*, edited by David Couzens Hoy, 123–48. Boston: Blackwell, 1996.

Hoy, David Couzens., ed. *Foucault: a Critical Reader*. Oxford: Basil Blackwell, 1996.

Hudson, David L. "The Secondary Effects Doctrine: 'The Evisceration of First Amendment Freedoms.'" *Washburn Law Journal* 37 (fall 1997): 55-94.

Hume, David. *A Treatise of Human Nature*. Edited by David Fate Norton and Mary J. Norton. Oxford: Oxford University Press, 2000.

Hunter, Howard Owen. "Problems in Search of Principles: The First Amendment in the Supreme Court From 1791-1930." *Emory Law Journal* 35 (1980): 59-137.

Hunter, Nan D. "False Promises: Feminist Anti-Pornography Legislation in the U.S. [Symposium: The Sex Panic: Women, Censorship and Pornography]." *N.Y.L. Sch L. Rev.*, 1993, 133.

Huppin, Mark, and Neil Malamuth. "Adult Entertainment: The Obscenity Conundrum, Contingent Harms, and Constitutional Consistency." *Stanford Law & Policy Review*, 2012. Retrieved from www.lexisnexis.com/hottopics/lnacademic.

Hyde, Alan. *Bodies of Law*. Princeton: Princeton University Press, 1997.

Itzin, Catherine, and Corrine Sweet. "Women's Experience of Pornography: UK Magazine Survey Evidence." In *Pornography, Women, Violence, and Civil Liberties: A Radical New View*, ed. Catherine Itzin, 222-35. Oxford, New York, & Toronto: Oxford University Press, 1992. Reprint, Oxford, New York, & Toronto: Oxford University Press, 1993.

Itzin, Catherine. "A Legal Definition of Pornography." In *Pornography, Women, Sexual Violence, and Civil Liberties*, ed. Catherine Itzin, 401-55. Oxford, New York, & Toronto: Oxford University Press, 1992. Reprint, Oxford, New York, & Toronto: Oxford University Press, 1993.

Jacobellis v. Ohio, 378 U.S. 184 (1964).

Jacobson v. Massachusetts, 197 U.S. 11 (1905).

Jacobson, Daniel. "Freedom of Speech Acts? A Response to Langton." *Philosophy Public Affairs* 24, no. 1 (1995): 64–78. https://doi.org/10.1111/j.1088-4963.1995.tb00022.x.

Jacobson, Daniel. "Speech and Action: Replies to Hornsby and Langton." *Legal Theory* 7, no. 2 (2001): 179–201. https://doi.org/10.1017/s1352325201072032.

Jameson, Jenna, and Neil Strauss. *How to Make Love like a Porn Star: a Cautionary Tale*. New York: It Books, 2010.

Jeffreys, Sheila. *The Industrial Vagina: the Political Economy of the Global Sex Trade*. London: Routledge, 2010.

Jennings, Jeremy, Edward Berenson, Vincent Duclert, and Christophe Prochasson. "Liberty," 95–102. *History, Values, Debates*. Ithaca, NY: Cornell University Press, 2011. http://www.jstor.org.online.library.marist.edu/stable/10.7591/j.ctt7zbwr.13.

Jensen, Robert. "Introduction." In *Pornography: The Production and Consumption of Inequality*, ed. Gail Dines, Robert Jensen, and Ann Russo, 1-7. New York & London: Routledge, 1998a.

_____. "Using Pornography." In *Pornography: The Production and Consumption of Inequality*, eds. Gail Dines, Robert Jensen, and Ann Russo, 101-46. New York & London: Routledge, 1998b.

Juson, Justin, and Brenda Lillington. "*R. v. Butler*: Recognizing the Expressive Value and the Harm in Pornography." *Golden Gate University Law Review* 23, no. 2 (1993). https://doi.org/https://digitalcommons.law.ggu.edu/ggulrev/vol23/iss2/7.

Kagan, Elena. "Pornography and Hate Speech Regulation After R.A.V." *University of Chicago Law Review* 60 (1993): 873–902.

Kaite, Berkeley. *Pornography and Difference*. Bloomington & Indianapolis: Indiana University Press, 1995.

Keeps, David. "Why Hollywood Asks Them to Strip." *New York Times Sunday Magazine*. June 25, 2000.

Kelly, Elizabeth A. *Education, Democracy, and Public Knowledge*. Boulder, CO: Westview Press, 1995.

Kernohan, Andrew. "Accumulative Harms and the Interpretation of the Harm Principle." *Social Theory and Practice*, 1, 19 (1993): 51–72.

Kimmel, Michael, and Michael Barron. "Sexual Violence in Three Pornographic Media: Toward a Sociological Explanation." *Journal of Sex Research* 37, no. 4 (2000): 161-168.

Kimmerle v. New York, 262 NY 99 (1933).

Kinsley, Jennifer M. "The Myth of Obsolete Obscenity." *Cardozo Arts & Entertainment Law Journal* 33 (2015): 607.

Koerner, Brendan I. "A Lust for Profits." *U.S. News & World Report*, 27 March 2000, 36 [online]; available from Lexis-Nexis, Academic Universe, News; accessed 1 March 2001.

Koppelman, Andrew. *Antidiscrimination Law and Social Equality*. New Haven, CT: Yale University Press, 1998.

———. "Free Speech and Pornography: A Response to James Weinstein." *New York University Review of Law & Social Change* 31 (2007): 899.

Kramar, Kirsten, and Richard Jochelson. "Governing Through Harm to Promote Liberal Values: The Canadian Approach to Obscenity and Indecency Following *R. v. Labaye*." *The Canadian Journal of Sociology* 36 (December 2011): 4.

Kritzman, Lawrence D., ed. *Michel Foucault: Politics, Philosophy, Culture: Interviews and Other Writings 1977-84*. New York: Routledge, 1988.

Kuhn, Thomas S. *The Structure of Scientific Revolutions*. Chicago, IL: The University of Chicago Press, 2015.

Kurylo, Bohdana. "Pornography and Power in Michel Foucault's Thought." *Journal of Political Power* 10 (2017): 71–84.

Laclau, Ernesto, and Chantal Mouffe. *Hegemony and Socialist Strategy: towards a Radical Democratic Politics*. London: Verso, 2014.

Lahey, Kathleen A. "The Canadian Charter of Rights and Pornography: Toward a Theory of Actual Gender Equality." *New England Law Review* 649 (1985).

Lane, Frederick S. *Obscene Profits: the Entrepreneurs of Pornography in the Cyber Age*. London: Routledge, 2001.

Langton, Rae. "Beyond Belief: Pragmatics in Hate Speech and Pornography." Essay. In *Speech and Harm*, edited by Mary Kate McGowen and Ishani Maitra, 126–47. Oxford: Oxford University Press, 2012.

———."Comments on A. W. Eaton's 'A Sensible Antiporn Feminism.'" http://web.mit.edu/sgrp. Cambridge: MIT Press, 2008. http://web.mit.edu/sgrp/2008/no2/Langton0508.pdf.

———. *Sexual Solipsism Philosophical Essays on Pornography and Objectification*. Oxford: Oxford University Press, 2013.

———. "Speech Acts and Unspeakable Acts." *Philosophy and Public Affairs* 22, no. 4 (1993): 293-330.

———. "Whose Right? Ronald Dworkin, Women and Pornographers." *Philosophy and Public Affairs* 19, no. 4 (1990): 311-59.

LaSelva, Samuel V. "Toleration Without Hate Speech: The Keegstra Decision, American Free Speech Exceptionalism, and Locke's Letter." *Canadian Journal of Political Science* 48, no. 3 (2015): 699–718. https://doi.org/DOI: https://doi.org/10.1017/S0008423915001043P.

Lawrence, Charles R. "If He Hollers Let Him Go: Regulating Racist Speech on Campus." Essay. In *Words That Wound: Critical Race Theory, Assaultive Speech, and the First Amendment*, edited by Mari J. Matsuda. Boulder, CO: Westview Press, 1993.

Leduc, Rita, President of Stringfellow's. Affidavit. New York: New York Supreme Court, Appellate Division, 1996. Photocopied, index number 103568/96, 103569/96.

Legislative Services Branch. "Consolidated Federal Laws of Canada, Access to Information Act." Canada Occupational Health and Safety Regulations, September 20, 2018. http://laws-lois.justice.gc.ca/eng/Const/page-15.html.

Lehman, Peter. *Pornography: Film and Culture*. New Brunswick, NJ: Rutgers University Press, 2006.

Lemley, Brandon K. "Effectuating Censorship: Civic Republicanism and the Secondary Effects Doctrine." *J. Marshall Law Review* 35 (2002): 189.

LePore, Ernest. *Truth and Interpretation: Perspectives on the Philosophy of Donald Davidson*. Oxford: Blackwell, 1993.

Levin, A. *Cost of Free Speech: Pornography, Hate Speech, and Their Challenge to Liberalism*. London: Palgrave Macmillan, 2014.

Levy, Ariel. *Female Chauvinist Pigs: Women and the Rise of Raunch Culture*. New York: Free Press, 2010.

Lewis, David. "Scorekeeping in a Language Game." *Journal of Philosophical Logic* 8, no. 1 (1979). https://doi.org/10.1007/bf00258436.

Lindsay, Jessica. "Why Are so Many Women Watching Male Gay Porn?" Metro. Metro.co.uk, July 17, 2018. https://metro.co.uk/2018/07/12/many-women-watching-male-gay-porn-7700321/.

Lochner v. New York, 198 U.S. 45 1905.

Locke, John. *A Letter Concerning Toleration*. Edited by Kerry S. Walters. Peterborough, Ontario: Broadview Press, 2013.

Macedo, Stephen. *Liberal Virtues*. New York: Oxford University Press, 1990.

MacKinnon, Catharine A. "Points Against Postmodernism." *Chicago-Kent Law Review* 75 (2000): 687.

MacKinnon, Catharine A. *Only Words*. Cambridge: Harvard University Press, 2002.

———. *Toward A Feminist Theory of The State*. Cambridge: Harvard University Press, 1989.

———. *Feminism Unmodified: Discourses on Life and Law*. Cambridge: Harvard University Press, 1987.

MacKinnon, Catharine A., and Andrea Dworkin. *In Harm's Way: the Pornography Civil Rights Hearings*. Cambridge: Harvard University Press, 1998.

MacNay, Lois. *Foucault and Feminism: Power, Gender and the Self*. Boston: Polity Press, 1997.

Mahoney, Kathleen. "The Canadian Constitutional Approach to Freedom of Expression in Hate Propaganda and Pornography." *Law and Contemporary Problems* 55, no. 1 (1992): 77–106. https://doi.org/https://scholarship.law.duke.edu/lcp/vol55/iss1/.

Maitra, Ishani, and Mary Kathryn McGowan. *Speech and Harm: Controversies over Free Speech*. Oxford: Oxford University Press, 2013.

Malamuth, Neil, and Mark Happen. "Drawing the Line on Virtual Child Pornography: Bringing the Law in Line with Research Evidence." *New York University Review of Law & Social Change* 31 (2007): 773.

Malloy, S. Elizabeth Wilborn, and Ronald J. Krotoszynski, Junior. "Recalibrating the Cost of Harm Advocacy: Getting Beyond Brandenburg." *William & Mary Law Review* 41 (April 2000): 1159-1245.

Malmer, Lisa. "Nude Dancing and the First Amendment." *University of Cincinnati Law Review* 59 (November 1991): 1275-1310.

Marbury v. Madison, 5 U.S. 137 (1803).

Martin, Biddy. "Feminism, Criticism, and Foucault." *New German Critique* 27 (1982): 3-30.

Martin, James P. "When Repression Is Democratic and Constitutional: The Federalist Theory of Representation and the Sedition Act of 1798." *University of Chicago Law Review* 66 (1999): 117-82.

Mason-Grant, Joan. *Pornography Embodied: from Speech to Sexual Practice*. Lanham, MD: Rowman & Littlefield, 2004.

Matsuda, Mari J, Charles R Lawrence, Richard Delgado, and Kimberle Williams Crenshaw, eds. *Words That Wound Critical Race Theory, Assaultive Speech and the First Amendment*. Boulder, CO: Westview Press, 1993 reprinted 2011.

Matsuda, Mari J. "Public Response to Racist Speech: Considering the Victim's Story." In *Words That Wound: Critical Race Theory, Assaultive Speech, and the First Amendment*, eds. Mari J. Matsuda, Charles R. Lawrence III, Richard Delgado, and Kimberle Crenshaw, 17-52. Boulder, San Francisco, & Oxford: Westview Press, 1992.

May, Larry. *Masculinity & Morality*. Ithaca, NY: Cornell University Press, 1998.

McClain, Linda C. "Symposium: Discrimination and Inequality—Emerging Issues Toward a Formative Project of Securing Freedom and Equality." *Cornell Law Review* 85 (July 2000): 1221-58.

Mcgowan, Mary Kate, and Bianka Takaoka. "Analytic Approaches to Pornography and Objectification." *Oxford Bibliographies Online Datasets*, 2015. https://doi.org/10.1093/obo/9780195396577-0263.

Mcgowan, Mary Kate. "On Pornography: MacKinnon, Speech Acts, and 'False' Construction." *Hypatia* 20, no. 3 (2005): 22–49. https://doi.org/10.1111/j.1527-2001.2005.tb00485.x.

———. "Oppressive Speech." *Australasian Journal of Philosophy* 87, no. 3 (2009): 389–407. https://doi.org/10.1080/00048400802370334.

———. "The Ethics of Free Speech." *The Routledge Companion to Ethics*, n.d. https://doi.org/10.4324/9780203850701.ch64.

McHoul, Alec, and Wendy Grace. *A Foucault Primer: Discourse, Power and the Subject*. New York: New York University Press, 1993.

Meehan, Johanna, ed. *Feminists Read Habermas: Gendering the Subject of Discourse*. New York & London: Routledge, 1995.

Metz, Cade. "The Porn Business Isn't Anything Like You Think It Is." *Wired*. Conde Nast, June 30, 2017. https://www.wired.com/2015/10/the-porn-business-isnt-anything-like-you-think-it-is/.

Meyer, Carlin. "Sex, Sin, and Women's Liberation: Against Porn-Suppression." *Texas Law Review* 72 (1994): 1111.

Miller v. California, 413 U.S. 15 (1973).

Mohanty, Satya P. *Literary Theory and the Claims of History: Postmodernism, Objectivity, Multicultural Politics*. Oxford: Oxford University Press, 1998.

Montag, Warren. "'The Soul is the Prison of the Body': Althusser and Foucault, 1970-75." *Yale French Studies* 88 (1995): 53-77.

Montigney, Yves de. "The Difficult Relationship between Freedom of Expression and Its Reasonable Limits ." *Law and Contemporary Problems* 55, no. 1 (1992): 35–52.

Moon, J. Donald. *Constructing Community: Moral Pluralism and Tragic Conflicts*. Princeton: Princeton University Press, 1993.

Morris, Betsy, Eileen P. Gunn, and Patricia Neering. "Addicted to Sex: A Primal Problem From The Shadows in a New—and Dangerous—Corporate Environment." *Fortune*, 10 May 1999, 66 [online]; available from Infotrac; accessed 1 March 2000.

Muller v. Oregon, 208 U.S. 412 (1908).

Munro, Neil. "The Web's Pornucopia." *The National Journal*, January 14, 1999, 38 [online]; available from Lexis-Nexis Academic Universe, News; accessed 2 March 2001.

Namaste, Ki. "Genderbashing: Sexuality, Gender, and the Regulation of Public Space." Environmental and Planning Development. *Society & Space* 14, April (1996): 223-39.

Nationalist Socialist Party v. Skokie, Illinois, 432 U.S. 43 (1977).

Neier, Areyeh. *Defending My Enemy*. New York: Dutton, 1979.

Neville, Brennan. "Anti-Pornography Legislation As Content Discrimination Under R.A.V.," 5 Kansas Journal of Law & Public Policy (Fall 1995): 121-30.

New York Times v. Sullivan, 376 U.S. 254 (1964).

Nieman, Donald G. *Promises to Keep: African-Americans and the Constitutional Order, 1776 to the Present*. New York: Oxford University Press, 1991.

Northend Cinema Inc. v. Seattle, 90 Wn. 2d 709 (1978).

Northrup, Christiane. *Women's Bodies, Women's Wisdom: Creating Physical and Emotional Health and Healing*. New York: Bantam Books, 1998.

Norton, Jody. "Bodies That Don't Matter: The Discursive Effacement of Sexual Difference." *Women and Language* 20, no. 1 (1997): 24-30.

Not a Love Story: A Film about Pornography. National Film Board of Canada, n.d. http://onf-nfb.gc.ca/en/our-collection/?idfilm=13558.

Note. "The Content Distinction in Free Speech Analysis after 'Renton.'" *Harvard Law Review* 102, no. 8 (1989): 1904. https://doi.org/10.2307/1341361.

Nussbaum, Martha C. *Sex and Social Justice*. New York & Oxford: Oxford University Press, 1999.

———. "The Professor of Parody." *The New Republic*, February 22, 1999. https://newrepublic.com/article/150687/professor-parody.

Obergefell v. Hodges, 576 U.S. _____ (2015).

Office, Attorney General's. *Report of the Attorney General's Working Group on the Regulation of Sexually Oriented Businesses*. Minneapolis, 1989.

Orren, Karen. "The Primacy of Labor in American Constitutional Development." *The American Political Science Review* 89, no. 2 (1995): 377-388.

Oser, Andrea. "Motivation Analysis in Light of Renton." *Columbia Law Review* 87 (March 1987): 344-67.

Paasonen, Susanna. *Carnal Resonance Affect and Online Pornography*. Cambridge: MIT Press, 2011.

Pateman, Carole, and Mary Lyndon Shanley. "Introduction." In *Feminist Interpretations and Political Theory*, eds. Mary Lyndon Shanley and Carole Pateman, 1-10. University Park: The Pennsylvania State University Press, 1991.

Pateman, Mary Lyndon Shanley & Carole, eds. *Feminist Interpretations and Political Theory*. University Park: The Pennsylvania State University, 1991.

Paul, Bryant, Bradley J. Shafer, and Daniel Linz. "Government Regulation of 'Adult' Businesses Through Zoning and Anti-Nudity Ordinances: Debunking the Legal Myth of Negative Secondary Effects." *Communication Law and Policy* 6, no. 2 (2001): 355–91. https://doi.org/10.1207/s15326926clp0602_4.

Paul, Pamela. *Pornified*. Ephrata, PA: Owl, 2006.

Pettit, Philip. *Republicanism: a Theory of Freedom and Government*. Oxford: Oxford University Press, 2010.

Pinsker, Joe. "The Hidden Economics of Porn." *The Atlantic*. Atlantic Media Company, November 29, 2016. https://www.theatlantic.com/business/archive/2016/04/pornography-industry-economics-tarrant/476580/.

Pinsker, Joe. "The Hidden Economics of the Porn." *The Atlantic Monthly*, n.d.

Plaxton, Michael. "What Butler Did." Osgoode Digital Commons. *The Supreme Court Law Review: Osgoode's Annual Constitutional Cases Conference*, 2012. https://digitalcommons.osgoode.yorku.ca/sclr/vol57/iss1/14/.

Plessy v. Ferguson, 163 U.S. 537 (1896).

Pornhub Insights. December 11, 2018 (d. "2018 Year in Review.") Pornhub Insights. Pornhub, January 31, 2019. https://www.pornhub.com/insights/2018-year-in-review#gender.

Procunier v. Martinez, 416 U.S. 396 (1974).

Putnam, Hilary. *Reason, Truth and History*. Cambridge: Cambridge University Press, 1998.

R. v. Butler, 1 SCR 452 (1992).

R. v. Keegstra, 3 SCR 697 (1990).

R.A.V. v. St. Paul, 505 U.S. 377 (1992).

Rabban, David M. "Free Speech in Progressive Social Thought." *Texas Law Review* 74 (1996): 951-1038.

———. "The Emergence of the Modern First Amendment Doctrine." *University of Chicago Law Review* 50 (1983): 1205.

Rabinow, Paul, ed. *The Foucault Reader*. New York: Pantheon Books, 1984.

Radin, Margaret Jane. *Contested Commodities*. Cambridge: Harvard University Press, 2001.

Rajchman, John. "Ethics after Foucault." *Social Text* 13/14 (1986). https://doi.org/www.jstor.org/stable/466209.

Rawls, John. *A Theory of Justice*. Dehli, India: Universal Law Publishing Co Ltd, 2013.

———. *Political Liberalism*. New York: Columbia University Press, 1993.

Raynaud, Philippe, Ann T. Gardiner, and Mark Lilla. "Constant," 82–90. Princeton University Press, 1994. http://www.jstor.org.online.library.marist.edu/stable/j.ctt7zvq8k.9.

Raz, Joseph. "On The Nature of Right." *Mind* 93 (1984): 194–214.

———. "Rights and Individual Well Being." *Ratio Juris*, no. 5 (July 2, 1992): 127–42.

Rochin v. California, 342 U.S. 165 (1952).

Roe v. Wade, 410 U.S. 113 (1973).

Rooney, Ellen. "Better Read Than Dead: Althusser and the Fetish of Ideology." *Yale French Studies*, no. 88 (1995): 183. https://doi.org/10.2307/2930107.

Rose, Joseph B. Adult Entertainment Study. New York: Department of City Planning, 1994, DCP# 94-08.

Rose, Joseph P. Affidavit. New York: New York Supreme Court, Appellate Division, 1996. Photocopied, index number 103568/96, 103569/96.

Roth v. United States, 354 U.S. 476 (1957).

Rouse, Joseph. *Knowledge and Power: Toward a Political Philosophy of Science*. Ithaca, NY: Cornell University Press, 1994.

Rubin, Edward L. "Nazis, Skokie, and the First Amendment as Virtue," review of *Nazis in Skokie: Freedom, Community, and the First Amendment*, by Donald Alexander Downs. *California Law Review* 74 (1986): 233-60.

Russell, Diana E. H. *Dangerous Relationships: Pornography, Misogyny, and Rape*. Thousand Oaks, London & New Dehli: Sage Publications, 1998.

Ryerson, James. "The Outrageous Pragmatism Of Judge Richard Posner." *Linguafranca*, May/June 2000, 26-34.

Saunders, Kevin W. *Degradation: What the History of Obscenity Tells Us about Hate Speech*. New York: New York University Press, 2016.

Sawicki, Jana. *Disciplining Foucault: Feminism, Power, and the Body*. New York & London: Routledge, 1991.

Saxonhouse, Arlene. "Aristotle: Defective Males, Hierarchy, and the Limits of Politics." In *Feminist Interpretations and Political Theory*, eds. Mary Lyndon Shanley and Carole Pateman, 32-52. University Park: The Pennsylvania State University, 1991.

Scalia, Antonin. "Originalism: The Lesser Evil." *University of Cincinnati Law Review* 57 (1989): 849-65.

Schauer, Frederick. *Free Speech: A Philosophical Enquiry*. Cambridge: Cambridge University Press, 1982.

———. "Speech and 'Speech'—Obscenity and 'Obscenity': An Exercise in The Interpretation of Constitutional Language." *Georgetown Law Journal* 67 (1979): 899.

Schenck v. United States, 249 U.S. 47 (1919).

Schlosser, Eric. "The Business of Pornography." *U.S. News & World Report*, February 10, 1997, 42 [online]; available from Lexis-Nexis, Academic Universe, News; accessed 1 June 2001.

Schwartzman, Lisa H. "Hate Speech, Illocution, and Social Context: A Critique of Judith Butler." *Journal of Social Philosophy* 33, no. 3 (2002): 421–41. https://doi.org/10.1111/0047-2786.00151.

Scott, Kathryn Leigh. *The Bunny Years*. New York: Gallery Books, 2011.

Shapiro, Ian, ed. *Abortion: The Supreme Court Decisions*. Indianapolis & Cambridge: Hackett Publishing Company, Inc., 1995.

Sherman, Jeffrey G. "Love Speech: The Social Utility of Pornography." *Stanford Law Review* 47 (1995): 661.

Skinner, Quentin. *Machiavelli*. Oxford: Oxford University Press, 1981.

Smart, Barry. "The Politics of Truth and the Problem of Hegemony." In *Foucault: A Critical Reader*, ed. David Couzens Hoy. Oxford & Cambridge: Blackwell, 1986.

Smart, Carol. *Feminism and the Power of Law*. London: Routledge, 2015.

Smith, Kimberly K. "Zoning Adult Entertainment: A Reassessment of Renton." *California Law Review* 79 (January 1991): 119-60.

Smith, Rogers. "Beyond Toqueville, Myrdal, and Hartz: The Multiple Traditions in America." *American Political Science Review* 87, no. 3 (1993): 549-66.

Smith, Steven B. *Hegel's Critique of Liberalism*. Chicago & London: The University of Chicago Press, 1989.

Spector, Horacio. "Four Conceptions of Freedom" *Political Theory* 38, no. 6 (2010): 780–808. http://www.jstor.org.online.library.marist.edu/stable/25749186.

Spicker, Paul. "Liberty," 5–42. In *Reclaiming Individualism: Perspectives on Public Policy*. Bristol University Press, 2006. https://doi.org/10.2307/j.ctt9qgkg5.6.

Stark, Cynthia A. Florida State University Department of Philosophy. "Is Pornography an Action?: The Causal vs. the Conceptual View of Pornography's Harm." *Social Theory and Practice* 23, no. 2 (1997): 277–306. https://doi.org/10.5840/soctheor-pract199723213.

———. "Rawlsian Self-Respect." In *Oxford Studies in Normative Ethics*, edited by Mark Timmons, vol. II: 238–61. Oxford Series in Normative Ethics II. Oxford: Oxford University Press, 2013. DOI:10.1093/acprof:oso/9780199662951.003.0010

Steinem, Gloria. "Erotica vs. Pornography." In *Transforming a Rape Culture*, eds. Emilie Buchwald, Pamela Fletcher, and Martha Roth, 31-46. Minneapolis: Milkweed Editions, 1993.

Sternhell, Zeev, and David Maisel. "The Anti-Enlightenment of the Cold War." In *The Anti-Enlightenment Tradition*, ed. Zeev Sternhell, 372–421. Yale University Press, 2010. http://www.jstor.org.online.library.marist.edu/stable/j.ctt5vm23x.12.

Stocker, Barry. "Wittgenstein's Paradox of Ordinary Language," *Essays in Philosophy* vol. 1, no. 2 (2000): 93–105.

Stone, Geoffrey R. *Perilous Times: Free Speech in Wartime: From the Sedition Act of 1798 to the War on Terrorism*, 1st Edition. New York: W.W. Norton & Co., 2004.

———. "Sex, Violence and the First Amendment." *Chicago Law Review* 74 (2007): 1857.

Stone, Geoffrey R. "Content Regulation and the First Amendment." *William and Mary Law Review* 25 (1983): 189.

Stringfellow's of New York LTD. v. City of New York, 653 N.Y.S. 2nd 801 (1996).

Sullivan, Andrew. "The He Hormone." *New York Times Magazine*, April 2, 2000 [online]; available from Lexis-Nexis Academic Universe, News; accessed May 4, 2001.

Sunstein, Cass R. *Democracy and the Problem of Free Speech*. New York: Free Press, 1995.

———. "The Supreme Court 1995 Term Foreword: Leaving Things Undecided." *SSRN Electronic Journal*, 1996. https://doi.org/10.2139/ssrn.2781624.

———. "Words, Conduct, Caste." *University of Chicago Law Review* 60 (1993): 836.

Sweatt v. Painter, 339 U.S. 629 (1950).

Talentino, Jia. "The Rage of the Incels." *The New Yorker*, May 15, 20118. https://www.newyorker.com/culture/cultural-comment/the-rage-of-the-incels.

Tannenbaum, Donald G. *Inventors of Ideas: Introduction to Western Political Philosophy*. Boston: Cengage, 2012.

Tanyi, Attila. "Self-Respect and the Demands of Equality," n.d. https://www.attilatanyi.com/uploads/2/5/0/0/25004408/respect.doc.

Tarrant, Shira. *The Pornography Industry: What Everyone Needs to Know*. Oxford: Oxford University Press, 2016.

Taylor, Charles. *Philosophy and the Human Sciences*. Cambridge: Cambridge University Press, 1985.

Taylor, Charles. "What is Wrong with Negative Liberty," In *Law and Morality: Readings in Legal Philosophy*, eds., David Dyzenhaus et al., 2003, pp. 359-69.

Taylor, Paul C. *Race: a Philosophical Introduction*. New York: Polity, 2013.

TenBroek, Jacobus. *The Antislavery Origins of the Fourteenth Amendment*. Berkeley: University of California Press, 1951.

Texas v. Johnson, 491 U.S. 397 (1989).

Theranian, John. "Sanitizing Cyberspace: Obscenity, Miller, and the Future of Public Discourse on the Internet." *Journal of Intellectual Property Law* 11 (2003): 1.

"Things Are Looking Up in America's Porn Industry." NBCNews.com. NBCUniversal News Group, n.d. https://www.nbcnews.com/business/business-news/things-are-looking-americas-porn-industry-n289431.

Thomas, Alexander, and Samuel Sillen. *Racism and Psychiatry*. Seacaucus, NJ: Carol Pub. Group, 1993.

Tinker v. Des Moines Independent Community School District, 393 U.S. 503 (1969).

Tong, Rosemarie. *Feminist Thought: a Comprehensive Introduction*. London: Routledge, 1997.

Tourkochoriti, Ioanna. "Should Hate Speech Be Protected? Group Defemation, Party Bans, Holocaust Denial, and the Divide Between (France) Europe and the United States." *Columbia Human Rights Law Review* 45, no. 552 (2014).

United States v. O'Brien, 391 U.S. 367 (1968).

Urbinati, Nadia. "Competing for Liberty: The Republican Critique of Democracy," *American Political Science Review* 106, no. 3 (2012): 607–21. http://www.jstor.org.online.library.marist.edu/stable/23275436.

Veyne, Paul, and Catherine Porter. "Foucault Revolutionizes History." Essay. In *Foucault and His Interlocuters*, edited by Arnold I. Davidson, 146. Chicago: University of Chicago, 1997.

Veyne, Paul. "Foucault Revolutionizes History." In *Foucault and His Interlocutors*, ed. Arnold I. Davidson, 146-182. Chicago & London: The University of Chicago Press, 1971.

Vinas, Tony. "X-Rated and on the A-List: Can the Web Make the Adult-Entertainment Industry Acceptable?" *Industry Week*, 21 September 1998, 11 [online]; available from Lexis-Nexis Academic Universe, News; accessed 2 March 2001.

Virginia v. Black, 538 U.S. 343 (2003).

Waldron, Jeremy. *The Harm in Hate Speech*. Cambridge: Harvard University Press, 2014.

Waltman, Max. "Rethinking Democracy: Legal Challenges to Pornography and Sex Inequality in Canada and the United States" 63, no. 1 (2010): 218–37. http://www.jstor.org.online.library.marist.edu/stable/27759897.

Watson, Bruce, and Shyla Rae Welch. "Just Harmless Fun? Understanding the Impact of Pornography." *Pornography*, http://www.enough.org/justharmlessfun.pdf , n.d.

Watson, Lori. "Pornography and Public Reason." *Social Theory and Practice* 33, no. 3 (2007): 467–88. https://doi.org/10.5840/soctheorpract200733318.

Watson, Lori. "Pornography." *Philosophy Compass* 5, no. 7 (2010): 535–50.

———. "Why Sex Work Isn't Work." *Logos: A Journal of Modern Society and Culture*, Summer, 14, no. 3 (2015).

Weinstein, James. "Democracy, Sex and the First Amendment." *NYU Review of Law & Social Change* 31 (2007): 865.

Weinstein, James. "Free Speech Values, Hard Core Pornography and the First Amendment: A Reply to Professor Koppelman." *New York University Review of Law & Social Change* 31 (2007): 911.

Weisberg, D. Kelly. "Butler v. The Queen," 110–17. In *Applications of Feminist Legal Theory to Women's Lives: Sex, Violence, Work, and Reproduction*. Philadelphia: Temple University Press, 1996. http://www.jstor.org.online.library.marist.edu/stable/j.ctt14bs8md.11.

Wertheimer, Aviva O. "The First Amendment Distinction Between Conduct and Content: A Conceptual Framework for Understanding Fighting Words Jurisprudence." *Fordham Law Review* 63, December (1994) [journal online]; available from Lexis-Nexis Academic Universe, Law Reviews; accessed January 29, 1999.

West Virginia State Board of Education v. Barnette, 319 U.S. 624 (1943).

West, Robin. *Progressive Constitutionalism: Reconstructing the Fourteenth Amendment*. Durham & London: Duke University Press, 1994.

West, Robin. "Toward an Abolitionist Interpretation of the Fourteenth Amendment." *West Virginia Law Review* 94 (1991): 111.

Whitney v. California, 274 U.S. 357 (1927).

Williams, Linda. *Hard Core: Power, Pleasure and "Frenzy of the Visible."* London: Pandora, 1990.

———. *Porn Studies*. Durham, NC: Duke University Press, 2004.

———. *Screening Sex / Linda Williams*. Durham, NC: Duke University Press, 2008.

Willis, Cylde E. "The Phenomenology of Pornography: A Comment on Catharine MacKinnon's Only Words." *Law and Philosophy* 16, no. 2 (1997): 177–99.

Wing, Adrien Katherine, and Jean Stefancic. *The Law Unbound!: A Richard Delgado Reader*. London: Routledge, 2016.

Wittgenstein, L. J. J. *Philosophical Investigations*. Edited by G.E.M Anscombe. Oxford: Blackwell and Mott, 1963.

Wolfson, Nicholas. "Free Speech Theory and Hateful Words." *University of Cincinnati Law Review* 60 (1991): 1-42.

———. *Hate Speech, Sex Speech, Free Speech*. Westport, CT: Praeger, 1997.

Wolin, Sheldon S. *Politics and Vision: Continuity and Innovation in Western Political Thought*. Boston & Toronto: Little, Brown and Company, 1960.

Yassky, David. "Eras of the First Amendment." *Columbia Law Review* 91 (1991): 1699-1755.

Yegennoglu, Meyda. *Colonial Fantasies: Toward a Feminist Reading of Orientalism*. Cambridge: Cambridge University Press, 1998.

Young v. American Mini Theatres Inc., 427 U.S. 50 (1976).

Young, Iris Marion. *Justice and the Politics of Difference*. Princeton: Princeton University Press, 1990.

Zeev, Sternhell and Maisel, David. "The Anti-Enlightenment of the Cold War," 372–421. New Haven, CT: Yale University Press, 2010.

Zemser, Amy Z. *Desiring Revolution: Second-Wave Feminism and the Rewriting of American Sexual Thought, 1920 to 1982*. New York: Columbia University Press, 2001.

Zimbardo, Philip G., and Nikita D. Coulombe. *Man Disconnected: How Technology Has Sabotaged What It Means to Be Male*. London: Rider Books, 2016.

Zizek, Slavoj. *The Sublime Object of Ideology*. 7th ed. London & New York: Verso, 1998.

———. *The Ticklish Subject: The Absent Centre of Political Ontology*. London & New York: Verso, 1999.

Index

About the Author

Lynn Mills Eckert is associate professor of political science at Marist College in Poughkeepsie, New York. Lynn is a graduate of the Maxwell School of Citizenship and Public Affairs at Syracuse University. Lynn lives in Rhinebeck, New York, with her spouse and three children.